Natural Resources of South-East Asia
General Editor: OOI JIN BEE

Conflict over Natural Resources
in South-East Asia and the Pacific

The United Nations University's Programme on Peace and Global Transformation was a major world-wide project whose purpose was to develop new insights about the interlinkages between questions of peace, conflict resolution, and the process of transformation. The research in this project, under six major themes, was co-ordinated by a 12-member core group in different regions of the world: East Asia, South-East Asia (including the Pacific), South Asia, the Arab region, Africa, Western Europe, Eastern Europe, North America, and Latin America. The themes covered were: Conflicts over Natural Resources; Security, Vulnerability and Violence; Human Rights and Cultural Survival in a Changing Pluralistic World; The Role of Science and Technology in Peace and Transformation; The Role of the State in Peace and Global Transformation; and Global Economic Crisis. The project also included a special project on Peace and Regional Security.

Conflict over Natural Resources in South-East Asia and the Pacific

Edited by
Lim Teck Ghee
and
Mark J. Valencia

UNITED NATIONS UNIVERSITY PRESS
1990

Singapore
OXFORD UNIVERSITY PRESS
Oxford New York
1990

Oxford University Press

Oxford New York Toronto
Delhi Bombay Calcutta Madras Karachi
Petaling Jaya Singapore Hong Kong Tokyo
Nairobi Dar es Salaam Cape Town
Melbourne Auckland
and associated companies in
Berlin Ibadan

Oxford is a trade mark of Oxford University Press

© The United Nations University 1990

Published in the United States by
Oxford University Press, Inc., New York

ISBN 0 19 588937 1

British Library Cataloguing in Publication Data

Conflict over natural resources in South-east Asia and the
    Pacific.– (Natural resources of South-east Asia.)
    1. Asia. South-east Asia. Natural resources
    I. Lim Teck Ghee, 1943–   II. Valencia, Mark J.   III. Series
    333.70959
    ISBN 0-19-588937-1

Library of Congress Cataloging-in-Publication Data

Conflict over natural resources in South-east Asia and the Pacific/
    edited by Lim Teck Ghee and Mark J. Valencia.
        p. cm.—(Natural resources of South-east Asia)
    "Arose out of a conference organized and supported by the United
    Nations University (UNU) project on 'peace and global
    transformation' in 1985"—P. v.
    Includes bibliographical references.
    ISBN 0-19-588937-1 (U.S.):
    1. Natural resources—Government policy—Asia.   2. Natural
    resources—Government policy—Pacific Area.   3. Asia—Economic
    conditions—1945–   4. International economic relations.   5. Natural
    resources—Law and legislation.   I. Lim, Teck Ghee.   II. Valencia,
    Mark J.   III. United Nations University.   IV. Series.
    HC412.5.C66   1990
    333.7'0959—dc20   90–31481
                                                                CIP

Printed in Malaysia by Peter Chong Printers Sdn. Bhd.
Published by United Nations University Press, The United Nations University,
Toho Seimei Building, 2-15-1 Shibuya, Shibuya-ku, Tokyo 150, Japan,
and Oxford University Press Pte. Ltd.,
Unit 221, Ubi Avenue 4, Singapore 1440

Acknowledgements

THIS book arose out of a conference organized and supported by the United Nations University (UNU) project on 'Peace and Global Transformation' in 1985 which brought researchers from the South-East Asian and Pacific regions together to discuss the problem of conflict over natural resources and its interlinkage with various aspects of the contemporary crisis in economic and social development.

We would like to acknowledge the assistance and encouragement given by Professor K. Mushakoji, Dr J. Golebiowski, and Dr T. Uchida from the UNU staff and Professor R. Kothari and Dr G. Deshingkar from the Peace and Global Transformation project of the UNU. We are also grateful to our respective institutions, Universiti Sains Malaysia (Penang) and the University of Malaya (Kuala Lumpur) in the case of Lim and the East–West Center in the case of Valencia, for supporting our involvement in the project and its output.

We would like to thank Dennis Lau for kindly giving us permission to use his photographs for the cover.

Kuala Lumpur and Honolulu   LIM TECK GHEE
July 1989   MARK J. VALENCIA

Contents

Tables

Figures

Notes on Contributors

James M. Anthony received his Ph.D. in Pacific History and Politics from the Australian National University. He has published widely on a range of policy issues related to Fiji and the Pacific. He is presently Director of the Pacific Research and Information Network located in Honolulu.

Yoko Kitazawa is a free-lance journalist specializing in Japanese–Asian affairs. She is a frequent contributor to major Japanese newspapers, including the *Asahi Shimbun*, and is on the editorial board of the journal *AMPO*.

Lim Teck Ghee is a Professor in the Institute of Advanced Studies, University of Malaya. He has written extensively on the socio-economic history and development of Malaysia and South-East Asia. His recent publications include *Agrarian Transformations: Local Processes and the State in Southeast Asia* (1989) and *Reflections on Development in Southeast Asia* (1988).

Eduardo C. Tadem is currently an Assistant Professor of Development Studies at the University of the Philippines, Manila. His most recent publications are 'Ethnic Self-Determination and Separatist Movements in Southeast Asia' (with Teresa S. Encarnacion) and 'The Aquino Government under Siege' (both 1989).

Mark J. Valencia is a Research Associate and Project Leader in Marine Resources and Development at the Resource Systems Institute, East–West Center, Honolulu. His interests and expertise centre on marine affairs and international relations in South-East Asia, East Asia, and the Pacific. His recent books include *Offshore North-East Asia* (1989), *Southeast Asian Seas: Oil under Troubled Waters* (1985), and *Marine Policy in Southeast Asia* (1985).

1
Introduction

Lim Teck Ghee and Mark J. Valencia

THE papers presented in this volume form part of the output of a larger programme of the United Nations University on 'Peace and Global Transformation'. That programme seeks to understand in a comprehensive way the underlying causes of conflict and tension as well as the diverse forms of struggle for peace. The director of the UNU's programme on 'Peace and Global Transformation' has argued that 'the control and use of natural resources lies at the heart of the deepening crisis in the world today', a crisis he describes as 'dividing the world into extremes of affluence and deprivation with concentration of poverty and scarcity and unemployment and deprivation in one vast sector of mankind and of overabundance and overproduction and overconsumption in another and much smaller section of the same species' (Kothari, 1979: 6). If this is so, it is important to understand how the two—natural resources and the contemporary crisis—are connected, and to arrive eventually at alternatives that can offer a way out of this crisis. The researchers engaged in the programme are trying to relate the issue of peace to the wide range of conflicts and various manifestations of violence at a number of different levels—local, national, and international.[1] Thus conflict over natural resources has been selected as the focus of the South-East Asian and Pacific component of the 'Peace and Global Transformation' programme.

There are several reasons why this topic is timely and important. First, while disputes over the control and use of natural resources have been linked to tension and violence in all parts of

1. A fuller description of the programme is obtainable from *UNU Focus*, United Nations University Information Services, No. 8, November 1985.

the world, the South-East Asian and Pacific regions are richly endowed with natural resources that are in demand in international trade and that have been the cause of many different types of conflict. It was the two regions' natural wealth that initially attracted the European powers during the period of colonial expansion and search for sources of raw materials in the eighteenth and nineteenth centuries. Just as industrialization changed the equilibrium between humankind and resources in the West, colonialism weakened indigenous cultures in South-East Asia and the Pacific, and introduced new approaches towards the environment and natural resources. The local cultures had fostered the development of life-styles that, in their essence, did not encourage competition for material gain or multiplication of possessions for their own sake, but stressed instead the aesthetic, cultural, and spiritual aspects of life. Wealth obtained was redistributed and the resources of the land were generally freely accessible to the people, whose needs were simple.

Industrialized societies, on the other hand, emphasized material needs, the maximization of production limited only by the ingenuity of science and technology, and the acquisition of material wealth for its own sake. They drew their social stratification from the unequal acquisition of material wealth. The transformation of natural resources into commodities for generating profits, and hence the control of access to natural resources, became a cornerstone of the capitalist economies that emerged in Europe. This system was transferred to states in Asia, the Pacific, and other parts of the world penetrated by colonialism. The result was a new round of conflict over the control and use of natural resources, quite different in scope and intensity from that which had existed prior to colonialism.

While competition over the sources of supply of spices, minerals, and other raw materials became the driving force of colonialism and imperialism at the regional and international levels, social classes and ethnic groups were pitted against each other for control of land, water, minerals, and other natural resources at the local level. The attainment of independence by countries in South-East Asia and the Pacific did not diminish in any substantial way the national and international conflict over natural resources. On the contrary, the burgeoning development programmes directed by the Westernized élites of the new states, and the increasing demands of the industrialized world, have imposed a new drain on natural resources, resulting in a more complicated pattern of competition among diverse groups, both local and foreign.

In the foreseeable future, the trend in South-East Asia and the Pacific is towards increased conflict over natural resources, especially those that are becoming scarce. Resources engendering conflict at the international level include extractive resources that have strategic or military value, such as metals, minerals, and fuels. Some of the countries in the two regions are among the world's foremost producers of tin, bauxite, nickel, natural gas, and petroleum. These resources are already deeply embedded in regional and international political rivalry, and conflict over them appears likely to intensify. At the same time, these and resources that are non-strategic but are of economic importance in the world's markets—for example, the products of plantation agriculture such as rubber, coconut, and palm-oil—are increasingly the focus of disputes over access to markets and price rivalries that are contributing to further economic tension and rivalry between states.

At the local level, conflict over natural resources among competing groups of users, including tribal communities, peasants, fishermen, miners, loggers, and corporations, has not only continued unabated but threatens to worsen in the coming years. This conflict is an immediate result of the dramatic increase in population and the corresponding increase in use of natural resources, the polarization of rival claimants, and the failure of many governments and authorities in the region to mediate effectively. This pessimistic assessment of likely future conflict over natural resources and the fact that events associated with the exploitation of natural resources in the two regions move so quickly make more discussion and research on the subject imperative. Baseline data are required to assist efforts to understand and reduce these conflicts.

Another reason for focusing on the subject of conflict over natural resources is that, in many countries in the two regions, there is a growing sense of resource nationalism and concern for the terms of resource development that are negotiated between states. From the perspective of a growing number of South-East Asian and Pacific states, the South–North trade in resources and North–South trade in manufactured products has a colonial character that is disadvantageous to the South. Resources, especially extractive minerals, are being mined or produced in large capital-intensive operations with little employment effects in the producing countries and shipped to the developed countries of the West and Japan for processing and manufacturing. If the resources are returned at all, they are in the form of expensive manufactured products, trapping the former colonies in a continuing exploitative relationship that can be broken only by drastic changes in the terms of resource development.

Meanwhile, a parallel environmental controversy is emerging over whether the two regions' economies should continue to be the suppliers of renewable and non-renewable resources to the developed countries. Many local environmentalists have criticized the environmental degradation and resource depletion of past development strategies and warn of an impending environmental crisis, should the natural wealth of their parts of the world be exposed to further indiscriminate exploitation. Apart from their impact on people and governments, the environmental consequences of the new phase of exploitation are likely to be severe, and could include widespread acid rain, depletion of stratospheric ozone, climatic deterioration due to increased atmospheric carbon dioxide, loss of tropical forests, pollution of estuaries and coastal waters, decreased supply of fresh water, species extinction, loss of valuable genetic resources, genetic defects from toxic chemicals, and spreading malnutrition and pestilence. The level of debate between the 'exploitation' and 'conservation' schools of national development as well as of that taking place between the proponents of an assertive rather than conciliatory resource nationalism can be improved by the documentation and analysis provided by this volume.

Peace is elusive and cannot be imposed or guaranteed militarily. The complexity of the subject of peace implies that fresh concepts and innovative methods are necessary to supplement the knowledge and insights provided by conventional research into conflict, i.e. through disarmament and military studies and international relations. This analysis of conflict through a focus on natural resources uncovers the linkages between resources and the role of the state in facilitating or preventing access to them, and the implications that the conflict over resources holds for human rights and cultural survival in the two regions. At the same time, the exploration of these and other more general linkages, such as the role of science and technology in the organization of resource extraction, distribution and utilization, and the impact of the world economic crisis on resource use, is a step towards a more holistic and integrated analysis of the root causes of conflict.

The studies contained in the volume are the results of research carried out at three different levels—regional, national, and local. Chapter 2 in the volume focuses on land-based resources in the ASEAN countries of the Philippines, Indonesia, Thailand, and Malaysia. Eduardo Tadem's study identifies some of the major conflicts over forests, agriculture, and minerals that have taken place in the region and examines the consequences. A major assumption of the study is that the conflicts are not accidents brought about by simple greed or survival instincts, but rather are the logical conclusions of historical and economic developments set into motion by social forces. Among these forces are multi-national corporations and state or bureaucratic corporations on the one side, and the victims of resource exploitation—tribal communities, peasants, and workers—on the other.

The second study, by Yoko Kitazawa on the Asahan aluminium project in Indonesia, provides an analysis of the strategies employed by Japan over the past twenty years to ensure its access to natural resources. She points out how, in response to criticism of Japan from Asian countries and the emerging international consensus in favour of a new economic order, Japanese enterprises launched an attempt to delineate a Japanese version of the new international division of labour. This strategy aimed at relocating some Japanese industrial sectors abroad, where utility rates and labour costs were low and where local sources of raw materials were plentiful. However, as she argues, the industrialization of the host has simply meant the creation of offshore production facilities for Japanese capital which neither the government nor the people in the country will ever own or control. Moreover, the host country is made to suffer the consequences of damage to the environment caused by pollution-intensive Japanese activities there. The study not only offers a prime example of the new Japanese role in the exploitation of natural resources in South-East Asia but also provides insights into the way in which élite political and economic interests in Japan and Indonesia converge to protect and enhance their own well-being at the expense of others.

The final three studies shift the reader's attention from land-based to marine-based resources. Marine resources, including fish, seabed minerals, and petroleum within the 200-nautical mile (nmi) exclusive economic zones (EEZs) of the Asian and Pacific countries, are a resource frontier with possibilities for improving the life of the masses. However, they have instead been and continue to be the focus of conflict, especially international conflict. This is the subject matter of two macro studies dealing with South-East Asia and the Pacific. Mark J. Valencia's study takes, as its reference point, the extended jurisdiction by coastal nations over the 200-nmi EEZs in the South-East Asian region which has left almost no marine area unclaimed and many areas where claims overlap. In this situation, the superimposition of national policies on trans-national resources has created possibilities for international competition and conflict as well as opportunities for co-operation and community betterment. The study focuses on competition for petroleum resources, fish, the environment, and ocean space itself in the form of sea lanes, from the viewpoint of the coastal states involved as well as that of the great powers—the United States and the Soviet Union—that have a long-standing interest in the military and economic development of the region.

There exists considerable documentation of the ways in which policy-makers in Asia and the Pacific are facing up to the politically sensitive and complex issues emanating from foreign exploitation of national natural resources, especially regarding the increasing sophistication of developing countries in negotiating the terms and conditions of oil and gas resource development. This, however, is often due not to any liberal government attitude or policy towards the release of information on national issues of importance but to a desire to mobilize local public opinion against foreign interests so as to enhance the local support base of ruling élites. Less easy to document because the political advantages of information release are considerably smaller, if not negative, is the manner in which policy-makers have tried to deal with claims to natural resources by competing local groups within the nation itself. Lim Teck Ghee's contribution adopts a historical approach to the study of the exploitation of fisheries resources in Peninsular Malaysia and the ensuing conflict between various interest groups, including small-scale fishermen whose economic livelihoods as well as ways of life are dependent on the well-being of their natural resource base. Placing the role of government and various government policies towards the fisheries sector under close scrutiny, Lim shows how a succession of misguided or narrowly opportunistic government policies over a period of thirty years have, in fact, created the conditions for the existing crisis in the

Malaysian fisheries industry. He also shows the importance of understanding the role of socio-economic and institutional forces (often operating over a prolonged time period) in determining the severity of what is sometimes misrepresented as a purely or wholly bio-ecological problem in the depletion or deterioration of natural resources.

Finally, James Anthony's study on the Pacific returns the reader to consideration of the involvement of outside powers in the present and future exploitation of Pacific marine resources, and assesses separately the consequences and ensuing dilemmas for small island states that do not have the strength—military, political, economic, or scientific—to contend with the outsiders, especially by themselves. A collective approach by the islanders to the management of marine resources would seem to hold the most promise in ensuring that the resources are used in the best interests of the majority of the islanders. But as the study points out, there is much actual and potential conflict within and between island states over questions such as disputed ocean boundaries, rates and terms of resource exploitation, and the allocation of responsibility for the protection of the environment.

Commonalities and Directions for Future Research

What the local and national case studies stress in common is that the state has not always managed its natural resource endowment in the best interests of its people. Indeed, the state often jeopardizes or is juxtaposed against those interests by serving as a facilitator for resource exploitation by foreign and domestic élites. This volume begins to document the emergence of a state system that is predatory—either directly through the proliferation of state institutions (the bureaucracy, military, state 'capitalist' agencies) which control access to natural resources or extract resources for the benefit of a small class—or indirectly through the aegis of a dominant foreign role in resource extraction in return for illicit payments to select national politicians and civil servants.

However, much more work is needed in this area. Much of the machinations of the state *vis-à-vis* natural resources (and other important aspects of economic activity) remains shrouded in secrecy. Research that examines closely the role of the state in managing or mismanaging natural resources, the neutrality or otherwise of state mechanisms established to resolve conflict over

natural resources, and the impact of state development programmes on natural resources is necessary to monitor that the
involvement of the state in the field of natural resources is in the
interests of the majority of the people.

The studies also show that when conflict over natural resources occurs, it has its greatest and most immediate impact on
small fishermen, tribal people, and peasants who draw their
physical and cultural sustenance directly from these resources.
Indeed, these groups often, in all too rapid succession, lose
their livelihood, are physically displaced, and become, in effect,
'deculturalized'. This is especially true of aboriginal peoples who
have been the hardest hit in the conflict over natural resources,
and are, in addition, often dominated and colonized by the major
ethnic group, as in Timor, Kalimantan, and Malaysia.

What has not been explicitly indicated by the studies is that a
turning point is often reached in the wake of conflict over natural
resources when there is growth of the state's armed forces and
the relegation of civilian officials (even corrupt and inefficient
ones) to a subordinate role *vis-à-vis* military officials. Military
involvement takes two, not necessarily exclusive, forms. One is
to act as the state agent of suppression against those sectors of the
population which resist government programmes on the utilization of resources. Secondly, once entrenched in a particular area
of conflict, the military often becomes legally or illegally involved
in economic activities. In this second instance, its physical presence
sometimes becomes a mere cover for its business activities in the
affected locality.

Of course, increased militarization occurs because government
policies and programmes often run counter to the interests of the
very people they are presumed to benefit. Mass resistance to
forced dislocation without adequate provision for the economic
and social well-being of the displaced is an understandable response
of communities. Such resistance is usually initially peaceful and
legal, such as village meetings, refusal to vacate houses and land,
petitions, delegations to the capital, and rallies and demonstra-
tions. If government representatives or agents of the private
concern are unable to convince the people to move, the next step
is to bring in the armed forces. The presence of the military and
the inevitable occurrences of abuse against the civilian population
often compel the people to take violent countermeasures. The
process is repeated in a seemingly never-ending cycle, since more

often than not, resource-based development projects of the state or private corporations are undertaken without consultation with the people resident in the area affected, and the main beneficiaries generally are an outside élite group. This hypothesis cries out for examination and documentation.

Natural resource exploitation in Asia and the Pacific is now entering a new phase of conflict with new actors and new mechanisms rising to the fore. In addition to renewed attention from the well-entrenched former colonial powers—the United States, France, Great Britain, and the Netherlands—business and commercial interests from natural resource-poor Newly Industrializing Countries (NICs) like Korea and Taiwan are now entering the fray. The most prominent resource exploiter in the region—Japan—is, with the co-operation of many of the region's governments, taking advantage of cheaper costs by transferring resource- (and pollution-) intensive industries to South-East Asian countries. In this connection, the changing economic relationship between Japan and the United States is an important factor. Driven by its high yen and protectionist tendencies in the United States, Japanese interests are likely to intensify their efforts to move some of their key export industries to South-East Asia.

On the other hand, foreign (mainly Western) ownership and control of some major land- and mineral-rich companies operating in the region, such as Harrisons & Crosfield, Sime Darby, Guthrie, East Asiatic, and London Tin, is passing to Third World governments. But national control of these giants does not necessarily mean equitable distribution of benefits. Indeed, if the transfer of ownership and control is only from a group of foreign shareholders to a local élite, it will merely further pit the state against its own people. Finally, new marine resources, such as strategic straits, petroleum, and fish, have come under national control, although the local interests have not been clearly identified.

Thus, the next generation of resource exploitation in South-East Asia and the Pacific might also see the rise of the NICs to pre-eminence as natural resource exploiters; the environmental 'cannibalism' of some countries as the holders of state power continue to reject ecodevelopment[2] and pursue growth without

---

2. Ecodevelopment induces desirable, soft change for a human social group, which is held to be not only better, but to contribute to an economic (broadly social) and ecological equilibrium.

equity and sustainability; the solidarity of the great powers in insistence on resource access to fish or sea lanes; and a breakdown of North–South divisions as Northern resource-extracting multinational corporations become ever more entwined with ruling élites from the South. This pattern of exploitation may intensify conflict between rich and poor, within and between countries and extend offshore into the new resource frontier—the oceans.

Whether South-East Asian and Pacific states will, in the future, become more sensitive to natural resource exploitation and its effect on the have-nots will depend on the growth of collective pressure and a collective conscience transcending narrow economic interests in each of the states. It will also demand imaginative approaches by concerned scholars, public-interest groups, and a vigilant mass media to define public rights and to dilute the notion of private property rights that have facilitated the inequitable exploitation of resources.

Among these new approaches could be the extension of the original common-heritage concept—that the resources in a particular area belong to all and should be used for the common good—to resource exploitation, management, and conservation on a national, subregional, or regional basis. The application of this idea to marine-based resources—that is, that all marine resources beyond national jurisdiction be administered by an international organization for the benefit of all mankind but particularly the peoples of developing countries—has already received widespread support from Third World nations, including those in South-East Asia. It would not be inconsistent to apply the same concept to natural resources at the local or national level by using the revenue from such newly gained resources to redress socio-economic inequities within the nation.

Another concept that may be directly applicable is compensation to those segments of society displaced, marginalized, or otherwise injured by developments adversely affecting their environment or natural resources. Thus, when a combination of industrial pollution, habitat destruction, and overly efficient foreign and domestic trawling deprives small fishermen of their livelihood, they could be compensated from the profits of the industries, land developers, and trawler fishermen. There is also a critical need to explore means to empower the poor to avoid and resist such deprivation. Such compensation should include education as to the causes and consequences of their dilemma and help in making the necessary adjustments.

For example, because of changes that follow 'development' of marine resources, it is clear that not all fishermen who want to continue fishing can make a living from it. Direct compensation to displaced fishermen may not be as drastic or as costly as a total ban on trawling, such as in Indonesia, or as strict and costly regulations and enforcement against industrial effluents and for coastal land use. Similarly, developers of coastal land for tourism could directly compensate displaced villagers with acceptable new land and a long-term percentage of the profits from the tourism development.

In the First World, schemes to compensate victims of onshore impact of offshore oil development are now commonplace and such suggestions would not be new to multinational corporations operating in the regions. Indeed, several companies have funded indigenously staffed environmental baseline surveys in the regions with the motive that, in the event of environmental damage caused by their operations, there will be evidence for a limit to their liability. Nowhere might this compensatory approach be more necessary and direct but also controversial as in the case of possible tolls for use of straits and sea lanes, particularly by oil-tankers and carriers of other potential pollutants. These tolls could be used to enhance safe navigation in the seas and to directly compensate coastal peoples for chronic pollution of their fishing grounds and shorelines.

The foregoing are preliminary suggestions on how to mediate in some instances of conflict over natural resources. Obviously, the wiser recourse is to prevent these conflicts from taking place through the implementation of prudent policies. However, when they do occur, there is a need to determine who might have to pay how much to whom and how. Not only should amounts and processes be researched, but the institutions and mechanisms for implementing more progressive management of natural resources at national and international levels should also be closely examined. In the field of ocean space, for example, studies could focus on the costs to coastal people of pollution, coastal land development, and overfishing in particular areas of South-East Asia and the Pacific, delineating feasible fees for users, compensatory amounts for those affected, and possible systems for efficient and equitable allocation of revenues among coastal groups. In this and other fields of natural resources, studies would be needed to identify which conflicts are important and what data are needed to quant-itatively assess them, and suggest management options for equitable and sustainable development of the regions' natural resources.

Also needed is exploration of realistic options for implementing ecodevelopment, which, when pursued by the First and Third Worlds, would alleviate the unequal relationship of resource utilization and reduce the potential for conflict. Pressure has to be brought to bear at the national and international levels for changes that would lead towards a life-style and economic system which conserves the environment, protects human health, produces durable and recyclable products and provides for the welfare of the masses of the people. Both developed and developing countries alike are beginning to grasp that responsibility for conservation and development and for a better balance between people and natural resources is very much a shared responsibility. Hopefully this new consciousness will lead to action that can bring about the sustainable and equitable development that alone can guarantee peace and thus the future of humankind.

References

Kothari, Rajni, 'The North-South Issue', *Mazingira*, No. 10, 1979.

UNU Focus, United Nations Information Services, No. 8, November 1985.

2

Conflict over Land-based Natural Resources in the ASEAN Countries

Eduardo Tadem

The Asean Region: Great Wealth and Great Strife

THE countries of the Association of Southeast Asian Nations (ASEAN) produce a major portion of some of the world's most essential natural resources. From the Philippines, Brunei, Indonesia, Thailand, Malaysia, and Singapore come 82 per cent of the world's production of natural rubber, 70 per cent of copra and coconut products, 70 per cent of tin, 56 per cent of palm-oil, and 50 per cent of hardwood. In addition, the region's seas and rivers account for a significant share of the world's supply of fish and other marine products. Thailand and the Philippines, for example, are major tuna exporters to the US market. Thailand is also one of the world's top rice exporters, and the Philippines boasts the largest pineapple plantation in the world.

Because of the abundance of vital resources in the countries of the ASEAN group, the area has been the scene of various local, national, and international conflicts centring on the use, control, and disposition of natural resources. As control over resources becomes a paramount issue in the drive for national and human survival, disagreements and differences in approaches, priorities, and philosophies emerge. Governments often clash over jurisdiction of lands containing valuable raw materials such as oil and minerals. On the other hand, a government often faces opposition from its own citizens regarding the issue of human rights violations committed by the state as it pursues certain national strategies of development. These conflicts are often portrayed in official pronouncements as being between modernity and tradition, but more often than not the conflict simply reflects the intransigence of institutionalized power and its propensity to impose bureaucratic and technocratic planning models.

The Historical Roots of Conflict

The ASEAN region has been a region of conflict. In varying degrees, the six member countries are continuing to experience social unrest born out of conflicts over the use of natural resources and the distribution of the economic product of this wealth. In the Philippines, a 12,000-man New People's Army (NPA) guerrilla army led by the Communist Party has been a major thorn in the side of the government, first to the Marcos regime and now to the Aquino administration, and a hindrance to the consolidation of power in that country. There has been a resurgence of land conflicts in Indonesia, raising the spectre of the pre-1965 agrarian unrest. In Malaysia, despite the low profile of the armed leftist movement, the government feels insecure enough to continue its Internal Security Act (ISA). Until recently, Thailand was the scene of various encounters between government troops and a well-equipped leftist guerrilla movement.

A common characteristic of the region is its history of colonial or semi-colonial rule. With the exception of Thailand, all of the ASEAN states underwent a period of direct colonial rule, a process that transformed native societies and incorporated their economies into a world capitalist system. Thailand's signing of the Bowring Treaty in 1855 put it into a situation similar to that of its colonized neighbours *vis-à-vis* the advanced Western nations (Chiengkul, 1983: 30–1). Colonial economic policies were based on the systematic plunder of the natural resources of the subjugated nations. The introduction of Western concepts of property, including private ownership of land, engendered major conflicts and was the cause of countless anti-colonial revolts launched by dispossessed peasants and ethnic groups. In the massive transfer of wealth generated by natural resources from the colony to the colonial power, nationalist élites also saw a justification for the launching of nation-wide anti-colonial movements, which eventually gained independence for their peoples. However, foreign exploitation of national resources did not end with the demise of direct colonialism. The Philippines was forced to accept the 'parity' agreement, by which American nationals were granted the right to exploit natural resources with as much ease as Filipinos. Malaya's tin, rubber, and oil-palm plantations continued to be controlled by the British long after the country attained independence. Under Sukarno, Indonesia tried to reverse the pattern by confiscating Dutch estates, but when he was toppled in 1966, his successor, Suharto, opened the economy to foreign participation and influence (Palmer, 1978: 82–3). Thailand became increasingly dependent on the United States for loans and investments. In short, the ending of colonialism did not result in the untying of the economies of the ASEAN region to the needs of the advanced industrial capitalist states.

The issue of conflict over natural resources must be situated in the political, social, and cultural contexts of the countries in which they occur, in this case the ASEAN states. The region as a whole will be examined in this chapter, but the emphasis will be on the Philippines.

The Plunder of Forest Resources

It has been estimated that nearly two-thirds of the world's tropical rain forests are to be found in South-East Asia, mostly in the Philippines, Sumatra, and Borneo. The Philippines, Indonesia, and Malaysia account for approximately 66 per cent of world-wide exports of hardwood; other tropical countries provide 16 per cent, and the remainder comes from temperate countries (*Asia Magazine*, 1984: 16).

Rapid depletion of Philippine forest resources began during the Spanish colonial period. The island of Cebu was completely stripped of its large hardwood trees to provide lumber to build the Spanish galleons plying the Manila–Acapulco trade route of the seventeenth and eighteenth centuries. American colonialists further developed forest extraction and engaged in the wanton exportation of logs to the home country. After the Second World War, a logging boom erupted in Mindanao, particularly in the north-eastern and southern parts of the island. Foreign companies, especially American multinationals, pioneered these ventures. Corporations such as Weyerhauser, Georgia–Pacific, Boise-Cascade, and Findlay Millar were active participants in the exploitation of Mindanao forest resources (Tadem, 1980: 46–7).

Environmental and Economic Implications of Depletion

The major issue on the extractive side is the depletion of the forest cover and the wide-ranging implications of this phenomenon.

Although tropical rain forests cover less than 10 per cent of the earth's surface, half of the world's plant and animal species populations are sheltered by them (*Asia Magazine*, 1984: 16). These forests are massive reservoirs of thousands of yet-undiscovered species.

Philippine forests have rapidly lost their trees. From 1952 to 1977 the rate of depletion of forest reserves was 61 per cent (Tadem, 1980: 47). Due to the half-hearted implementation of conservation laws, the rate of forest destruction exceeds reforestation by a margin of nine to one. In 1981 a series of floods brought about by constant heavy rains in north-eastern Mindanao left 283 people dead, 14,000 injured, and thousands homeless (*Asia Magazine*, 1984: 16). This part of Mindanao had been the site of the logging boom of the 1950s and 1960s, and its forest area has been virtually denuded.

The pulp and paper mills that accompany the logging industry are notorious sources of pollution from chemically contaminated wastes, which are often simply dumped into the rivers and seas. The chemicals used in the mills also cause air pollution, and fishing villages along coastal areas are adversely affected on both counts. Fish producers in Agusan del Norte have filed a resolution opposing the establishment of the Manila Paper Mills because the resulting pollution of the Agusan River and the Mindanao Sea will damage the livelihood of thousands of fishpond operators and individual fishermen (*Bulletin Today*, 1980). It had been noted that Paper Industries Corporation of the Philippines (PICOP), the country's sole newsprint producer, dumps its waste into Bislig Bay in Surigao del Sur with little or no treatment.

The Philippines was the first of the ASEAN group to be extensively exploited for its forest resources and it will likely lose all its virgin forest designated for production purposes by 1990 at the latest, according to a survey by the United Nations Food and Agriculture Organization (FAO). Logging and wood-processing companies are aware of this, and their response has been to shift their attentions to neighbouring Malaysia and Indonesia.

But resources there are also running short. A 1977 national forest inventory ordered by the federal government in Kuala Lumpur reported that 'the country's timber resources will be depleted in about twelve years unless reforestation measures are carried out urgently' (Rowley, 1977: 47). Sabah, which accounts for 46 per cent of Malaysia's total log production and exports 80 per cent of its production, is expected to log its virgin forests

within a period of ten years if current rates of felling are maintained. Peninsular Malaysia, which had drastically cut its log
exports to only 2 per cent of production in 1979, has begun to
court log imports and may have to compete with Japan for
Sabah's logs (Gigot, 1979a: 52–3). Of Peninsular Malaysia's total
land area of 35.2 million acres, only 17 million (48 per cent) are
still covered with some form of forest, according to the Penang-
based environmental group, Sahabat Alam Malaysia (SAM).

Despite the establishment of reforestation programmes by the
Kuala Lumpur government, log production declined by only
3 per cent overall in 1980, and this was due almost entirely to the
17.8 per cent decline in Sabah (SAM, 1981: 2). Timber output in
Peninsular Malaysia declined by only 1.1 per cent, while in
Sarawak timber production rose by 15.1 per cent. In March 1981,
the Ministry of Primary Industries announced a government plan

TABLE 2.1

Indonesian Timber Output, 1970–1977

Product Type and Year	Production ('ooo cu. m)	Export Volume ('ooo cu. m)	Export Value (US$'ooo)
Logs			
1970	10 899	7 350	100,568
1971	13 706	10 761	168,635
1972	17 717	13 891	230,849
1973	26 197	19 433	583,345
1974	23 380	18 082	725,651
1975	16 296	13 921	499,976
1976	22 741	18 549	780,879
1977 (January–June)	n.a.	9 500	450,000
Sawn Timber			
1970	568	46.6	1,691
1971	470	80.6	2,804
1972	840	132.2	3,754
1973	1 380	337.9	18,226
1974	1 919	353.9	26,534
1975	1 708	410.4	31,695
1976	1 900	643.9	49,053
1977[1]	n.a.	713.0	29,500

Source: *Far Eastern Economic Review*, 2 December 1977, p. 66.
[1]Projection.
n.a. = not available.

to reduce the tree-felling rate from 922,000 acres per year to 385,000 by 1985 (SAM, 1981: 2). The Ministry planned to re-plant, in Peninsular Malaysia, 65,000 acres by 1985 and a total of 500,000 acres from 1985 to 2000. This programme is considered insignificant in the face of a national logging rate of almost 1 million acres per year.

Indonesia's forests contribute its second highest export earnings, after oil. Overseas sales in 1976 totalled US$830 million. The country has approximately 120 million ha of tropical rain forest, 47 million ha of which is production forest. However, excesses, such as rampant illegal logging, have endangered this vast re-source. Logging companies cut indiscriminately in many areas, and in the process they cut down trees of only 40 to 45 cm, in violation of the legal minimum of 50 cm, at times with the tacit approval of forestry officials (Jenkins, 1977: 66). Thus, in many areas 'the whole forest canopy is being or has been destroyed'. The irresponsibility of companies working their concessions, coupled with overharvesting, will soon cause irreversible damage to East Kalimantan's forests.

Widespread logging in Indonesia's outer islands did not occur until the late 1960s, when the new Suharto government adopted an open-door policy towards foreign investors. Timber exports rose 1,500 per cent from 1966 to 1971, and one-third of foreign capital inflow was to logging through US, Japanese, and Filipino companies (Grossman and Siegel, 1977: 2–3). Indonesia was widely advertised as the alternative to the Philippines for an unrestricted supply of timber for export. A total of 5.6 mil-lion ha were offered to investors for exploitation. Weyerhauser, which has closed its operations in Mindanao, quickly moved into Indonesia and occupied a one million acre concession, which it plans to thoroughly deplete by 1990, the year its contract expires (Grossman and Siegel, 1977: 7–8).

Effects of Logging on Agriculture

Logging operations inevitably come into conflict with traditional upland farmers, many of whom belong to non-majority ethnic groups. Relying on slash-and-burn agricultural systems, these hillside farmers depend on their age-old farming practices for survival. Despite the propensity of officials to place equal blame on them for the loss of forest lands, it is an incontrovertible fact that many generations of swidden farming cannot equal the de-

TABLE 2.2
Foreign Investments in Indonesia's Forests, 1970

Nationality of Control	Amount Invested (US$ million)	Number of Firms Counted in Previous Column	Area of Concessions (million ha)	Number of Firms Counted in Previous Column	Total Number of Firms
United States	62.0[1]	6	2.726	9	9
Japan	70.0	9	2.464	8	12
Philippines	256.0	9	1.647	9	9
Philippines-US	238.0	2	1.2	1	2
Malaysia	15.5	14	1.92	14	14
Hong Kong	13.5	4	0.50	4	4
British-controlled	2.0	2	?	—	2
South Korea	53.0	2	0.49	2	2
France	2.5	3	0.37	4	4
Panama	1.5	1	0.10	1	1
Netherlands	1.1	1	?	—	1

Sources: *Indonesian Observer*, 7 March 1969; 'Loggers Locked in a Scramble', *Philippine Lumberman*, Vol. 15, No. 10, 1969, pp. 22–4; 'Indonesia: Forest Paradise for Foreign Capital', *Pacific Basin Report*, December 1970; 'List of Foreign Companies Investing in Indonesia', *Indonesian Perspectives*, September 1970; 'Wilds of Borneo Lure U.S. Lumbermen', *Business Week*, 27 June 1970, p. 51.
[1] The *Japan Lumber Journal* ('Indonesian Forest Development', Vol. 11, No. 4, 1970, pp. 2–4) gives a figure for US investments of US$88 million.

struction wrought by logging corporations in only a dozen or so years.

Thus, tribal groups are being squeezed out of their ancestral lands and deprived of their means of livelihood in the name of development. The Manobos of eastern Mindanao have been pushed out of the lowlands and into the forests by settlers, agricultural companies, and ranchers. Now in their last area of retreat, they are still being hounded out of existence. Farmers in one part of East Kalimantan have been ordered not to grow rice to force them to rely on work in the logging concessions (Grossman and Siegel, 1977: 7–8). In South Kalimantan, natives were ordered to desist from continuing with their traditional methods of farming or felling trees to build homes; otherwise, they risked being accused as thieves.

Long-term effects of indiscriminate logging on the soil have also been documented. Abundant tree cover reduces the speed at which rains hit the ground. Without forests, the force of rains strips off the topsoil in which the necessary nutrients that sustain plant life abound (SAM, 1981: 25). What remains is a barren piece of ground with as much potential to support plants as a desert. Siltation of rivers also takes place, blocking water passageways. The 1981 floods in north-eastern Mindanao were caused by heavy rains spilling off barren mountains into the Agusan River. As the river's outlet was blocked by large silt deposits, the flood-waves simply went back upstream, submerging homes and fields to a depth of about 7 metres (*Asia Magazine*, 1984: 17).

Communities bordering areas where logging concessions operate are often victims of the negative effects of company operations. Many of them have occupied these areas for generations prior to the entry of the loggers. On the other hand, communities built around the timber operations, where logging workers and their families live, are nothing more than temporary camps whose existence depends on the continued supply of timber. Once the resource is exhausted, these communities are abandoned. Many families continually experience this uprooting and dislocation as they follow the companies for the work they provide.

Reforestation sometimes takes the form of encouraging the development of 'industrial tree farming'. Farmers growing food crops are being urged to grow *falcatta*, giant *ipil-ipil*, rubber, and other fast-growing but mainly softwood trees instead, to supply the large timber processing plants being built by both foreign and local investors, usually in partnership with the government. In Mindanao, hundreds of thousands of hectares of land have been reserved for tree farms. Corporations not wanting to deal with small farms have undertaken the cultivation of softwood trees for their own pulp and paper mills.

Tree farms are cropping up in the north-eastern Mindanao provinces of Agusan del Norte and Agusan del Sur and in the southern Mindanao province of Davao del Norte. Various conflicts have emerged. Applications by two large companies, Manila Paper Mills (MPMI) and the Aguinaldo Development Corporation (ADECOR), for the lease of tens of thousands of hectares have already been approved, with thousands of hectares more to be added later. Settler farming communities will most likely be evicted from their lands as a result. The companies are trying to entice farmers into giving up their claims by offering them jobs on the tree plantations or in the pulp and paper plants. The settlers are resisting, however, and are working against the clock to have their claims titled at the Bureau of Lands. The process is time-consuming as well as financially draining, and both money and time are in short supply for the farmers.

PICOP has been the most aggressive in contracting small-scale farmers to grow *falcatta* with loans available through funds provided by the World Bank and channelled through the Development Bank of the Philippines (DBP) (Tadem, 1980: 48–9). But farmers cannot go full-time into tree farming, as it takes seven years before any income can be earned. Also, the terms of the contract tie the farmers to PICOP, with the company dictating the purchase price. Earlier promises by PICOP of large incomes have turned out to be false, and many farmers have actually incurred losses due to the delays by PICOP in collecting the cut trees. Although the farmers are totally dependent on PICOP, the company does not rely on them completely for supplies of pulp because it operates its own 33 000-ha tree plantation.

The tragic consequences of denudation can be observed in the case of the 24 500-ha watershed of Pantabagan in Nueva Ecija

TABLE 2.3

Industrial Tree Plantations and Tree Farm Agro-forestry Farm Leases by Region in the Philippines, 1980 (area in ha)

Region	Total		Industrial Tree Plantations		Tree Farms		Agro-forestry Farms	
	No.	Area	No.	Area	No.	Area	No.	Area
Philippines	115	47 800	12	87 759	101	9 111	2	930
Region 9	1	324	—	—	1	324	—	—
Region 10	6	49 657	50	48 987	10	670	—	—
Region 11	3	28 843	20	28 103	1	740	—	—
Region 12	1	460	—	—	—	—	1	460
4 Regions	11	79 284	70	77 090	12	1 734	1	460

Source: Philippines, Bureau of Forest Development, *1981 Philippine Forestry Statistics*.

province in Central Luzon (*ARC Newsletter*, 1981: 3). Some 14,000 families were relocated there to make way for the huge Pantabagan Dam, inaugurated in 1976, and the area has been completely denuded. The cause, according to a World Bank study, was excessive logging operations. A number of government-built houses have slid down from the hillside as heavy rains eroded the soft clay under the houses. These farming families crowd the upper slopes of the watershed and try with little success to plant for soil erosion is too swift and extensive. This area is located high above the dam, so they cannot even make use of the irrigation from the project that caused their resettlement and dislocation from lowland homes.

The Social Costs of the Wood Industry

Conditions in both logging areas and wood-processing plants leave much to be desired. Wages are low, legally stipulated benefits are often withheld, and housing facilities are inadequate. In this situation, labour–management conflicts often arise, with workers demanding a greater share of the profits reaped by the corporations.

In 1979 the US-owned Findlay Millar Timber experienced a year-long strike by its 1,000 workers, who were demanding the three months' wages withheld from them by the company (Reyes, 1984). This confrontation between wood-industry workers and the corporation was bitter, with management resorting to standard tactics of harassment and deception to force the workers back to work. Other major strikes in Mindanao-based wood companies were at Zamboanga Wood Products—40 per cent of which was then owned by Boise-Cascade—and at Sta. Clara Lumber in Davao. These conflicts rarely end favourably for the workers, because their unions are short on funds and some labour leaders sell out to management.

If the workers insist on carrying on their fight for higher wages and better working and living conditions, the company can always close down its operations and move to other places. Such decisions are also influenced by the fact that with the rapid depletion of forests, companies would have to move on anyway. When this happens, the workers are the hardest hit. Not having benefited from the logging booms of the 1950s and barely able to eke out a marginal existence in the succeeding decades of logging declines, workers have been left to fend for themselves. The first casualties of the death of any industry are the workers and their families, just as they are always the last to taste the benefits of any upturn.

Conflicts between Producers and Consumers

On the international level, there is conflict between the producing countries and the consumers, the latter comprising countries from the developed world. Most of the vital information regarding the world wood market is in the hands of the consumers, and producers have little influence in shaping consumers' demands (Khan, 1984: 4). Asian lumber, for example, is a buyer's market, with Japan exercising a dominant role. Market-access problems increase with the degree of processing. The European Economic Community (EEC) charges 13 per cent tariffs on imports from South-East Asia; the United States excludes from its Generalized System of Preferences (GSP) the most important species of South-East Asia, the *dipterocarps*; and Japan totally excludes timber from its GSP (Khan, 1984: 4). Log exports, on the other hand, usually enter duty-free.

One aspect of the problem is the low storage prospect of timber because of its susceptibility to fungal and insect attacks. Retention of trees is deemed impractical because of the need to respond effectively and promptly to market changes, and the long distances between the producers and the market (Khan, 1984: 4). High transport costs also cut export earnings.

Japan has come under fire from timber-producing countries in the Asia–Pacific region for 'plundering resources without replacing them and without regard for the impact on local economies'; entering into agreements with 'comprador concessionaires who [have] little loyalty to the producing countries'; and 'undermining the independence of these countries through ... economic imperialism' (Awanohara, 1979: 88).

Japan has also been criticized for perpetuating the primary level of production in wood-exporting countries and failing to accommodate the 'desire to add increasing amounts of processing; and hence, value, to their products before exporting them' (Awanohara, 1979: 88). Only after incessant and impatient demands from the producing countries was some positive response from the Japanese forthcoming; even then, movement has been slow. From the point of view of Japan's own timber-processing industry, the development of local processing in South-East Asia, for example, does not make sense. Japan's own industry is large and labour-intensive, and thus carries some electoral clout. It is also protected by tariff barriers that 'encourage imports of unprocessed timber but [put] a damper on value-added imports' (Awanohara, 1979: 88). According to Awanohara, the Japanese government charges the following import duties on wood:

Unprocessed logs = 0 per cent
Sawn timber = 5 per cent within GSP quota and 10 per cent for remainder
Veneer = 7.5 per cent within GSP quota and 15 per cent for remainder
Plywood = 20 per cent.

Such barriers to trade only increase the distrust of developing countries towards the First World, a feeling carried over from the colonial past in which an international economic order highly favourable to the developed world was fashioned and has largely continued to the present. However, the Third World is becoming more aware of how to deal with a system that works against its interests. Since the 1970s, calls for a new international economic order have been growing louder, and the developed world has been forced to listen and respond. The successes of the Organization of Petroleum Exporting Countries (OPEC) and the UN Convention on the Law of the Sea (UNCLOS) have inspired others.

Like other producers of essential commodities exported mainly to First World countries, timber producers have attempted to restructure the international wood market. Private log producers in Malaysia, Indonesia, the Philippines, and Papua New Guinea banded together to form the Council of Southeast Asian Lumber Producers Association (SEALPA) in 1974. The group has reached specific agreements on limiting log exports in order to stabilize prices and, for the longer term, '[has] agreed to minimize log exports and maximize the export of finished wood products' (Rowley, 1977: 47). The more ambitious plan, however, is to ultimately regulate world prices and protect the earnings of the producing countries. SEALPA's supply–demand scenario for timber projected a growth in demand far exceeding the supply for a three-year period from 1978 to 1980 (*Asia Yearbook*, 1980: 91–3). This was calculated to encourage the importation by Japan of processed wood products. From 1975 the proportion of logs in

TABLE 2.4

Supply/Demand Scenario for South Sea Logs, 1978–1980 (million cu. m)

	1978	1979	1980
Demand			
Japan	21.8	22.0	21.0
South Korea	6.9	7.2	7.5
Taiwan	7.0	7.3	7.7
Singapore	1.7	0.9	0.7
Others	1.0	0.9	0.7
	38.4	38.3	37.6
Supply			
Indonesia	18.9	18.0	16.5
Sabah	12.4	10.0	8.0
Sarawak	4.2	4.5	5.0
Philippines	1.9	0.8	0.5
Others	0.4	0.5	0.5
	37.8	33.8	30.5

Source: Southeast Asian Lumber Producers Association (SEALPA), as reproduced in *Asia Yearbook*, 1980.

total wood imports had fallen at the rate of 1 per cent per year to 64 per cent in 1979.

Japan's reaction to the formation of SEALPA was typical of the attitude of developed countries to calls for a new international economic order. In 1975, SEALPA decided to control the export and production of logs for that year to forestall an expected slump in log prices (Sta. Romana, 1979: 88–90). Confidently holding a five-month stockpile of logs and lumber, Japan unilaterally slashed the buying prices of logs and lumber 'to break up any wood and forest product cartel in the region' (Sta. Romana, 1979: 87). It limited its purchases to low-grade logs from Indonesia, the Philippines, and Malaysia and cut the prices of Philippine logs from US$35/cu. m to only US$25/cu. m, reportedly US$7 below production costs. Although a week after the cut-back the Japan External Trade Organization (JETRO) announced an acceptance of SEALPA's decision, imports were still to be lower in 1975.

Since then, SEALPA has been registering its impact more as a forum than as a cartel. A more effective group has been Komasi,

TABLE 2.5

South-East Asian Log Production and Exports, 1979

Country	Log Production (million cu. m)	Percentage of Log Production Exported	Log Exports as Percentage of Total Exports
Peninsular Malaysia	10.2	2	9
Sabah	11.1	90	52
Philippines	6–7	23	—
Indonesia	31.8[1]	59	—

Source: Far Eastern Economic Review, 7 December 1979.
[1]Figure is a goal. Total 1978 log production was 26 million cu. m, of which almost 70 per cent was exported.

comprising plywood producers from Malaysia, South Korea, and Singapore, which has succeeded in setting a minimum world price for plywood made from tropical logs (Gigot, 1979b: 53).

An international cartel was in the making in 1979 when a member of the International Islamic Fund approached a major supplier of sawmilling equipment in Singapore (Gigot, 1979b: 53). Claiming to represent a range of Islamic interests, this Singaporean businessman broached the idea of setting up a huge timber-processing complex on the Batam Islands and other islands in the Riau group in Indonesia. To ensure initial supplies, loggers from Sumatra would be brought in. Processed timber would be sold and released at the best possible prices. Malta would provide alternative storage for the timber. Later, loggers in Sabah, Sarawak, the southern Philippines, and Kalimantan would be invited to join in, and log exports to Japan, South Korea, and Taiwan would be stopped altogether. All of these areas have substantial Islamic populations; therefore prospects for co-operation are enhanced. Although there is no clear connection with this plan, Kuwaiti investors had that same year bought into a 300,000-acre concession in Sabah, a Saudi group was negotiating for another concession, and a Saudi prince bought interests in Philippine sawmills.

An international wood cartel is not as easy to set up as one for oil (Gigot, 1979b: 53). Most South-East Asian exporters are private entrepreneurs, so unpleasant government intervention is needed to enforce the decisions of the cartel. In addition to storage problems, timber has not been relatively underpriced as long as oil had been. Substitutes also abound for tropical timber, such as softwoods from temperature countries.

The Transformation of a Natural Resource: From Agriculture to Agribusiness

The distinction between forestry and agriculture is sometimes a fine one. Shifting cultivators often follow in the wake of commercial loggers, and because of the marginal character of the logged-over land, farming becomes a tedious and unproductive undertaking. In 1974, the Philippine government attempted to turn denuded forest lands into rice-growing areas by requiring logging concessionaires 'to develop areas within their concessions ... for the production of rice, corn, and other basic staples to take care of the consumption requirements of their workers and the people within their areas' (Tadem, 1978). This law, which was known as Presidential Decree No. 472, was never really implemented because it also granted exemptions to firms in 'financial distress'.

When the Philippines became a rice-exporting country in 1977, it appeared on the surface that Marcos' agricultural policies were working after all. In the midst of the euphoria surrounding the dramatic turnabout, official propaganda conveniently disregarded the costs that accompanied the statistics of increased production. As public awareness gradually grew about the reality—that the economic and social costs far outweighed the benefits of the rice exports—a severe economic crisis, beginning in 1983, suddenly cast the country back into the familiar role of rice importer. This reversal underscored the fragility of a food-production programme that was highly dependent on imports.

Indonesia does not rely on the importation of fertilizers for its rice industry because it is an oil exporter, and the major fertilizers used are oil-based. Yet, until 1986, the country was one of the world's major rice importers. For fiscal year 1983–4, imports were estimated to reach 900 000 tonnes, a 172 per cent increase over the 1982–3 level. Indonesia's rice imports reached the stage at which they affected the world market prices for the commodity. This situation existed for a long time despite the fact that 51 per cent of food-crop land was devoted to paddy fields and yearly growth stood at 4.8 per cent (Sajogyo, 1982: 48).

Thailand's case is different. Traditionally a rice exporter, the

TABLE 2.6
Production of Agricultural Commodities in ASEAN Countries, Various Years ('000 tonnes)

Country	1969–1971	1977	1978	1979
Indonesia				
Coffee	173	198	223	267
Tea	65	85	89	93
Sugar	10 322	14 709	14 880	15 995
Rubber	838	835	900	851
Jute	1 189	1 288	1 497	1 445
Rice	19 136	23 356	25 781	26 350
Palm-oil	218	525	610	640
Philippines				
Coffee	48	82	105	122
Sugar	16 271	23 126	20 273	20 348
Banana	893	2 125	2 390	2 430
Pineapple	251	427	465	480
Rice	5 225	6 895	7 318	7 000
Malaysia				
Cocoa beans	4	19	24	26
Rubber	1 285	1 613	1 607	1 617
Rice	1 696	1 922	1 527	2 161
Palm-oil	457	1 778	2 184	2 600
Thailand				
Sugar	5 856	23 658	20 561	20 000
Banana	1 200	1 700	2 000	2 082
Pineapple	187	1 250	2 000	2 000
Rice	13 475	13 921	17 530	15 640

Source: *FAO Monthly Bulletin of Statistics*, various issues.

country has long been considered a yardstick for determining the quality of rice traded in the world market by other countries. The government relies heavily on foreign exchange from rice exports to support a basically agrarian and primary-product economy. The three years from 1982 to 1985, however, brought the rice industry to a critical point. World market prices had been deteriorating: from a peak of US$500/ton in mid-1981, the price had fallen to as low as US$220/ton by January 1985, a 56 per cent decline (Sricharatchanya, 1985: 48).

Meanwhile, in the Philippines and Thailand and, to a lesser extent, Indonesia, agribusiness and commercial farming have been growing. This is related to the modernization drive in agriculture in which various actors, both local and foreign, are playing neatly assigned parts. Changes in the social, economic, cultural, and political spheres are also taking place. As is inevitable, the introduction of new methods of production, new philosophies of growth, and new means of surplus generation have engendered conflicts on various levels. The competition for land, for access to its product, and for shares of the surplus lie at the roots of conflicts arising in the agricultural sector. The issues are seldom clear, particularly when judgements have to be made regarding the effects of new methods. For example, it is still widely believed that the dislocation of thousands of small farmers to make way for massive hydroelectric projects is justified. The assumption is that the immediate disruption of the productive lives of peasants is only temporary and that in the long run, everyone will benefit from electricity. Narrow-minded as this perception may be, it is enough to convince other sectors of the population not directly affected by these projects that sacrifices such as the dislocation of communities must be accepted. Even the affected peoples are made to go along with the scheme through a combination of persuasion, coercion, and intimidation.

The various conflicts that now characterize the competition for land can be traced to the breakdown of subsistence farming in favour of commercialized production, or in some cases, the subsumption of the former to the latter. Subsistence production has its own contradictions, but since this type of agriculture is no longer the dominant mode in the underdeveloped areas in South-East Asia, it is more relevant to examine instead the widespread 'commoditization' that has become the characteristic trend.

The Modern Agricultural Context: Agribusiness

A pervasive characteristic of rural South-East Asia is the inequality in the distribution of land. In Java, 55 per cent of 4.6 million farming families own only 22 per cent of the land while 4 per cent or approximately 400,000 families control 24 per cent (Sajogyo, 1982). Sixty per cent of Javanese households have an average of only 0.2 ha. Tenancy rates in Thailand's Central Plains were as high as 40 per cent as of the late 1970s and continue to be so in the

1980s. Farmers engaged in commercial crop production are often in debt, and failure to repay on time can mean loss of their lands. In the Philippines, rural poverty has continuously risen, with almost 80 per cent of rural families falling below the poverty line in the late 1980s. Landlessness has also increased, and dispossessed workers presently form the majority of the Philippine rural labour force.

A relatively recent phenomenon is the development of large plantations by multinational corporations, the state, or local capitalists for the cultivation or processing of export crops. In the Philippines, multinationals such as Del Monte, Dole, and United Brands pioneered and controlled the banana export industry in Mindanao. Dole joined Del Monte in the production and processing of pineapple for export. Dole also expanded its pineapple operations into Thailand. Transnational agribusiness has exacerbated the conflict between the production of food crops and export crops. Officially welcomed by host governments, this type of agriculture represents a higher level of foreign and local exploitation of resources with minimal benefits for the poor sectors of society.

Agricultural modernization and increasing commercialization have not necessarily meant social progress and economic prosperity. Agribusiness expansion often results in the physical eviction of the actual cultivators. Food-producing communities have been displaced by the development of the banana and pineapple export industries in Mindanao. A Philippine corporate farming programme launched in 1974 also resulted in displacement. In the early 1980s, the Philippine government joined with local entrepreneurs and Malaysian transnationals to introduce large-scale palm-oil production in eastern Mindanao. Several thousand settler-farming households were displaced to make way for Guthrie's 8 000-ha plantation. As late as 1976, the 50-year-old Del Monte subsidiary, Philippine Packing Corporation, forcibly ejected 371 farmers in the Pontian Plains in Bukidnon province by ploughing through five barrios (PPI, 1983: 1). In 1980, on the 13 000-ha Hacienda San Antonio-Sta. Isabel in Ilagan, Isabela, 300,000 people were threatened with eviction by a large corporation owned by businessman Eduardo Cojuangco, a Marcos crony (PPI, 1983: 1). Anca Corporation wanted to transform the newly purchased hacienda into an agribusiness plantation growing coconut and *ipil-ipil* pulp trees.

The shift from food crops to export crops raises the issue of priorities for agricultural production. Given severe problems of malnutrition among the majority of the population, it would have been more beneficial if emphasis had been placed on food production for domestic consumption rather than on exports. Ironically, ASEAN countries are also food importers. Philippine and Indonesian wheat imports from the United States under Public Law 480 constitute a drain on local resources. Although PL 480 allows importing countries to pay in their local currency, the process has the overall effect of creating a need for a product that previously was not in the local diet. Even during the years of rice exportation, poor Filipino farmers subsisted on meagre diets that were often nutritionally inadequate.

Agribusiness versus Land Reform

Agribusiness development brings about conflict between itself and land reform and equity-oriented rural programmes. Large-scale plantations necessarily involve the concentration of land in the hands of a few individuals and corporations. In the Philippines, a land reform programme initiated upon the declaration of martial law in 1972 has been proceeding slowly. Covering only 33 per cent of tenanted lands and 6.8 per cent of total crop area, the Operation Land Transfer (OLT) programme had, as of 1983, benefited only 9 per cent of its targeted number of farms (MAR, 1983). In Indonesia, since the Suharto coup, the land reform programme has been frozen, and those clamouring for its implementation are invariably said to be communist-inspired.

A successful land reform programme is a necessity in a country where feudal and semi-feudal relations of production persist. These relations are sources of serious social conflict. Agrarian movements in South-East Asia, and in other areas where similar conditions prevail, revolve around issues of oppressive pre-capitalist land tenure arrangements such as share-cropping, exorbitant land rent, and usury. Although agribusiness sometimes does away with the old mode of production, it often replaces it with more exploitative structures. In many cases, agribusiness exists alongside old subsistence or feudal modes, the reason being that companies can keep the cost of production low by making the producer directly responsible for reproducing its labour power. Thus labour reproduction does not enter into the determination of plantation wages, which can then be maintained at levels lower than subsistence. This can be observed in both the Philippine and Thai experiences. Wages of Filipino sugar workers are often below subsistence, and if relied on solely, cannot sustain a worker's existence. But since field-work is seasonal, the worker can return to his home (frequently an outlying island) and engage in subsistence or share-cropping cultivation.

Even if plantations are able to completely transform tenants into full-time agricultural workers who depend wholly on their wages, conflicts still arise. Workers discover that their living conditions are no better and are sometimes worse. The highest yearly income of a Filipino plantation worker in 1983 (as legislated by a presidential wage order) would amount to ₱8,600. If two family members are working (and this is rare), the total income would still fall below the estimated minimum subsistence income of approximately ₱20,036 a year required for a rural family (Almazan and Ibanez, 1984). Unlike tenants, plantation workers have no alternative sources of food and income. To add to the gravity of the situation, few plantations pay the minimum legislated wage to their workers. Corporations can easily apply for and secure exemptions from the minimum-wage rule by pleading insolvency or a distressed situation. Another way by which companies circumvent the law is to hire non-permanent contractual or probationary workers and renew their contracts every few months.

Agribusiness and the National Economies

Agribusiness also leads to a monopolistic type of capitalism. Huge capital resources and extensive international marketing contacts are needed for a successful operation. Only the largest corporations, often multinationals, have access to or control over such resources. Conflicts arise between these huge monopolies or oligopolies and the aspirations of local entrepreneurs for a greater share of production and the market. Often local competitors are pushed out after being driven to bankruptcy. Those who manage to survive inevitably enter into joint-venture arrangements with the foreign firms and end up as junior partners. The dominance of multinational agribusiness over certain types of agricultural products in underdeveloped countries serves as a hindrance to the full development of local industries under the control of national capitalists. Indigenous development and nationally oriented growth do not take place at all.

In some instances, however, the transfer of control from foreign to local firms results in the substitution of native, often state-controlled, companies for foreign monopolies. In the Philippines, marketing monopolies in the sugar and coconut industries were established with the aid of government decrees. Ostensibly the monopolies are private firms, and private individuals sit as board directors. However, the presence of government officials and the fact that marketing control was achieved only through state intervention makes government denials ring hollow. Public outcry against this anomalous arrangement, the disenchantment of a significant section of local entrepreneurs left out of the lucrative market, and demands by no less than the International Monetary Fund and the World Bank for the dismantling of the monopolies led to certain steps being taken by the Marcos government to accommodate other local businessmen. The individuals who controlled both the sugar and coconut industries were leading Marcos cronies. However, it remains to be seen whether these arrangements can be overturned under the Aquino government.

Even as agribusiness firms and state monopolies are developing highly integrated and large-scale agricultural systems, with deleterious effects on society and the national economy, small-scale farming (especially of rice and maize) has had to cope with the technological changes brought about by the Green Revolution that began in the 1960s (Feder, 1983). Green Revolution technology involves the extensive use of high-yielding varieties of seedlings (HYVs), massive inputs of fertilizers and chemical pesticides, a degree of mechanization, and, in some cases, supervised credit.

Although the new technology may have increased crop production, this has been achieved at the cost of damaging the natural ecosystem of paddy fields. Rivers and farm animals are poisoned and extra sources of food (fish and snails) are lost to the farmers (Fegan, 1982). The import-dependent character of the new system poses even greater problems and conflicts. Studies in the Philippines have shown that the tremendous increase in the costs of production due to the expensive inputs have exceeded crop-yield increases by a margin of five to one. In the Philippines, the prices of fertilizers and pesticides increased by more than 100 per cent in 1983–4 alone. Farmers in Central Luzon cut down on fertilizer use or planted less to minimize costs. The result was a decline in rice production and the government had to begin importing rice.

Government support prices for rice farmers have been inadequate to meet rising costs in Thailand as well. In 1985 Thai farmers were demanding a paddy price of B3,500 a *kwien* (ton), which is B500 more than the national average farmgate price. Declining paddy prices in the Thai central plains have forced farmers into greater indebtedness running into tens of thousands of baht each (Sricharatchanya, 1985: 49). The government's dilemma is that it must maintain low farmgate prices for rice in order to subsidize the urban consumer. Instead of taking steps to lower the costs of farm production as an alternative to raising rice prices, governments are apparently locked into the narrow perception that the only factors subject to state intervention are the farm support price and the retail price of rice. Thus the consumer is pitted against the farmer, and both groups are protesting. Farmers' groups are asking why the fertilizer and pesticide companies (mostly multinationals) are not being made to bear some of the costs. Besides, the farmers argue, they are consumers, too.

The Political Consequences

The conflict between agribusiness interests and farmers in the Philippines was brought to a climax when some 5,000 farmers belonging to the Alliance of Central Luzon Farmers (AMGL) staged protest marches in several provinces on 4–5 February 1985, ending at the Ministry of Agriculture office in Metro Manila. The peasants were joined by hundreds of supporters from the student, worker, urban poor, and professional sectors in a camp-in demonstration in front of the ministry. The AMGL presented the following demands:

1. A drop in fertilizer and pesticide prices to the 1 October 1983 level;

2. A new small-farmer credit scheme in which interest rates do not exceed 12 per cent per year;

3. A write-off of all small-farmer debts incurred in the government Masagana 99 programme.

4. Strengthening of the *palay* (paddy) support price without increasing the price of rice;

5. Lowered gasoline and electricity costs in order to minimize irrigation fees; and

6. Establishment of a nationalistic agro-industrialization programme and implementation of genuine land reform (AMGL, 1985).

A series of dialogues between peasant leaders and the Agriculture Minister during the demonstration ended in a stalemate as officials contended they were powerless to act on the demands and that only the President could help the peasants. The peasants then demanded to meet with Marcos himself, but before this confrontation could be arranged, government troops moved in and violently dispersed the peasants in the early morning hours of 13 February 1985. The farmers and their supporters were chased 3 km to the nearby campus of the University of the Philippines, where they were sheltered by students and the Catholic Church. Though none of their demands were granted, the farmers had made their point and had been heard.

A resurgence of peasant unrest is also brewing in Thailand. Deteriorating conditions for the Thai peasantry set the backdrop for a three-day demonstration by 3,000 farmers joined by members of the opposition Chart Thai Party in front of Government House on 8–10 January 1985 (Sricharatchanya, 1985: 49). The peasants came mostly from the central and upper central plain provinces. Prime Minister Prem Tinsulanond averted a major political crisis by paying the demonstrators a predawn visit on 10 January. In this instance, Prem handled the farmers in a better way than his Philippine counterpart; while the Thai farmers remain dissatisfied, an immediate crisis was averted.

These two examples bring up the issue of peasant organizations and their role in the process of rural change. ASEAN governments generally regard independent rural organizing efforts with suspicion and try to set up state-sponsored groups that champion the maintenance of existing conditions. The extreme case is Indonesia, where the government takes an almost paranoid attitude towards peasant organizations formed independent of state supervision (Mortimer, 1975). Suharto's fear is that there will be a revival of the militant Parti Komunis Indonesia-led organizations that disrupted Javanese society during Sukarno's rule with their revolutionary calls for change among the hundreds of thousands of peasants they mobilized. Because of this history and the government's attitude, minimal rural organizing is undertaken in Java and outer islands.

In the Philippines, there has been a long history of peasant organizing dating from the American colonial period (Constantino, 1975). National organizations arose concurrently with the founding of the Communist Party in 1930, with heaviest activity in Central Luzon, a traditional area of agrarian unrest. Despite the proscription of the CPP, these organizations survived, but they were finally made illegal shortly after the Second World War. The final burst of activity was the abortive Huk peasant rebellion from 1946 to 1954, which was violently suppressed and ended a traumatic first phase in radical peasant organizing. In the years that followed, only moderate and church-sponsored peasant groups were active. Radical groups did not re-emerge until 1964, and a split within the CPP in 1967 led to the birth of a new communist party and the NPA. The NPA currently numbers around 10,000–15,000 armed regulars scattered all over the country. Its main aim is to carry out an agrarian revolution in the Philippines with the peasantry as its main force. The major political conflict in the Philippine countryside today is that between the NPA and the Armed Forces of the Philippines. The NPA platform is based on the issues of lowering land rent and eliminating usury and, in the long term, the implementation of a comprehensive land reform programme that will redistribute land to the landless and organize production around co-operatives and collective farms where feasible.

Conflicts over Mineral Resources

The struggles over the world's mineral resources by various countries has often provided impetus for wars, whether of a limited scope or world-wide. Shortages of iron and steel for Germany's industries and the spectre of 4 million workers going jobless are said to have influenced the decision of the Kaiser to participate in the First World War (Eckes, 1979). Japan in the Second World War coveted the rich mineral resources of East and South-East Asia to support an industrial expansion programme.

South-East Asia, particularly the ASEAN countries, holds major reserves of some of the world's most important and strategic minerals (*Balai Asian Journal*, 1981: 14–17). The Philippines is the third largest producer of chromite after South Africa and Zimbabwe; it has the third largest reserves of cobalt after Zaire and New Caledonia; it was the ninth largest producer of copper in 1980; and it is a major producer of nickel and silver. Indonesia has the highest reserves of tin in the world—24 per cent of 10 million tonnes. Malaysia, which ranked fifth in reserves, produced the most tin in 1980—25.36 per cent of the world total. Bauxite deposits are found in both Indonesia and Malaysia; zinc is found in

TABLE 2.7

ASEAN: Mineral Production and Exports, 1976

	ASEAN	Indonesia	Malaysia	Philippines	Singapore	Thailand
Tin Concentrate						
Production[1]	115	23	64	—	—	28
Export Volume[1]	102	13	69[3]	—	—	20
Export Value[2]	692	83	463[3]	—	—	146
Copper Concentrate						
Production[1]	1 158	223	78	857	—	—
Export Volume[1]	1 158	223	78	857	—	—
Export Value[2]	381	86	29	266	—	—
Nickel Concentrate						
Production[1]	29	14[4]	—	15	—	—
Export Volume[1]	21	9[4]	—	12	—	—
Export Value[2]	83	24	—	59	—	—
Iron Ore						
Production[1]	1 196	292	308	571	—	25
Export Volume[1]	883	207	9	667	—	—
Export Value[2]	5.36	0.16	0.2	5	—	—

Sources: Asian Development Bank; Land and Mines Department,
Malaysia; SGV–Utomo, Indonesia; SGV–Na. Thalang & Co.,
Thailand.

[1]Thousand tonnes.

[2]US$ million.

[3]Net export figures, i.e. export of tin concentrates from ore mined
locally only.

[4]Figures estimated on basis of ore production.

both Thailand and the Philippines. Thailand also produces tungsten ore, lead ore, antimony, iron ore, and manganese.

International Disputes

The potential for conflict lies in the relationships between these countries and the world's major industrial powers, which are heavily dependent on the supply of raw or lightly processed minerals to fuel their economies. Data compiled by the Japanese Ministry of International Trade and Industry (MITI) show that Japan's degree of dependence on other countries for key minerals in 1982 was as follows: coal (81.8 per cent), iron ore (98.7 per cent), copper (96.0 per cent), lead (83.9 per cent), zinc (68.5 per cent), tin (98.4 per cent), aluminium (100 per cent), and nickel (100 per cent) (MITI, 1982: 100). Asian countries are the main source of Japan's raw materials, particularly minerals.

In 1974 a major trade crisis arose between the Philippines and Japan (Sta. Romana, 1976: 88–90). In December 1974 the three major buyers of copper concentrates in Japan—Mitsubishi, Nippon, and Mitsui Smelting—announced a 30 per cent cutback on purchases of Philippine copper effective the following month. Japan's dumping of refined copper in the international market reduced foreign demand for the Philippine produce while internal recession resulted in a slump in domestic sales. Since 80 per cent of Philippine copper was sold to Japan at that time, the cutback severely affected the country's trade balance, which showed a larger deficit compared to the previous year. The Philippine government tried to invoke the newly ratified Treaty of Amity, Commerce, and Navigation with Japan in urging Tokyo to withdraw the cutback, but the Tanaka government rejected the proposal and the crisis was extended up to the middle of 1975.

Another aspect of international disputes over minerals is related to the moves towards industrialization made by developing countries, as seen in the plans to set up mineral-processing facilities in their own areas. The Philippines' plans to set up an integrated steel mill have been on the drawing board for many years but have not been implemented because of the lack of co-operation from Japan. Instead, what the Philippines obtained through Kawasaki Steel, a Japanese conglomerate, is the now-infamous iron-ore sintering plant. Thirty-two per cent of the US$250 million copper smelter's equity ended up in the hands of a consortium of Japanese firms, which also constructed the plant from funds provided by the Export–Import Bank of Japan (Tadem, 1983: 107–8). Fifty-eight per cent of the plant's output is committed for export to Japan. In order to repay the loan—at a high 18 per cent interest—refining charges have been set at a level higher than that charged by Japanese plants. Filipino mining companies, which have been ordered by presidential decree to sell a fixed percentage of their production to the smelter, have repeatedly complained about this imposition. Lately, it was discovered that the plant's facilities were faulty, and a few months into production it had to shut down for major repairs.

Another case in point of Japan's exploitation of the Third World's need for technological and financial support and mineral resources is the Asahan aluminium project in North Sumatra, which includes an aluminium refinery and a hydroelectric plant, costing US$1 billion. The second largest Japanese investment in Asia, this project has raised a host of issues touching on national development, resource extraction, social dislocation, and environmental degradation which are discussed more fully in Yoko Kitazawa's chapter in this volume. Fears have also been expressed that the project will only reinforce the dependence of the Indonesian economy on Japan.

Foreign exploitation of the natural resources of Third World countries is also exemplified by the Gunung Bijih copper mine in Irian Jaya (Seigel, 1976). The first mining venture approved by the Suharto government, it is a transnational venture involving US, West German, and Dutch corporations. Freeport Minerals, a Texas-based American firm, is the main beneficiary of the project and was awarded a generous work contract by the Indonesian government, which gives it a virtually free hand in the 38 square mile contract area, in addition to granting a three-year tax holiday.

The mine began operations in February 1973, and during the next 23 months it earned profits amounting to three times Freeport's original equity investment. Because the firm's contract specified that it need not pay dividends until 1 January 1987, the Indonesian government sought a renegotiation of terms in order to cash in on the windfall. The resulting adjustments, however, did not cause any substantial loss for Freeport, even though it agreed to forgo the second and third years of its tax holiday.

Effects of Mining on Local Communities

Large-scale foreign-supported mining operations and their expansion not only affect Third World economies at the national level but would also have an impact on the livelihood of farming communities who are forced out by the companies. A case study of the growth of Atlas Consolidated Mining and Development Corporation in Cebu province in the Philippines shows the gradual takeover by the company of agricultural lands (McAndrew, 1983: 53–5). Atlas is reported to be one of the top five mining firms in the world. In the town of Toledo, where Atlas has its main copper-mining operations, data from the Bureau of Census and Statistics show a marked decrease in the number of farms planting maize (the province's staple food) and the area planted to the crop. In 1960, 5,074 Toledo farms were planting maize over an effective crop area of 12 549 ha. Eleven years later, only 1,570 farms were still operating on an effective crop area of only 2 500 ha. Total maize production also dropped from 149,794 *cavans* (1 *cavan* = 50 kg) in 1960 to 18,715 *cavans* in 1971. In 1960 more than half of Toledo's total population were considered to be farmers, but this dropped to only one-fourth by 1970–1 (McAndrew, 1983: 53–5).

The McAndrew study cited here also revealed that few farm families displaced by Atlas were taken on by the company as employees. Citing a survey by a University of the Philippines team, the study pointed out that only 14.5 per cent of Atlas rank-and-file workers lived in Toledo. Most of the farmers displaced by the mine simply migrated out of the town.

Mining operations often pose grave dangers to the safety of mine workers and surrounding communities. Inadequate safety measures could result in landslips, the bursting of bunds, and other mishaps. In Malaysia, a single landslide in Gunung Ceroh in 1973 killed 30 people, and 29 more died in twelve landslips from September 1974 to November 1976 (CAP, 1978). The gravel-pump method used by more than 55 per cent of Malaysian tin mines is often responsible for accidents resulting in deaths. Malaysian tin mining had its blackest week in March 1981 when 27 people died in three separate landslips within a period of 8 days: in Puchong (19 deaths), Kampar (5 deaths), and Tanjung Tuallang (3 deaths). From 1963 to 1981, there were fifteen major mining disasters in Malaysia, with a total of 157 lives lost.

Environmental hazards are also a by-product of the extraction and processing of minerals. Mining generates a high percentage of waste materials. Only a small portion of pulverized rocks is extracted—e.g. 0.05 per cent of gold and 0.5 per cent of copper. The rest is impounded in tailing ponds and rock dams. Thus, more than 99 per cent of extracted earth and rocks turn to waste or silt. The adverse impact of these wastes on local communities is receiving increasing documentation. For example, in 1980, some 3,000 farmers in La Union province in Northern Luzon filed for damages to an area of farmland comprising some 3 782 ha that had been affected by mine tailings from three mining firms (Danguilan-Vitug, 1980: 19, 23). The farmers asked for ₱1,300 each as compensation for the loss of one year's harvest. A team from the Ministry of Agriculture inspected the damage and estimated the loss caused by the mine tailings at 20 *cavans*/ha/yr. Thus, instead of harvesting 60–80 *cavans*/ha/yr, the farmers produced only 40–60 *cavans*/ha/yr.

In the Ilocos region, also in Northern Luzon, four major rivers are heavily polluted, thus affecting the livelihood of nearly 500,000 farming families (Belena, 1980: 9). The Bureau of Soils has confirmed that mine wastes discharged into these rivers cement soil in irrigated ricelands and thus choke the rice paddies. Moreover, waste from mines, unlike eroded topsoil, renders rice-fields infertile. An *ad hoc* committee on pollution created by the Provincial Regional Office for Development discovered that 75 000 ha of farmland in Pangasinan and La Union provinces are directly affected by pollutants from the mines in Benguet. Nineteen towns in these two provinces receive fine sand, cyanide, and mercury from the mines every year. Rice harvests have dropped between 5 and 40 per cent yearly with the damage in the two provinces estimated at ₱388 million/yr.

Traditional fishing grounds also suffer from pollution from mining. Aquatic life has all but disappeared from the Agno River. In 1980 a team of researchers from Silliman University conducted an underwater study of marine life in and around the tailing discharge area off the coast of Toledo in Cebu (McAndrew, 1983: 60–1). It was discovered that within the vicinity of the pipeline, all the animals found were dead, and the ocean bottom was heavily silted and devoid of benthic organisms. The report stated that 'it is difficult to attribute the death of these animals to factors other than the acute sedimentation of the bottom brought about by the dumping of mine tailings' from the Atlas Consolidated Mining and Development Corporation (McAndrew, 1983). Dr A. S. Alcala, head of the research team, concluded forcefully that 'in the light of recent data on marine pollution by mine tailings dumped directly to the sea, such as those of Atlas ... it is a mistake to consider disposal of copper mining wastes to the sea a safe procedure' and that 'sea disposal of mine tailings is inimical to sea life, especially the benthic forms' (McAndrew, 1983).

The Social Costs of Mining Activities

Mine workers receive relatively low wages in spite of the hard physical work and danger they face. In the Benguet gold mines in Northern Luzon, miners strip to their underwear before they enter or leave the underground mines and are subjected to the radioactive rays of a metal detector. Constant daily exposure to these harmful rays has resulted in various ailments to the miners, including rapid ageing, general malaise, and loss of sexual potency. In 1978, 1,138 Benguet workers resigned for health reasons. Conditions in the mines are appalling, as described in the following report:

Crawling into the mine tunnel is a whole new nightmare. Extending some 60 miles, the labyrinth weaves into the core of the earth from 3,000 to 5,000 feet underground. At that depth, temperatures soar to a blistering 100 degrees Fahrenheit, so hot that miners don nothing but briefs and helmets for work. Like overheated machines, these miners are cooled periodically by dousing from a water hose. The dark and dank tunnels also expose them to dust, grime and toxic gases. Inadequate oxygen is another risk.... The biggest spectre that haunts them, however, is the dreaded cave-in. Blasting rocks to ferret out the ore, miners expose themselves constantly to landslides, falling rocks, and the very real possibility of being buried alive (*Balai Asian Journal*, 1981: 24).

Conditions for the families of miners are just as bad. At Benguet, the 'free housing' means a 'one-room affair, 3 by 7 meters, shared by two families, totalling 10 to 17 persons', and a family of six 'sleeps in an area the size of a dining table, elevated from the floor ... while another family sleeps underneath' (*Balai Asian Journal*, 1981: 24).

The low wages and poor working conditions have precipitated many conflicts between mine workers and mine owners. Perhaps the longest mine workers' strike in South-East Asia occurred at the Atlas copper mines in Cebu (McAndrew, 1983). Started in 1966 with a walk-out by almost the entire work-force, it continued into 1985, with some 800 to 1,000 workers of the original 4,000 still on strike. The workers originally asked for housing allowances, more decent transportation to and from work sites, salary increases, and safety equipment. The conflict dragged on because the company, which was largely owned by foreign nationals and corporations, consistently refused to negotiate with the union and instead invited another union to organize in an effort to break the strike. The company even specially constructed a camp for two companies of Philippine Constabulary (PC) troops to police the strike. Scabs flown in by helicopter continued the work of the strikers. Despite the dispute, Atlas that year (1985) experienced its most profitable season ever, and although reluctant to share this windfall with its workers, it declared a stock dividend of 25 per cent.

Development and Tribal Peoples: Resistance to Displacement

The survival of a large number of tribal peoples in South-East Asia is increasingly being threatened by the development and implementation of large-scale infrastructure projects that are designed to maximize the extraction and utilization of natural resources. On one side of the conflict are ranged the national government and its economic planners, international funding agencies, giant foreign corporations and their local partners, and the military. Against the enormous power wielded by the forces of the establishment stand the relatively small communities of tribal peoples with their 'pre-modern' concepts of property ownership, their simple modes of production and self-sufficient economic systems, and their communal styles of living. They often are fighting a losing battle.

In Belaga, Sarawak, there have been plans for two hydroelectric dams financed by the Federal government to be constructed across the Balui River in Gian Bakun (SCS News, 1984). At a total cost of M$9 billion with a power output of 2 400 MW, and covering an area of 600 sq. km, the project will be the largest in South-East Asia. The power to be generated will be more than enough for Sabah and Sarawak's projected industrial power needs, so it is also proposed that electricity from the project be sold to the Philippines,

Indonesia, and Singapore, as well as Peninsular Malaysia. This would involve the laying of the longest cable in the world—672 km.

For the 10,000–12,000 people living in the area, however, the hydroelectric project can only mean an end to their way of life with no bright prospects for the future. The people comprise the Kayan, Kenyah, Kejaman, Ukit, Penan, and other ethnic groups. They were never informed or consulted about the project, and they are apprehensive about what the dams will do to the rivers that are their chief means of communication and transport. The rivers have already been polluted by the activities of logging companies, which have refused to pay compensation for the damages.

In Northern Luzon, in the Kalinga–Apayao and Mountain provinces, tribal hill peoples are struggling against the incursions of giant dam projects that will mean their extinction as a people (Carino, 1980). The Chico River is the longest and most elaborate river system in the Cordillera mountain ranges in Northern Luzon. Four dams, with a total capacity of 1 010 MW, are to be built with funds from the World Bank. Officially named the Chico River Basin Development Project (CRBDP), it would cover an area of 1 400 sq. km. Total affected population is estimated at 100,000 in six towns in Mountain Province and four towns in Kalinga–Apayao. These people belong to the Kalinga and Bontoc tribal groups. The lands in question are the ancestral properties of the communities and are considered sacred.

Chico IV alone would uproot more than 5,000 Kalingas from their ancestral villages, destroy 1,200 stone-walled rice terraces, and ruin 500 ha of valuable fruit trees. Traditionally involved in tribal wars among themselves, the people saw the need to unite in order to safeguard their homes, families, and heritage. Thus in 1975 began the struggle of the Kalinga and Bontoc peoples against the Chico dam project. The local movement became a national symbol of protest against similar projects in other regions of the country and an international issue that drew the attention of people all over the world facing similar problems. The area was heavily militarized as the tribes prepared to resist the dam at all costs. Inevitably, the NPA began gathering support and was able to win over many of the tribal residents. The government tried to gain the support of tribal leaders through bribery, intimidation, and force, but the Kalingas and Bontocs persisted. Finally, the government relented under local and international pressure and the World Bank itself decided to postpone the dam project. In the meantime, more than 100 people had died.

While attention was being showered on the Chico dam, the government was quietly building an even bigger project farther north in Kalinga–Apayao (*Ibon Facts and Figures*, 1979). Known as the Apayao–Abulug River Hydro-Electric Development Project, it was projected to cost about ₱5.2 billion to construct and will inundate 9 400 ha where some 18,000 members of the Isneg tribal group live in the town of Kabugao. It appears the National Power Corporation (NPC) has learned the wrong lesson from the Chico experience. Instead of becoming more open about development plans and how they affect the people in Apayao, the NPC seems to have become more secretive, in the hope of avoiding another public outcry of the same magnitude as the Chico controversy.

In Abra province, also in Northern Luzon, some 55,000 Tingguian tribal peoples were involved in confrontation beginning in 1977 with the Cellophil Resources Corporation (O'Connor, 1981: 5). Owned by a close friend of President Marcos, Cellophil began operations on its 200,000-acre logging concession which it had acquired in 1972 and 1974. The company set out to construct a pulp and paper mill and planned to expand into a rayon-staple fibre plant in neighbouring La Union province. Life was made difficult for the villagers by Cellophil. Those who refused to sell their lands had to fence off their property or were accused of trespassing; bulldozers filled up irrigation and drainage ditches; the mill rapidly destroyed fishing, one of the Tingguian's alternative sources of livelihood; pasturelands for the water buffalo were lost; and the people faced the depletion of their forests as well as the likelihood of erosion, landslips, floods, and drought.

Like their neighbours the Kalingas, the Tingguians fiercely resisted Cellophil, and the Marcos government responded by launching a military campaign against the protestors beginning in March 1977. Sympathetic church leaders were hunted down and persecuted. One parish priest, a native Tingguian named Fr. Conrado Balweg, was forced to go underground and later joined the NPA. Many farmers have been detained, and numerous military abuses, including the killing of civilians, have been committed. Because of the intensified military campaigns, hundreds of residents have evacuated into towns in the northern part of Mountain Province (Biag, 1983).

These cases point to the seeming irreconcilability of the many conventional viewpoints regarding national development and the interests of tribal peoples in South-East Asia. Governments must recognize the rights of tribal groups and strive to preserve and develop their societies within the context of their centuries-old systems, instead of pursuing a policy of extermination of traditional cultures in the name of modernization and progress. Otherwise, national unity can never be achieved.

Natural Resource Abuses: A Time for Change

The extraction, transformation, and utilization of natural resources have resulted in great damage to the environment and spawned conflicts at various levels between labour and capital, corporations and tribal communities, and governments of the developed and the developing worlds. The role of the state as the primary agent for the supervision and disposition of natural resources is a crucial factor in the analysis of these conflicts. Related to this is the rise of militarization, especially in areas where the victims of development have begun to fight back and assert their rights.

The depletion of forest and, to a certain extent, mineral resources has already reached crisis proportions in South-East Asia. The degradation of the ecosystem only emphasizes the critical nature of the problem. The displacement of local communities, including tribal peoples, from their homes and traditional sources of livelihood without adequate alternatives being offered is a violation of human rights. While corporations reap large profits from their operations, the workers and their families subsist below the poverty line and endure poor living conditions. Labour conflicts are immediately traceable to the exploited condition of the workers in the forest and mineral industries. In agriculture, which is a transformation of a land-based resource, peasant land rights are constantly being violated by the expansion of agribusiness concerns as land reform programmes are half-heartedly implemented, if at all. Food crops are being replaced by export crops, and malnutrition remains a major problem.

Industrialized countries are heavily dependent on raw material-producing countries for mineral and forest products, but they also control international trade and dictate the prices as well as the traffic in such goods. Capital and technology are also monopolized by the First World. These countries are generally indifferent to the development of the processing capabilities of the primary-product producing countries, and in cases in which transfer of technology is undertaken, it has been confined to the less desirable types such as heavy-polluting or energy-consuming ones.

There is obviously a need to change existing priorities for development in the ASEAN countries. A stronger position must be taken against the monopolistic control being exercised by the developed countries over local resources. Considering that ASEAN countries possess sizeable forest and mineral reserves, the possibilities for these states to come together and demand a revision of trade and investment patterns are bright and attainable. Presenting a unified position, ASEAN countries can enter into negotiations with raw material-importing countries and arrive at mutual agreements. The industrial countries must be made to realize that unless they agree to negotiate for change, their traditional sources of primary products may be lost or unilateral restructuring may have to be undertaken.

Internal conflicts are a different matter, however. The governments of the ASEAN states range from mildly to overtly authoritarian. In many cases, internal sources of tension such as labour conflicts and peasant unrest have been dealt with by state repression. In this way, governments lose their credibility with the population and popular sympathy shifts to opposition groups, including those promoting radical alternatives. Bureaucratic anomalies, financial scandals, widespread corruption, and foreign-biased economic programmes all serve to erode the government's position. The state becomes identified with the interests of logging and mining companies, usurious international funding agencies, and foreign agents. It is not surprising that official policies are perceived to have benefited only these interests while causing great harm to the peasantry, workers, and tribal communities.

References

Afrim Resource Center (ARC), *ARC Newsletter*, Vol. 5, No. 1.

Almazan, Alejandro and Ibanez, Carol (1984), 'Determining Poverty Thresholds', *Business Day*, Manila, 25 May.

AMGL (Alyansa ng mga Magsasaka sa Gitnang Luzon [Alliance of Central Luzon Farmers]) (1985), 'Magbubukid, Pahigpitanang Pagkakaisa Laban sa Pagsasamantala!' (Peasants: Strengthen Our Unity against Exploitation), Manifesto issued 4 February.

Asia Magazine (1984), 'Timber', Vol. 22, No. Y-17, 20 May, pp. 16–17.

Asia Yearbook (1980), 'Commodities', pp. 91–3.

Awanohara, Susumu (1979), 'Japan's Unequal Timber Partnership', *Far Eastern Economic Review*, 7 December, p. 88.

Balai Asian Journal (1981), 'The Miners' Plight: A Case Study', Vol. II, No. 1, March 1981, pp. 6–10, 14–17, 24.

Belena, Abe (1980), 'Pollution Perils 4 Rivers', *Times Journal*, Manila, p. 9.

Biag, Ando (1983), 'Reign of Terror in Villages in the Philippines', *Japan–Asia Quarterly Review*, Vol. 15, No. 2.

Bulletin Today (1980), 'Paper Mill in Mindanao being Mulled', 6 March.

Carino, Joanna K. (1980), 'The Chico River Basin Development Project: A Case Study of National Development Policy', paper presented at the Third Annual Conference of the Anthropological Association of the Philippines, Manila, 22–27 April.

Chiengkul, Witayakorn (1983), *The Effects of Capitalist Penetration on the Transformation of the Agrarian Structure in the Central Region of Thailand (1960–1980)*, Bangkok: Chulalongkorn University Social Research Institute, pp. 30–1, 37–8, 45, 47.

Constantino, Renato (1975), *The Philippines: A Past Revisited*, Quezon City, Philippines: Tala Publishing.

Consumers Association of Penang (CAP) (1978), *The Malaysian Environment in Crisis*, Penang.

Danguilan-Vitug, Marites (1980), 'Environmental Issues Raised: Mine Wastes', *Business Day*, 27 November, pp. 19, 23.

Eckes, Alfred E. Jr. (1979), *The United States and the Global Struggle for Minerals*, Austin and London: University of Texas Press.

Feder, Ernest (1983), *Perverse Development*, Quezon City, Philippines: Foundation for Nationalist Studies.

Fegan, Brian (1982), 'Land Reform and Technical Changes in Central Luzon: The Rice Industry under Martial Law', paper presented at the Fourth Conference of the Asian Studies Association of Australia, Monash University, 10–14 May.

Gigot, Paul (1979a), 'The Fall of the Forests', *Far Eastern Economic Review*, 30 November, pp. 52–3.

—— (1979b), 'An International Plan for Control', *Far Eastern Economic Review*, 30 November, p. 53.

Grossman, Rachael and Siegel, Lenny (1977), 'Weyerhauser in Indonesia', *Pacific Research*, Vol. IX, No. 1, pp. 2–3, 7–8.

Ibon Facts and Figures (1979), 'Isnegsa and the Abulug Dam', 15 October.

Jenkins, David (1977), 'Indonesian Warning', *Far Eastern Economic Review*, 2 December, p. 66.

Khan, Kabir-Ur-Rahman (1984), 'Agricultural Raw Materials under the UN Integrated Programme for Commodities', *Raw Materials Report*, Vol. 2, No. 4.

McAndrew, John P. (1983), *The Impact of Corporate Mining on Local Philippine Communities*, Davao City: ARC Publications, pp. 53–5, 60–1.

Ministry of Agrarian Reform, Philippines (MAR) (1983), 'Status Report on Land Reform', Manila.

Ministry of International Trade and Industry (MITI) (1982), 'White Paper on International Trade', Tokyo: Government of Japan, p. 100.

Mortimer, Rex (1975), 'Strategies of Rural Development in Indonesia: Peasant Mobilization vs. Technological Stimulation', paper presented at the SEADAG Conference on 'Peasant Organizations in Southeast Asia', New York, 25–27 September.

O'Connor, David (1981), 'The Cellophil Corporation in Abra', *ARC Newsletter*, Vol. 5, No. 1, March, pp. 3, 5.

Palmer, Ingrid (1978), *The Indonesian Economy since 1965: A Study in Political Economy*, London and New Jersey: Frank Cass and Co., pp. 82–3.

Philippine Peasant Institute (PPI) (1983), 'Landgrabbing: An Assault on the Countryside', Manila, p. 1.

Reyes, Johnny (1984), 'The Mindanao Wood Industry: A Stripped Land, An Uprooted People', *Showcases of Underdevelopment in Mindanao*, Davao City: Alternate Resource Center.

Rowley, Anthony (1977), 'Forests: Save or Squander', *Far Eastern Economic Review*, 2 December, p. 47.

Sahabat Alam Malaysia (SAM) (1981), 'The State of the Malaysian Environment 1980/81', Penang, pp. 2, 25.

Sajogyo (1982), 'Rural Technologies and Institutions', paper presented at the Kuala Lumpur UNESCO Workshop on 'Cultural Changes in Communities Resulting from Economic Development and Technical Progress', 4–6 October.

SCS (Student Catholic Service) News (1984), 'Current Report on the Minorities Project in Belaga, Sarawak', December.

Siegel, Lenny (1976), 'Freeport Mines Indonesian Copper', *Pacific Research*, Vol. VII, No. 2, February.

Sricharatchanya, Paisal (1985), 'The Last Straw', *Far Eastern Economic Review*, 31 January, pp. 48, 49.

Sta. Romana, Elpidio (1979), 'Dependency and the Philippine–Japan Treaty of Amity, Commerce, and Navigation: Focus on Trade and Investments', unpublished MA thesis in Asian Studies, University of the Philippines, pp. 88–90.

Tadem, Eduardo C. (1978), 'Peasant Land Rights and the Philippine Corporate Farming Program', *Philippine Social Sciences and Humanities Review*, Vol. XLII, Nos. 1–4.

———— (1980), *Mindanao Report*, Davao City: Afrim Resource Center, pp. 46–7, 48–9.

———— (1983), 'The Japanese Presence in the Philippines: A Critical Assessment', *Anuaryo: Journal of History and Political Science*, Vol. 2, Nos. 1–2, pp. 107–8.

3
The Japanese Economy and South-East Asia: The Examples of the Asahan Aluminium and Kawasaki Steel Projects
Yoko Kitazawa

The Japanese Miracle

POST-WAR overseas investment by Japanese corporations began in the mid-1960s, when Japan experienced a major sustained burst of rapid economic growth. Japanese textile, electrical appliance, and food-processing industries began production in Taiwan, South Korea, Hong Kong, and other Asian countries. In most instances, the manufacturing was undertaken by factories subcontracted to produce parts and components for parent companies in Japan. In the synthetic textile and auto industries, Japanese companies supplied raw materials or auto parts to their subsidiaries in the host countries, where finished goods were produced and sold in local markets. These operations were financed by Japanese 'export-substitution' investment, designed to replace the export of finished goods from Japan by local production. In every case, Japanese direct investment in manufacturing in these industries and countries was designed to exploit cheap Asian labour.

Japanese overseas investment in the mid-1960s featured small amounts of capital committed per project and a concentration in the light industries. Consequently, these Japanese manufacturing operations competed with already-developed local industries, driving them out of business. In particular, since a large part of Japanese direct investment overseas was located in Asia (Table 3.1), the Japanese presence in the region was strongly resented and attacked. Popular opposition to the penetration of Japanese corporations culminated in 1974 in the massive anti-

TABLE 3.1

Trends in Japan's Direct Overseas Investment (US$ million)

Region/ Country	1974[1]			1983[1]			Percentage Change
	Cases	Amount	Per Cent	Cases	Amount	Per Cent	
United States	3,345	2,571	23.8	10,846	16,535	27.5	6.7
Indonesia	443	1,190	10.9	1,237	7,641	12.7	1.8
Hong Kong	819	274	2.5	2,180	2,387	4.0	1.5
South Korea	813	495	4.6	1,150	1,442	2.4	-2.2
Singapore	316	226	2.1	1,557	1,705	2.8	0.7
Philippines	241	190	1.8	603	786	1.3	-0.5
Malaysia	374	250	2.3	816	904	1.5	-0.8
Thailand	468	194	1.8	926	593	1.0	-0.8
Taiwan	649	174	1.6	1,317	582	1.0	-0.6
Asia Total	4,123	2,993	27.7	9,786	16,040	26.6	1.1
Middle East	96	780	7.2	295	2,654	4.4	-1.9
Western Europe	164	189	1.7	3,338	7,136	11.9	3.7
Brazil	691	1,253	11.6	1,244	3,955	6.6	-3.4
Latin America	1,405	2,510	23.2	3,924	10,730	17.9	2.3
Australia	330	524	4.8	1,067	3,048	5.1	0.9
Total	10,154	10,820	100.0	30,500	60,098	100.0	100.0

Source: Ministry of Finance, Japan.
[1]Year-end.

Japanese uprisings which broke out in Indonesia, Malaysia, the Philippines, and Thailand.

That same year, at the United Nations, the developing countries of the 'South' demanded that the industrialized countries of the 'North' establish a 'new international economic order'. Transnational corporations reacted to this request by creating a 'new international division of labor'. In response to these criticisms of Japan from Asian countries and the emerging international consensus in favour of a new economic order, Japanese corporations launched an attempt to develop a Japanese version of the new international division of labour. This effort evolved into the Pacific Basin Economic Cooperation concept

The rapid economic growth of the 1960s was driven by expansion of energy-consuming industries based on lavish use of cheap Middle East oil. The leaders of this spurt in growth were the raw material-processing industries. Iron ore, copper ore, bauxite, and other minerals, as well as lumber and petroleum, were imported in huge volumes and processed in Japan. From 1963 to 1973,

TABLE 3.2

Annual Growth Rate of Consumption of Natural Resources,
1963–1972 (per cent)

Resource	Country				
	Japan	United States	West Germany	France	United Kingdom
Energy (total)	10.0	4.6	4.1	5.9	1.3
Oil	16.1	5.1	11.0	13.5	6.8
Copper	13.4	3.9	4.0	5.2	2.2
Copper ingots	12.8	2.9	5.2	5.4	0.4
Lead ingots	6.8	4.5	1.8	2.3	0.1
Zinc ingots	9.8	3.2	4.6	4.8	1.4
Aluminium	20.8	8.1	10.5	6.4	4.4
Tin	9.2	0.5	3.1	0.3	1.6
Nickel	17.3	5.0	10.4	6.5	1.3
Wood	5.6	3.8	0.5	2.3	0.2
Meat	8.2	2.5	2.8	1.2	0.3
Wheat	2.5	4.3	2.7	0.0	0.6
Maize	9.2	3.9	10.6	9.9	2.8

Source: World Energy Supplies, Metal Statistics, FAO Production Yearbook (various issues).

Japan consumed much more raw materials than the Western economies. In that period, the consumption of oil, copper, aluminium, and nickel in Japan increased more rapidly than in the United States and West Germany, growing at double the pace of GNP (Table 3.2).

End of the Miracle?

With the oil crisis in the 1970s, these industries became an economic shackle. Direct and indirect oil consumption for raw material-processing industries—petrochemicals, cement, nonferrous metals, steel, paper and pulp, and synthetic textiles—was much higher than that in assembly industries like machinery and automobiles (Figure 3.1). The Japanese industries were hard hit by the increase in the price of raw materials in the 1970s. Japan relied almost exclusively on oil as its source of energy, and almost all of it had to be imported. Moreover, close to 70 per cent of the crude oil imported by Japan is converted into heavy oil, and heavy oil is supplied mainly to steel and other primary processing industries and to electric power utilities.

The Movement Overseas

Until the oil price hike, the strong competitiveness of Japanese goods was due to the supply of cheap energy from overseas, and the rapid growth of the Japanese economy was due to the expansion of energy- and raw material-intensive industries. The slump that plagued these industries was, therefore, structural. In the mid-1970s, these vulnerable industries began to be scrapped. By ordinance, the Japanese government subsidized companies, which then closed down factories to cut their losses. Other administrative measures were taken to encourage factory closures. Corporations involved in the vulnerable industries actively relocated their factories overseas.

Aluminium manufacture was the most typical raw material-processing and energy-consuming industry. The aluminium industry obtained 100 per cent of the bauxite it needed from overseas sources, and the aluminium-smelting process consumed considerable amounts of electricity. Japan produced 2 million tons of aluminium ingots in 1972, making it the world's second largest aluminium producer, second only to the United States. By 1977

FIGURE 3.1

Rate of Oil Consumption (Direct and Indirect) by Different Industrial Sectors

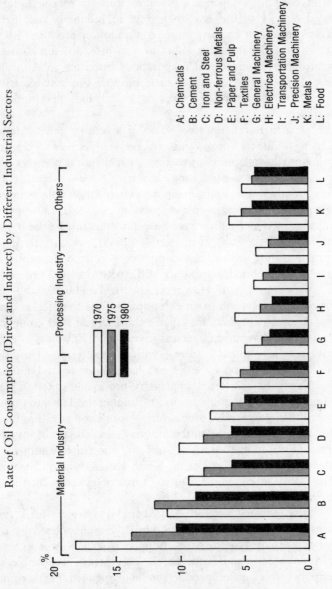

A: Chemicals
B: Cement
C: Iron and Steel
D: Non-ferrous Metals
E: Paper and Pulp
F: Textiles
G: General Machinery
H: Electrical Machinery
I: Transportation Machinery
J: Precision Machinery
K: Metals
L: Food

Source: MITI (1985), 'White Paper'.

Japan's aluminium output had fallen to 1.2 million tons. Output dropped further, to 660,000 tons in 1981 and to 300,000 tons in 1983. Accordingly, Japan's aluminium imports rocketed. Japan invested heavily in the Asahan project in Indonesia and in the Amazon project in Brazil to import aluminium produced by its joint ventures. Japanese corporations also provided funds to US and European multinational corporations operating in Australia, securing agreements to import their products on a stable basis. This investment–import formula is called the 'development-import' scheme.

The petrochemical industry was also a leading raw material-processing industry promoting overseas investment. Japanese corporations have been constructing petrochemical complexes in oil-producing or oil-processing countries such as Iran, Saudi Arabia, South Korea, and Singapore, where large-scale refineries have sufficient capacity to provide feedstock. (A Japanese petrochemical project in Iran has been suspended because of the Iranian revolution and the subsequent Iran–Iraq war, which interrupted construction just before the complex was to be completed.) Ethylene, an intermediate product of the petrochemical process, is then shipped to Japan. However, the steel industry, although experiencing a recession, is an exception. Of the five steel majors, Kawasaki Steel Corporation, Japan's third largest steel company, is the only one favouring overseas investment. Kawasaki is eager for overseas investment because—with the exception of mills in Chiba and Mizushima—it does not have modern steel mills at home. Kawasaki transferred its primary-processing sintering plant to Mindanao in the Philippines and is running the Tubarao project in Brazil. Nippon Steel Corporation—Japan's top steel producer, with a monopolistic hold on the industry—has so far not invested overseas. Even in its two major steel-mill construction projects in Kaohsiung, Taiwan, and Pohan, South Korea, Nippon Steel has invested only in engineering in the form of government-funded technical co-operation.

The steel industry has not invested heavily overseas for several reasons. First, steel production is virtually monopolized by five major companies: Nippon Steel, Nippon Kokan, Kawasaki Steel, Sumitomo Metal, and Kobe Steel. This makes it possible for monopoly prices on steel products to be maintained. Furthermore, since the monopoly of the five giants is not limited to production but extends to distribution involving wholesalers and export-import trading firms, the big producers can limit the import of cheap steel products from abroad (especially from South Korea, Taiwan, and Brazil) despite high prices in Japan. Thus the steel industry differs from the aluminium and petrochemical industries. Although the import of crude steel products from these countries— which was less than 100,000 tons per year until 1977—grew to 1.34 million tons in 1981, 1.89 million tons in 1982, and 2.4 million tons in 1983, the 1982 amount represents only 3.8 per cent of all crude steel products consumed that year.

Second, the demand for steel products is concentrated in major automobile, shipbuilding, and electrical companies. Both the suppliers of the five steel majors and the buyers, the majors themselves, are in a position where monopolistic prices can be maintained external to market mechanisms. Moreover, since in this supply–demand relationship the suppliers are much stronger, high prices can be imposed. Nippon Steel, which generally has the biggest share of the five majors, holds the chairmanship of Japan's two major economic organizations which influence general business and political decisions.

Thus the strong economic and political power of the steel industry is a factor enabling it to maintain monopolistic high prices and delay overseas investment, despite the effects of recession and the large gap between lowered production capacity and demand. Actual crude steel production was 99.95 million tons in 1982—below the 100 million ton level that has served the industry as a yardstick. Other reasons for the special situation of the steel industry are that the coke ratio used by Japan's steel industry is lower than that of other advanced industrial countries; its international competitive position is stronger because of its high productivity per worker; and since the first oil crisis of 1973, the industry has promoted energy conservation. Its energy dependency is also lower than oil- and electricity-dependent industries, such as aluminium and petrochemicals.

Emerging as the alternative leaders of industrial growth in the 1970s were the machinery and automobile industries. They were followed in the 1980s by new knowledge- and technology-intensive processing industries based on high technology. These industries filled the vacuum left by the relocation abroad of the primary-processing industries. Industrial trends from the 1960s to the 1980s indicate that the new processing and assembling industries are recording higher productivity than the raw material-processing industries. It is in these industries that Japanese products outperform West German and US commodities on the world market.

Where have all the scrapped industries gone? Japanese capital has been freed, and industrial relocation to the Third World countries has been encouraged by the government with generous subsidies. In September 1974, the Industrial Structure Council, an advisory body to the Ministry of International Trade and Industry, presented a policy recommendation entitled 'A Long Term Vision of Industrial Structure', covering the period 1976–85. This recommendation officially approved the trend already initiated by private business.

A New Vision of Economic Development

The 'Vision' characterized the world following the oil crisis as plagued by inflation coupled with an economic slump, which, it said, has caused trade deficits in a series of advanced industrial countries and produced large external debts in developing countries. The Vision also referred to the 1974 declaration of a new international economic order as resource nationalism, a new trend among developing countries. From this it was concluded that Japan, dependent on foreign sources for raw materials (Table 3.2), could no longer dream of rapid economic growth and should therefore pursue long-term 'stable growth' instead. The Vision recalled that growth in the 1960s had been dependent on the expansion of equipment investment by private firms at home, but warned that this pattern of growth would not work in the future. Instead, future growth would rely on the expansion of personal consumption and government spending, which would help private firms invest in new equipment. In other words, the government and the Japanese people were being asked to spend more to ensure the expansion of private business.

A second countermeasure was also recommended; that is, the development of sophisticated high-technology industries and energy conservation. The steel, non-ferrous metals, petrochemicals, and paper and pulp industries were urged to relocate overseas; machinery, final processing, assembling, and other knowledge- and technology-intensive industries were encouraged to stay in the country. The Vision specifically recommended that the former industries relocate to Asian and other Third World countries with abundant cheap labour and rich natural resources. It was proposed that these industries should undertake primary processing of local raw materials to produce, for example, pig iron, aluminium ingots, ethylene, and plywood and chips. Intermediary products would either be imported to Japan for final processing or sold by Japanese firms on the world market. This strategy was called 'offshore production aimed at establishment of a new division of labor with resources-rich countries'. The policy recommended a rapid increase in Japan's overseas investments, increasing sevenfold from US$12,666 million in 1974 to US$80,700 million in 1985.

Because the primary processing of raw materials usually involves heavy pollution, the 'new international division of labor' means, first and foremost, the export of pollution. Most of the governments of the host countries in South-East Asia welcome foreign capital and do not tolerate open opposition to foreign investment. Thus criticism of the behaviour of foreign firms by the local press is prevented. This is an ideal environment for offending companies. Moreover, most of these countries are ruled by authoritarian governments that repress non-government labour movements. When the world market stagnates, Japanese companies operating in these countries can dismiss workers far more easily than would be possible in Japan. In this sense, relocation also means the export of recession.

But the main aim of the new international division of labour is to enable Japan to control the supply of the resources in the host countries. Iron ore, bauxite, lumber, and crude oil have been imported for some time (Table 3.3). The strategy of moving the industrial processing of these raw materials to the resource-producing countries will forestall and circumvent the formation of cartel-like arrangements by raw-material producers. If Japan has at its disposal raw materials produced by Japanese factories in the resource-supplying countries, it can simply dump these products on the world market, driving down the price and eventually destroying any cartel arrangement.

Furthermore, the 'offshore-production' schemes are not integrated production systems. Final products are not made locally—raw materials are processed only into intermediary goods, and the intermediary products are brought to Japan. To make such 'development–import' projects possible, host countries must spend enormous amounts for the building of necessary infra-

TABLE 3.3

Japan's Imports of Primary Resources (US$ million)

Resource	Overseas Dependency (1981)	Imports (1982)	Source					
			Number 1 Supplier	Per Cent	Number 2 Supplier	Per Cent	Number 3 Supplier	Per Cent
Energy (total)	84.8							
Crude Oil	99.8	46,274	Saudi Arabia	39.0	Indonesia	15.9	UAE	14.4
Coal	83.4	5,782	Australia	37.4	USA	36.9	Canada	13.1
Natural Gas	90.9	n.a.	Indonesia	49.0	Brunei	31.5	UAE	13.0
Iron Ore	99.6	3,630	Australia	40.7	Brazil	23.8	India	12.1
Copper	95.9	1,419	Philippines	24.2	Canada	20.2	n.a.	
Bauxite	100.0	n.a.	Australia	46.9	Indonesia	21.4	Malaysia	13.3
Wood	68.3	4,546	USA	30.2	Malaysia	29.2	Indonesia	10.1
Wheat	90.5	n.a.	USA	57.5	Canada	27.4	Australia	15.1
Cotton	100.0	n.a.	USA	44.3	USSR	12.6	Egypt	5.7

Source: Ministry of Finance, Japan.

n.a. = not available.

structure. They have also to provide cheap labour, cheap land for factories, and cheap electric power. Primary processing generates much less value-added than final processing, which is done in Japan. Thus, the development–import scheme has little to do with genuine industrialization in the host countries. The host countries could consider nationalizing the Japanese plants at some point, but nationalization would have little meaning since the plants produce only intermediary goods, which in order to be useful and marketable must be made into final products in Japan.

The strategy of overseas relocation entails the vertical, pyramidal integration of the entire production process, from the provision of raw materials and primary processing to final processing, with Japan at the top of the pyramid. The division of labour recommended in the Vision is the diametric opposite of the new international economic order being demanded by the developing countries. It is thus a counter-revolutionary new international economic order.

By relocating stagnant industries to the Third World, Japan has been able to maintain the strong competitiveness of its products in the markets of other advanced industrial countries, and in the process, Japan's overseas investment grew 3.6 times between 1974 and 1981. Japan's overseas investments have a remarkable feature: Japan invests heavily in the developing countries, especially Asia, whereas the United States and Western Europe invest overwhelmingly in other advanced industrial countries. This preference for the Asian region became more pronounced as industrial relocation proceeded. The targets of Japanese private investment coincide with the recipients of Japanese official development aid (ODA).

A similar tendency is found in trade patterns. For some years after the Second World War, the Japanese government maintained that since Japan was a resource-poor country, it should live on trade. Under the banner of trade-oriented nation-building, export promotion became the priority task. The consequence has been that Japan imports almost 100 per cent of its raw materials and exports only industrial products. In the 1980s, energy-related raw materials accounted for about 50 per cent of Japan's total imports, and the products of assembly and high-technology industries accounted for 65.2 per cent of its exports.

This pattern is distinct from that of the United States and Europe. For example, the United States is a major exporter of grain and an importer of industrial products. In Western Europe, European Economic Community (EEC) trade is high, and EEC members both import and export large amounts of industrial goods. Taking each of the Western European countries in turn, dependence on trade is much higher than in Japan, but only because they trade with each other within the EEC. This comparison shows that the trade relations between the United States and Western Europe are more or less complementary, whereas the Japanese trade relationship is totally one-sided. Japan increases without limit the exports of high-value-added products of assembling and high-technology industries to all countries. This is why trade conflicts are bound to occur and why they cannot be mitigated.

The real contradictions in Japan's trade are with other Asian countries. There are many newly industrializing countries (NICs) in East and South-East Asia. South Korea, Taiwan, Singapore, and Hong Kong are the primary NICs; Thailand, the Philippines, and Malaysia are the secondary NICs. In the 1980s, the share of light industrial products in their exports has invariably increased as they have begun to export these products to advanced industrial countries. However, Japan does not buy their products in significant amounts and indeed recently has drastically reduced the import of industrial products from these countries. Consequently, Japan's share in their exports has become smaller than that of the United States and Europe. The serious economic crisis besetting the Philippines stems partly from this type of trade policy, in addition to the special vulnerability of the NICs to world recession.

The Vision in Action: Asahan

Japanese private business made its first major step towards the implementation of development–import schemes in the South-East Asian region on 7 July 1975 when a consortium of Japanese companies signed an official contract with Indonesian President Suharto for the Asahan Aluminium Smeltery Project, which the press described as unprecedented both in the amount of money involved and in its size among Japanese overseas investment projects. The Asahan Aluminium project is a comprehensive development project for power plants and an aluminium smelter. The plan was to build two hydroelectric power plants with a total productivity of 604 000 kilowatt-hours (kWh) from Lake Toba in the northern part of Sumatra. The power produced by the plants was to be sent to a 225,000 ton-per-year aluminium smelter constructed in Kuala Tanjung, about 95 miles south-east of Medan.

The consortium[1] is investing a total of US$900 million through the Japan Asahan Aluminium Company. At a cabinet meeting on 4 July 1975, only three days before the contract was signed, the Japanese government decided to provide 85 per cent of necessary funds to the consortium. At this meeting, the project was described as economic co-operation, in a major part of Indonesia's Second Five Year Plan, and its purpose was stated to be to secure for Japan a stable supply of aluminium.

The Asahan project is highly controversial. First, the funding process written into the Master Agreement—whereby funds from the Overseas Economic Cooperation Fund and other Japanese government financial institutions were to be provided directly to Japanese companies rather than to the Indonesian government—is in contravention of existing Japanese financial regulations. Second, there is no clear source of the needed raw material (bauxite) available. When the Asahan project was initiated, it was assumed that an American firm, the Aluminium Corporation of America (ALCOA), would provide bauxite from its new mines in Kalimantan and Bintan. But according to officials of the Japan Asahan Aluminium Company in Tokyo, there has been no clear decision by ALCOA to go into bauxite production in Kalimantan and the attempt to secure bauxite from Bintan has been terminated.

The Japanese investment in the Asahan project is thus not a new ideal form of overseas economic co-operation, breaking away from the profit-oriented investment project, but is in fact an investment in another nation's power resources and environment. Not only will this project use US$900 million of public money for private gain, but there are also grave new suspicions that it would not add to the value of Indonesia's mineral resources but would become merely an export platform for Japanese industry to process bauxite from elsewhere for Japan. In the name of national development, foreign aid resources from Japan were mobilized to pay for a project that would bring little if any direct benefit to Indonesia while it drained the power of its most important river

1. The consortium consists of twelve firms with five aluminium smelters—Sumitomo Chemical as the representative of the consortium, Nippon Light Metal Company, Showa Denko, Mitsui Aluminium, and Mitsubishi Chemical Industries—together with seven trading firms.

to serve Japanese business. In fact, the Asahan project could best be described as a capital- and pollution-intensive Free Trade Zone, or as a case of extraterritoriality for Japanese companies. It would only reinforce the dependency of the Indonesian economy on Japan.

The History of Asahan

The history of the Asahan project began when Indonesia was a Dutch colony. With an annual rainfall of more than 2 000 mm, and an elevation of 900 m, water from Lake Toba becomes a rapid stream within a short distance. The Dutch colonial authority, realizing that Lake Toba would be one of the best sites in the world for hydroelectric power development, carried out a survey of the area in 1908.

Japan planned Indonesia's post-war development during its military occupation of Indonesia in the 1940s. Kubota Yutaka, who was in pre-war days a managing director of Nihon Chisso Hiryo (presently the Chisso Corporation, infamous for the Mina-mata pollution) and concurrently the president of Korea Hydro-electric Power Company, carried out a survey of the water power of the Asahan River and began preparation for construction of a power station and an aluminium smelter. This plan halted with Japan's defeat. After Indonesia won its independence, the Soviet Union began a feasibility study of the same project in 1960, but this was also suspended due to Sukarno's downfall.

Kubota Yutaka is now chairperson of Nippon Koei Co., Ltd. As soon as the Foreign Investment Act was passed in January 1967 after Suharto had come to power, Nippon Koei proposed a comprehensive Asahan development project to the government of Indonesia. On 5 August of the same year, Nippon Koei concluded a contract for operations with the Indonesian government and began a feasibility study. At that stage, it was planned that Nippon Koei would be responsible for construction of a hydro-electric power plant; and Sumitomo Chemical, Nippon Light Metal, and Showa Denko would be in charge of an aluminium smelter. However, Kaiser and ALCOA indicated that they would compete to build the aluminium smelter.

In May 1972, a Japan–US joint consortium was organized to undertake the project. The international consortium consisted of seven firms—from Japan, Mitsubishi Chemical Industries and

Mitsui Aluminium in addition to the above-mentioned three firms, and, from the United States, ALCOA and Kaiser. These firms subsequently decided to jointly tender for the project. Sumitomo Chemical was the principal member of the consortium at this stage.

To secure a source of bauxite, the Japanese aluminium industry had to include the two US firms as partners in the Asahan project. The Japanese aluminium industry depended almost totally on Australia, Malaysia, and Indonesia for bauxite; imports from Indonesia constituted only one-fifth of the total amount imported. Development of bauxite resources in these countries was mono-polized by a multinational aluminium cartel, the 'Big Four' of the United States and Europe. The Big Four announced suddenly in 1972 that production of bauxite would be decreased to 84 per cent as a self-imposed quota to prevent price reduction (*Pacific Basin Report*, August 1974: 68).

In tendering for the Asahan project, the Japan–US consortium attached a condition that the construction of a hydroelectric power plant should be separated from the aluminium smelter project, and that it should be carried out by the Indonesian government by means of a separate government loan. This condition was pro-posed mainly by the two US firms. The Indonesian government, on the other hand, insisted that the project should be a package investment including both the smelter and the power plant. The scheduled date for tendering, 15 July 1972, passed without any compromise between the international consortium and the Indonesian government.

Similar situations have often occurred in other foreign invest-ment projects concerned with the development of resources. However, the Asahan project initiated a new era in Japanese overseas investment. In August 1972, immediately after the Tanaka cabinet was formed, Indonesia sent a governmental envoy to request Japan to finance the Asahan project with govern-ment funds in one package including both aluminium smelting and power development. At the same time, Indonesia announced its Second Five Year Plan to begin in April 1974. It was said that the very survival of the Suharto regime depended on the success of the Five Year Plan, which totalled US$20 billion. The Asahan project was of primary importance in the plan. On 15 January 1974, when then Prime Minister Kakuei Tanaka was visiting Jakarta, he discussed the Asahan project with Indonesian leaders as one of his many 'national projects'. Because he promised to provide President Suharto with low-interest loans, the project suddenly became practical.

As a result of several rounds of negotiations between Sumitomo Chemical and the Indonesian government, a basic agreement on the project was officially signed between the two parties on 7 January 1974, one week prior to Tanaka's visit. In the agreement, it was stated that within six months of that date, the Japanese party should talk 'the Japanese government into providing low-interest loans' to finance the project (*Far Eastern Economic Review*, 14 February 1975: 40–3). In spite of the progress made on both governmental and private levels, negotiations for implementing the project went on for nearly two years due to several difficulties. The two US companies decided to pull out of the consortium in August 1974 on the grounds that to include construction of the hydroelectric power plants 'would make the project unprofitable'. The US companies seemed to have been more interested in obtaining the right to develop the bauxite resources necessary for the Asahan aluminium smelter than in building the power plants. ALCOA had already begun a feasibility study on the development of a bauxite mine in North Kalimantan and had also begun negotiations with the Indonesian government regarding bauxite resources on Bintan Island (*Pacific Basin Report*, August 1974). This pull-out presented a problem of where to obtain funds to replace the US companies' 30 per cent share. It was decided to include seven more Japanese-affiliated trading firms in the project in addition to the original five smelters. Thus the Asahan project became a Japanese investment project consisting of a private twelve-company consortium. The second major difficulty was the rising cost of construction due to inflation. In January 1974 construction costs were estimated at US$600 million, but they were projected to eventually be as much as US$900 million, a 50 per cent increase (*Far Eastern Economic Review*, 4 March 1974: 49–50).

A third difficulty was that Premier Tanaka, who was the strongest promoter of the Asahan project, in September 1974 promised President Geisel of Brazil that Japan would invest in the Amazon aluminium project. This project is a joint venture consisting of five Japanese smelters, including Mitsui Aluminium, and Rio Doce, a Brazilian state-owned mining company. The total investment amounted to US$3 billion, US$1.2 billion of which was to be financed by Japan. The project was expected to produce 320 000 tonnes of aluminium per year. However, the Tanaka cabinet resigned due to the bribery scandal before either project could be finalized.

The fourth obstacle arose from the fact that when it came to financing this enormous amount with government funds, the Ministry of International Trade and Industry (MITI), which was promoting the project, was opposed by other ministries. The financing plan MITI proposed, based on the requests of the five aluminium smelters, was: (1) that the government loan cover 85 per cent of the total business costs; (2) that the aluminium smelter be financed by the Export–Import Bank of Japan, the power plants by the Overseas Economic Cooperation Fund, and the infrastructure by the Japan International Cooperation Agency (JICA), which was established in August 1974; and (3) that the financing terms for the power plants entail an annual interest rate of 3.5 per cent over 30 years and those for the smelter be set at 6.75 per cent over 20 years (*Toyo Keizai*, 28 June 1975: 54–7).

The Export–Import Bank considered this plan feasible. The Finance Ministry, which administers various funds, stated that it was not able to extend public loans of such amounts at such low interest and with such long terms for a specific overseas investment by private corporations. However, the real reason for the opposition was the fact that the aluminium industry was in a serious depression. The five Japanese smelters were in the midst of the worst slump in their history, and thus were in no position to offer security on the enormous loans. When public loans are provided for domestic investment projects of private firms, the plant facilities to be built or other properties must be mortgaged. This practice was not applicable for the Asahan project because the investment was not domestic but overseas, and thus the plants or other properties could not be mortgaged. The Foreign Ministry was reluctant to approve the plan, saying that a loan of US$300 million beyond the limit set by the IGGI (Inter-Governmental Group on Indonesia) for importing crude oil from Indonesia had just been given to the country in 1972, and because the Asahan project exceeded that amount, it would be unfair to other IGGI member countries.

The Japan–Indonesia Master Agreement

In December 1974, a draft of the master agreement concerning the Asahan project was signed in Tokyo between Sumitomo Chemical and the Indonesian government. On 30 April 1975, MITI Minister Komoto Toshio arrived in Jakarta with a signed letter from Premier Miki Takeo, assuring Suharto of the Japanese government's commitment to the Asahan project. The Indonesian government, however, was concerned about the rival Amazon aluminium project and sent a special envoy to try to change Japanese policy. On 4 July 1975, a Takeo cabinet meeting classified Asahan as a 'national project' and decided to finance about 85 per cent of the cost with government funds, calling it an 'exceptional measure'. At the same time, it was called a 'politically oriented' decision, designed to coincide with the scheduled visit of Suharto to Japan.

MITI's support was crucial in reaching this decision. The major promoting force of the Asahan project was the group of senior MITI officials of the Tanaka faction called the 'internationalist group'. To the criticisms of the other ministries, MITI replied that Japan had already cancelled other projects—such as plans for investment in a petrochemical plant in Thailand and the contract for subway construction in Hong Kong—using economic depression as an excuse, and that the scrapping of the Asahan project could only result in serious damage to Japan's reputation in South-East Asia. MITI claimed also that Premier Tanaka had made a commitment to President Suharto on the Asahan project and that, therefore, it was actually a national project. As for the problem of the mortgage that was holding up government financing, MITI proposed to the Finance Ministry the following 'unprecedented' financing terms: (1) that the mortgage be on assets overseas such as the power plants and smelter to be constructed in Indonesia; (2) that MITI ask the participating trading firms to assume joint liability for the loans; (3) that the five Japanese smelters ask the OECF to participate in the planned investment company on the Japanese side; and (4) that the five smelters persuade the Indonesian government to assume some form of liability (*Toyo Keizai*, 28 June 1975: 54–7).

On the other hand, MITI informed the aluminium industry that the ministry had already established a basic agreement with the Finance Ministry and the Export–Import Bank for the financing of the Asahan project and requested the industry to proceed with negotiations with the Asahan Technical Committee in Indonesia. However, after the ratio of investment of each of the twelve companies was decided and the official contract with Indonesia was about to be concluded, it was revealed that there was no concrete agreement on government financing between MITI and the OECF, the Export–Import Bank, and JICA. The aluminium industry spokesmen then criticized MITI for going too far alone (*Nikkei Sangyo Shimbun*, 23 July 1975).

The Asahan project agreement that was hurriedly signed on 7 July 1975 stated that it was an unprecedented national project because of the amount of money involved and its size among post-war Japanese overseas investments. However, this project was not an example of Japanese economic co-operation with Indonesia; rather, it was an example of an investment consortium established across the boundaries of financial circles then being backed by the government.

The master agreement establishes an unprecedented pattern of financing. Japan established a private investment company, Japan Asahan Aluminium, which is jointly owned by twelve companies (Tables 3.4 and 3.5). The company was capitalized at US$14.5 million. Half of this capital was provided interest-free as a loan from OECF. The balance was divided among the companies. However, 70 per cent of this amount was provided directly by the government's Export–Import Bank in loans at 6.75 per cent interest; the remaining 30 per cent was loaned by a

TABLE 3.4

Breakdown of Japanese Funds Invested in the Asahan Project
(US$ million)

Item	Total Construction Cost	Funds from Japan
Power Plant	270	225.00 (OECF 83%; City Banks 17%)
Refinery	431	345.00 (Export–Import Bank 80%; City Banks 20%)
Infrastructure	82	27.00 (Export–Import Bank 100%)
Research	5	1.67 (JICA 100%)
Operation	56	18.67 (JICA 100%)
Total	844	617.34 (Japanese Government Funds 82.6%; City Banks 17.4%)

Sources: Monthly Bulletin of Keidanren, September 1975; *Far Eastern Economic Review*, 14 February 1975.

TABLE 3.5

Financing Terms of the Asahan Project

Source	Annual Interest Rate (Per Cent)	Term
OECF	3.5	30 years after a grace period for construction
Export–Import Bank	6.75	15 years
JICA	0.75	30 years

Source: Mainichi Shimbun, 7 April 1976.

consortium of twenty-three Japanese city banks. These twelve parent companies invested nothing in this project, yet control is entirely in their hands. Also, Hasegawa Norishige, president of Sumitomo Chemical, is president of Japan Asahan Aluminium.

In December 1975, PT Indonesia Asahan Aluminium (INALUM) was established with a capital of US$2.5 million, 75 per cent of which was covered by Japan. The remaining 25 per cent—which Pertamina was originally expected to finance—was covered by the Indonesian Regional Government Fund, because Pertamina was in financial difficulties. Within the first year, however, real investment by Indonesia was reduced to 10 per cent. According to the master agreement, Indonesian capital was supposed to increase by 1.5 per cent every year after operations began, reaching 25 per cent within ten years.

PT Indonesia Asahan Aluminium was expected to purchase alumina from ALCOA Indonesia, which was supposed to have developed mines in Kalimantan, and to sell the aluminium ingots produced. However, this part of the plan was in doubt. Nippon Koei was in charge of the construction of the smelter, and Tokyo Electrical Power Co., Ltd., was responsible for both the construction and the technical aspects of the power plants. The feasibility study for the project was completed in 1975, and construction began in 1976.

Total construction expenses, taking inflation into account, exceed US$1 billion, doubling the total Japanese investment in Indonesia, which at the end of 1974 was US$1.1 billion. When the investment of US$1.4 billion for another massive project on liquefied natural gas (LNG) development is included, Japan is the largest foreign investor in Indonesia, surpassing the United States.

The Benefits of Asahan

President Suharto called the Asahan project 'an imperishable monument of friendship between Japan and Indonesia'. What benefits would the project bring to both countries? What did the promoters claim? Hasegawa Norishige, president of Sumitomo Chemical and the representative of the Japanese consortium, stated, 'What should be pointed out first is that the purpose of the project is to secure an abundant and inexpensive power source . . . since the oil crisis, a sharp rise in the price of crude oil raised the cost of electrical power greatly. Considering that the power cost, which used to be about 3 yen/kWh, is now nearly 8 yen/kWh, the Asahan project is very appealing.' (*Monthly Bulletin of Keidanren*, September 1975: 38–41.) MITI asserted, 'The power cost of the Asahan project can be held down to less than 3 yen/kWh.' (*Toyo Keizai*, 28 June 1975.) This is important, because electric rates constitute about 40 per cent of the production cost of aluminium ingots, and 15 000 kWh of electric power is consumed per tonne of metal.

The second projected benefit was the securing of bauxite resources. Indonesia has bauxite deposits and it is possible to use deposits on Bintan Island and northern Kalimantan as raw material for aluminium.

The third benefit was to be that, since the whole Japanese aluminium industry would participate in the project, which would be administered under Japanese management with Japanese technology, it would be valuable as the first self-sufficient overseas development of aluminium resources. It was also argued that in view of the world demand for and supply of aluminium, the project would enable Japan to become more active internationally in this field.

The merits of the project for Indonesia were also pointed out. The Asahan plan is 'vital for the successful implementation of [Indonesia's] second Five Year Plan, and the key for the development of Sumatra. By the construction of infrastructure such as electric power plants, harbors and roads, the project will promote the development not only of the aluminium industry, but also of other industries in the area . . .' and will help by enhancing 'effective use of resources, promoting employment, improving the level of technology, and increasing exports' (*Monthly Bulletin of Keidanren*, September 1975). In addition, officials of MITI stressed that the project represents a completely new Japanese policy for overseas economic co-operation, moving away from the past pattern of profit-first investment. Now the results bear examination.

The Asahan project has many characteristics of a Free Trade Zone (FTZ). PT Indonesia Asahan Aluminium has the right to develop and operate in the project area, and the right to own the land. Administration and business transactions are to be conducted between the company and the Asahan Authority, which is to be set up in this area by the Indonesian government. Stocks cannot be offered to the public. The period of operation is 30 years, after a construction period of 7–9 years. The period of operation of the smelter, if it is expanded, is 30 years after the completion of the expansion work. Eighty per cent of the electricity produced by the Asahan hydroelectric power plants is to be supplied to the smelter at a cost determined by the Japanese company. Even after 30 years, when the power plants are transferred to Indonesia, the electricity would still be provided at cost.

Construction materials, foreign employees' personal effects, and the alumina, if imported from outside Indonesia, are duty-free. The company will decide the price of ingots produced and where to export them, and even if the domestic demand for ingots increases in Indonesia, no more than one-third of the products will be supplied to the domestic market. At least 75 per cent of the work-force must be Indonesian within five years of the commencement of operation. This five-year term, however, is extendable. Foreigners (i.e. other than Japanese) can be employed only as administrators.

A lump-sum payment of US$2 million shall be paid to the Indonesian government within 30 days after the agreement is signed. A compensation fee of US$6 million shall be paid to the Indonesian government for the expenses of land acquisition, compensation for relocated residents, registration fee for surface rights, toll for roads, and a harbour entry permit. An annual fee for a water concession of US$650,000 is required after commencement of operation of the power plants, with US$520,000 added to this per year for six years.

The corporate tax will be 37.5 per cent for ten years after commencement of operations (the normal corporate tax is 45 per cent). The stoppage at source will be half the normal practice for dividends and royalties. The personal income tax will be half of the usual rate for a foreigner for the first ten years. The project is exempt from all export and import duties and local taxes. Money subscribed for stocks and loans in foreign currency can be held outside Indonesia, as can 60 per cent of income from exports. Freedom of foreign remittance will be guaranteed.

In sum, A. R. Suhud, the head of the Indonesian Asahan Negotiation Team, stated that 'Indonesia is not going to draw any major direct benefit from the project. Apart from providing a steady, if small, source of revenue in the form of company tax and water rights, the project will provide employment for 10,000 people during construction stage and for 2,000 in the smelting plant.' (*Far Eastern Economic Review*, 14 February 1975.)

The Costs of Asahan

The project is likely to cause several problems. Although it was argued that this project is vital for the development of Sumatra, 80 per cent of the electricity generated by the Asahan hydroelectric power plants is consumed by the smelter and cannot be used for other development in Sumatra. By committing to the Asahan project, the development of northern Sumatra will be controlled by Japan for as long as 30 years, and the whole area, including its resources and assets, will be placed under the control of Japanese enterprises, hindering the independent economic development of Sumatra.

The Asahan project is record-breaking for Japanese overseas investment, both in scale and in form. Such an enormous investment will surely affect Indonesia beyond northern Sumatra. For instance, at the smelter site, there is a small fishing village of about 300 families. However, the plan involves the building of a factory town of 20,000 people, together with a loading port; 2,000 will be employed at the smelter. The number to be employed in the construction of the smelter is 10,000, and a labour force of 30,000 will be required during the busiest period (*Mainichi Shimbun*, 12 June 1976). To build a factory town of 20,000 people and the hydroelectric power plants, it will be necessary to recruit workers from other parts of Indonesia. To fill this need, the Indonesian government would probably make use of people displaced by its Transmigration Programme. They would probably be farmers from Java, who would be moved off the land where they and their ancestors have long lived, and employed as construction workers in Sumatra, which has a different climate and

environment from Java. Unless there is adequate planning for
their employment after the construction phase is completed, life
will be hard for them there.

Japan's aluminium industry has been given privileged power
rates since the pre-Second World War period, because the aluminium is of strategic military importance. Yet the practice continues
even today. Before the power rate was raised due to the oil crisis
in late 1973, electric power companies in Japan were spending
3–3.5 yen to generate 1 kWh of power and were charging
14 yen/kWh for household use and 7 yen/kWh for industrial use.
However, power was supplied to aluminium smelters at a bargain
rate of 1.8 yen/kWh, whereas the steel industry, which was
generally criticized for obtaining power at an unreasonably low
rate, was paying 2.8 yen/kWh. Nevertheless, Japanese aluminium
producers complain that due to the rise in the power rate to nearly
8 yen/kWh in 1975, their international competitive position has
deteriorated. Canadian companies pay less than 1 yen/kWh
and the United States and Australian competitors pay only
1.5 yen/kWh.

MITI says that the power cost for the Asahan project can be
held down to 3 yen/kWh. However, President Hasegawa of
Asahan Aluminium later announced that the power cost would be
1.2 yen/kWh (*Nihon Keizai Shimbun*, 12 June 1976). With the
rise in construction costs due to inflation, this rate seems unreasonably low even in comparison with the current power
generating cost in Canada. One of the motives for Japan's investment in the Asahan project is the guarantee of a cheap electric
power supply when smelter operations begin, thus enabling Japan
to be internationally competitive again.

The Japanese requested a complete exemption of corporate
taxes during the ten years of construction and of income tax of the
workers on several hundred thousand man-days, on the grounds
that OECF money was 'to be provided to developing countries on
the basis of complete tax exemption, and that in the case of the
Asahan project the fund was an extra-soft loan at an annual rate of
3.5 per cent'. The Indonesians, however, insisted on only a partial
tax reduction, as prescribed in the Agreement (*Mainichi Shimbun*,
12 June 1976).

During the basic survey, separate bathrooms were built for
Japanese and Indonesian workers. This was reported in some local
newspapers in Indonesia, and, according to the *Mainichi Shimbun*

(12 June 1976), some students said, 'The next flash point of the anti-Japanese movement is Asahan.' Lie Tek Tjeng, an Indonesian scholar and the director of LIPI (National Institute for Cultural Studies), pointed out in his paper, 'The Asahan Project and the Future of Indonesia–Japan Relations', that northern Sumatra will be flooded with Japanese in the next few decades, and there is a possibility that tension will increase between the Japanese and the local population.

To secure the land for the project, the Indonesian Army evicted the residents, and the Indonesian government compensated them. Kuala Tanjung, where the smelter was built, was a fishing village of about 300 households. There were about 100 households on the factory site who were compensated for their losses. However, the other 200 households that were in the area used for the project's roads and other infrastructure were not compensated. Although the 20 households of a village on the site of the power plants were compensated for their eviction, an aboriginal ethnic minority group of 20,000 people living downstream were not supplied electricity from the power plants, and some were evicted.

The difficulty of finding locations for heavy industries in Japan was one of the rationales stated by MITI in proposing that the aluminium smelter be built overseas. This difficulty arises not only because of scarcity of land, but also because the citizens' movement of the 1960s against environmental destruction caused by development has become increasingly active. The principle of the aluminium-smelting process has not changed since it was developed in 1885. When cryolite is added in the second process, hydrofluoric gas is generated. Hydrofluoric gas is highly poisonous to humans and plants. In producing one tonne of aluminium, 25–35 kg of hydrofluoric gas are produced, 60 per cent of which is discharged from the furnace as gas. The toxicity of hydrofluoric gas is demonstrated by the fact that no vegetation grows within a radius of 10 km of the smelter at the Kambara Plant of Nippon Light Metal (Shizuoka prefecture), which started its operations 30 years ago on an annual production scale of 120,000 tons, due to hydrofluoric gas pollution. If caustic soda, used in the first process, is to be produced in Indonesia, a large amount of mercury would be discharged from that factory. It is obvious that the Asahan project would pollute the environment but the Japanese consortium, MITI, and the Indonesian government have not taken any measures to prevent pollution.

According to the proposal, the first justification for overseas investment was that aluminium smelting consumes large amounts of electric power. This, in addition to the fact that pollution controls had been strengthened and the price of land had risen, led the Aluminium Section of the Japanese Industrial Structure Council to believe that it had become impossible to begin construction of new smelters in Japan (The Aluminium Section of the Industrial Structure Council, 12 August 1975). The Council's proposal concerning the next ten years for the aluminium industry (1976–85) recommended finding overseas locations and vertically integrating the smelting and rolling fields. The Council estimated the total Japanese consumption of aluminium in 1985 at 3.1 million tonnes, based on the assumption that the Japanese economy would maintain its annual growth rate at 7 per cent for the following ten years. Of this demand, the Council estimated that only 1.8 million tonnes could be produced domestically in 1985, and the balance would have to be imported from abroad. The

TABLE 3.6

Aluminium Supply and Demand in Japan, 1979 and 1981 (tonnes)

	Year		Percentage Change
	1979	1981	
Supply			
Production	1 188 294	666 053	−44
Import	471 579	1 061 898	125
Demand			
Rolling	1 817 477	1 225 134	13
	81 114	90 572	12
	31 960	29 503	−8
Others	100 695	92 900	−8
	34 248	56 888	66
	47 021	81 597	74
	26 587	32 298	21
Domestic Consumption	1 409 094	1 608 892	14
Export	103 353	8 993	−91
Producer's Stock	278 013	268 088	−4
Total Stock	416 828	795 241	91

Source: Resource Statistics Yearbook, Japan.

Council then proposed to bring semi-processed products to Japan from overseas factories constructed by the Japanese aluminium industry. Sites at Asahan in Indonesia and the Amazon in Brazil were specifically recommended.

However, it was obvious in late 1975, when the Council announced its policy, that the aluminium industry was beginning its deepest recession ever. Furthermore, for more than two years it had reduced its annual output from a capacity of 1.5 million tonnes to 1.0 million tonnes, and its stockpile still remained at 400 000 tonnes (Table 3.6). For example, the Toyo plant, which Sumitomo Chemical had built in 1974, had to reduce its operations by 80 per cent. The construction industry was hit most severely by Japan's economic recession at the time of the first oil crisis, and the aluminium industry is dependent on the construction industry for more than 50 per cent of its demand. The five aluminium-smelting companies which are members of the Asahan Consortium recorded recurring deficits of 100 billion yen (US$334 million) for April–September 1976 alone. There was no sign of recovery for the aluminium industry in the foreseeable future, and since Japanese industry would not need the semi-processed aluminium to be produced by the Asahan and Amazon projects, the Council's long-term plan for the aluminium industry was unrealistic indeed.

The Goals of the 'Asahan Method'

So why was the aluminium industry promoting the Asahan project while it was suffering from a recession that was causing a reduction of domestic operations and stockpiling? In addition, why was the project guaranteed a high profit rate through 85 per cent financing by government funds, guaranteed cheap power rates, an FTZ-type investment environment, a cheap labour force, and no pollution control? In the first place, Japan, as the world's second largest consumer of bauxite, was under pressure to secure its sources of this vital material, because bauxite was becoming the next target of resource nationalism. As with oil, Japan had to import nearly 100 per cent of its bauxite, the production of which had been monopolized by the United States and the European major mining companies. The Jamaica Treaty, concluded among the bauxite-rich countries, seemed the first step towards the eventual formation of an international resource cartel among the bauxite-exporting countries in the Caribbean. Japan wanted to secure a long-term, stable supply of bauxite from Indonesia and

Brazil—the bauxite-supplying countries in the developing world which were not parties to the Jamaica Treaty. The Asahan project would smelt aluminium using bauxite produced in Indonesia or Australia as the raw material and export it to Japan as semi-processed products. This system was guaranteed for 30 years. This strategy—not to oppose Third World resource nationalism with force but to penetrate and subvert it from within—is a true Japanese-style strategy.

The Asahan project was vital to the political life of the Indonesian élites. Pertamina was on the verge of bankruptcy, with debts of US$10 billion, and Indonesia's national debt was US$8.2 billion. As a result of Pertamina's economic crisis, most basic projects of the Second Five Year Plan were shelved. The Asahan project was the only one that survived.

For the Indonesian government, facing a general election in May of that year and a presidential election in 1978, the foreign exchange pouring into the Asahan project was not only a direct relief but was expected to become a political fund for the President himself. For instance, the 26.25 billion yen (US$85 million) from the OECF that had been loaned to PT Indonesia Asahan Aluminium for the construction of the hydroelectric power plants first went through the Indonesian Central Bank and then the Indonesian National Bank, which added an extra 0.5 per cent interest. The Indonesian government then made the actual loan. It was also a boost to Indonesia's investment climate that Japanese corporations would put nearly US$1 billion into a project with the Suharto government.

Recent Developments in the Asahan Project

The most recent developments in the Asahan project indicate that even the short-term viability of the project is questionable. Until 1988, aluminium prices at the London Metal Exchange had remained well below the estimated breakeven price for operation (US$1,500 per tonne). Thus, within the first four years of operation, the aluminium plant (INALUM) incurred a cumulative loss of US$160 million. To save the project, the Export–Import Bank of Japan granted it a two-year moratorium on the repayment of principals on its loans in 1986. An additional 56 billion yen was injected into the aluminium project in 1987 (32 billion yen from Indonesia and 24 billion yen from Japan). Japan also stretched out maturities on its loans to the project and lowered its interest rate from 7 per cent to 5 per cent, which allowed the project, for the first time, to post a profit of US$50 million in 1987.

But while Japan appeared happy with the operation of the project, the continued strengthening of the Japanese yen against the US dollar (Indonesia's foreign exchange earnings are mostly in US dollars from the sale of gas and oil) raised Indonesia's original debt of 320 billion yen incurred in the project (or US$10.4 billion at the 1975 rate) by more than one-third in US dollar terms by the mid-1980s. This put severe strains on the Indonesian economy which was already hard-hit by the falling petroleum prices. The planned alumina-producing plant at nearby Bintan Island was shelved indefinitely as it was felt that it would be cheaper to import the raw material from Australia.

On the technical side, the project has been threatened by the declining water-level of Lake Toba, which feeds the two hydro-electric stations. Crucial to the aluminium plant is a cheap and abundant power source but deforestation following the construction of a pulp and rayon plant up-river from the hydroelectric stations has greatly reduced the water-catchment area. The lake's water-level has fallen in recent years to a point where serious doubts exist as to the sufficiency of power available through the stations. In 1987, the 225 000-tonne-capacity smelter managed to produce only 191 000 tonnes of aluminium due to power constraints.

Indonesia is also beginning to assert for a more equitable share in the joint venture. The Master Agreement entitled Indonesia to a 33 per cent share of the aluminium produced in return for its 25 per cent equity stake. Under the 1987 restructuring, the Indonesian government converted 32 billion yen of government debts into equity to raise its stake from 25 per cent to 37 per cent in the Asahan project (there is pressure from domestic aluminium users to raise it to 50 per cent) but its request for a third of the aluminium produced for domestic use plus 41 per cent of the remainder was rejected. This dispute over distribution culminated in the suspension of aluminium shipments to Japan in July 1987. Although an interim agreement was made in December 1988 which resumed regular shipments to Japan, no solution had been reached so far. It is possible that a prolonged dispute may well upset the 'economic cooperation' of the two countries which the Asahan project purportedly tried to promote.

Japan's Overseas Steel Industry

Until the early 1970s, the investment of the Japanese overseas steel industry was only US$200 million, mostly in joint ventures in processing and manufacturing of secondary and tertiary steel products such as galvanized sheet, tin plate, and steel pipe in South-East Asia, Latin America, and Africa. Most of these plants were relatively small in scale and processed materials from Japan. The main purpose of this investment was to secure the market in those areas and not for an international division of labour or cheap labour such as that of the textile or electronics industry. Usiminas in Brazil and Malayawata Steel in Malaysia, both financially supported by the Japanese government, are exceptional. The former was set up in January 1958 and the latter in August 1965 by Yawata Steel (now Nippon Steel). Neither has been very successful.

With the slowdown of the high economic growth of the 1960s, the steel industry in Japan had to cope with several negative factors—a dimunition of domestic demand, a standstill in exports to Europe and the United States, environmental damage caused by air pollution and industrial wastes, and difficulties in finding sites for expansion. As a result, the industry decided to shift its focus to Third World countries. According to the International Iron and Steel Institute, the annual growth rate of steel and iron demand in Asia (except Japan, China, and India), the Middle East, and Latin America was high—12.0 per cent, 9.4 per cent, and 6.5 per cent respectively (*Toyo Keizai*, 8 November 1972: 104–10). The Industrial Structure Council felt that direct export from Japan should decrease, and that more overseas steel plants exporting semi-finished products to Japan or other countries should be constructed. In this way Japan could co-operate with and further the self-sufficiency efforts of the developing countries. The Council gave several reasons for its forecast of a rapid increase in overseas investments by the Japanese steel industry:

First, there is a strong request from the developing countries. In recent years, these countries have increasingly aimed at fostering labor-intensive basic industries in an attempt to promote their own economic development, but now they fully expect to develop steel industries which would provide large employment as well as stimulate other industries.

Second, because of the rise in labor costs and scarcity of construction within Japan, investment for new construction within Japan is becoming less advantageous compared to overseas investment. On the other hand, resource-rich countries want to level up their processing capacity. These factors, both external and internal will level off the cost of steel production abroad in the long run.

Third, Japan as an advanced steel-producing country should contribute to securing the supply of steel for international demand. In terms of the future of steel supply and demand on the world market, Japan is not expected to continue to increase its production as it has in the past in response to world demand because of the limitation of domestic construction as well as stronger regulation on pollution. Also the developing countries are unlikely to expand their steel production without technical and financial cooperation from advanced countries. Meanwhile, the demand for steel in the developing countries will increase rapidly as industrialization proceeds and income levels rise. Therefore there will be an increased demand for steel worldwide, and by around 1985, the shortage of supply will amount to more than ten million tons. Thus, it is necessary for Japan's steel industry, with its highly advanced technology and abundant experience to cooperate with steel production in developing countries and contribute, along with the Western steel industries, to an increase in the steel supply through overseas investment.

Fourth, from a long term viewpoint, overseas investment should be expanded in order to secure resource imports which in turn will stabilize supply and demand in Japan. Thus, it is expected that overseas investment will rapidly increase, and the total sum of steel industry investment will reach US$500–1,000 million. By 1985, the cumulative sum will amount to US$4.5 billion. (*Sangyo Kozo Shingikai*, September 1974.)

Not all steelmakers in Japan are following this course and actively entering Third World countries to construct integrated steel mills. Nippon Steel and NKK, the two largest steel companies in Japan, are attempting to expand abroad through international consortia. But Kawasaki Steel decided to follow the first course.

Kawasaki in Mindanao: The Export of Pollution

The Kawasaki Steel project is another example of Japan's overseas industrial relocation of pollution-intensive processing industries. In August 1974, Kawasaki Steel Corporation began to construct a sinter plant with an annual production of 5 million tonnes of sinter ore in Mindanao in the Philippines. The total construction cost was US$214 million. In December 1974 Kawasaki Steel established the Philippine Sinter Corporation, a fully owned subsidiary with an initial capital of ₱50 million (around US$7 million), which was increased to ₱485 million (US$70 million) at the end of January 1975. The plant was completed in April 1977.

The project was one of the largest overseas plants in the steel industry, the first to use the sintering process outside of Japan and to make iron sinter for export to Japan. The entire process—from the application for the sinter plant project to the granting of permission, the acquisition of the land, the granting of beneficial treatment, and thence to construction—demonstrated characteristics typical of the behaviour of Japanese firms in South-East Asian countries. Both the Philippine government and Kawasaki Steel promised that the sinter plant as well as the proposed industrial estate would improve the quality of life in the region. However, many people in the Villanueva and Tagoloan areas in Misamis Oriental Province and near Cagayan de Oro City, who used to live by farming and fishing, were deprived of their means of making a living. The anger and disappointment of the people who were forcibly relocated by the project have forged strong public opposition to Kawasaki's entry into the area. In Japan, too, there is increasing criticism of Kawasaki Steel for its 'pollution export' (Kido Junko, 1977).

Kawasaki Follows the Vision

Kawasaki Steel Corporation is eagerly pursuing overseas expansion congruent with MITI's vision. The company not only plunged into construction of an ultramodern sinter plant in the midst of coconut trees, small barrios, and a population dependent on subsistence agriculture and fishing, it also decided to launch another project, the Tubarao in Brazil. This project involves the construction of slab and blooming plants in Tubarao with a production capacity of 6.8 million tonnes a year. Kawasaki Steel has invested US$820 million for the construction of the plant jointly with Siderbras, a Brazilian state-owned steel investment company, and Findider International, an Italian steel firm. The total investment amounted to US$3.1 billion, and the plant was completed in April 1983.

Locating such projects in pristine natural areas is not new to Kawasaki Steel. It boasts of transforming the Chiba coastal area in Japan, with its small fishing villages, into an industrial area—'like building a factory in the middle of the desert'. Starting as an open-hearth-furnace steelmaker, after the Second World War it purchased pig and scrap iron to be refined into steel, rolling and producing steel products without a blast-furnace. With its huge profits from war procurement contracts during the Korean War, Kawasaki Steel expanded in 1950 into reclaimed area along the Chiba coast north-west of Tokyo Bay, a calm shoaling beach that residents had hitherto found ideal for shell-gathering, farming, fishing, and swimming. Although common sense in the steel industry dictates locating a blast-furnace near the site of iron-ore and coke production, Kawasaki Steel built an integrated steel mill with a strip mill at this 'playground for children', and, through drastic rationalization and decreasing transportation costs, expanded annual crude steel production at its Chiba plant from 2 million to 4 million tonnes between 1958 and 1961, to 5 million tonnes in 1965, and to 6 million tonnes in 1966. The company now has nine blast-furnaces with an annual crude steel production of 15 million tonnes. 'High productivity and profit' became the Kawasaki Steel slogan.

Establishment of infrastructure was fully supported by the Chiba prefectural and city governments, which were eager to invite industrial capital. The advancement of Kawasaki Steel into the Chiba coastal area triggered a boom in construction of steel mills along sea coasts by major Japanese steelmakers with blast-furnaces. By the 1960s, this process had become the normal pattern—even to the extent of being referred to as the 'Chiba method'—for setting up plants in undeveloped areas. The main feature of the method was that the land was sold to private companies which had to promise to pay the costs in advance. Funds for large-scale development can be raised more easily when several big enterprises want to locate in an area. Reclamation in Chiba was aimed strictly at attracting industry rather than at benefiting the people living there. Of course, it was claimed the industries would make the whole prefecture prosperous and people would thereby enjoy a happy life.

In 1960, a 'Plan to Construct the Keiyo Coastal Industrial Area' was announced, in which huge tracts of reclaimed land were given to big businesses such as the Mitsui and Mitsubishi groups. In 1968, spacious oil-storage stations appeared in the area. Furthermore, Nippon Steel moved on to another reclaimed land site, stating that it would construct the largest steel mill in Asia there. There are now more than 30 big companies located in 4 340 ha of reclaimed land. The sky and land soon became completely covered with smoke and waste waters. Crude oil and industrial wastes turned the sea a coffee colour and the air is a reeking, dirty, violet haze. The deadly fruit of industrialization was pollution.

From the early 1970s, increasing numbers of Chiba residents began to realize that their health had been seriously undermined. By the end of August 1976, more than 30 known pollution victims had died. The management of Kawasaki Steel must have taken into consideration the demands for compensation from pollution victims and the growing popular movement against pollution when it made its decision to move the sinter plant, one of the major sources of pollutants, out of Chiba to Mindanao. In 1972, a Kawasaki executive expressed the company's intention to leave the country: 'With pollution becoming an issue, Kawasaki Steel is to build sinter plants within the resource-producing countries. However, it wouldn't pay to manufacture half-finished products such as slub, steel ingot at overseas plants and then bring them back to Japan.' (*Toyo Keizai*, 8 November 1972.) Kawasaki therefore decided to build on its experience in Chiba and move to Mindanao to cut costs. It is now much cheaper to build a plant outside the country than within Japan because of the rise of environmentalism there.

In October 1973, Kawasaki Steel's President Fujimoto visited the Philippines to meet with President Marcos and Industrial Minister Paterno and applied for permission to construct a sinter plant there. The process, from the application to the formal granting of permission, was accompanied by political negotiations.

In the Philippines, Kawasaki Steel had been operating a pellet plant since 1967—Pellet Corporation of the Philippines. The plant had to be closed in June 1974 when the iron resources in Ralap, Luzon, were exhausted. The company used to produce 700 000 tonnes of pellet annually, all of which was exported to Japan. According to Kawasaki Steel, the Philippine government recommended that the company stay and begin other industries (*Kokusai Keizai*, July 1976: 107).

The Selling of the Project

On 8 January 1979, at the summit meeting between Japan and the Philippines, President Marcos told visiting Premier Tanaka, 'Industrialization is what we are aiming for. We expect strongly Japan's support and aid.' He also reassured Japan on its pollution problems: 'If it gets difficult to expand plants in Japan, we are willing to accept them.' (*Asahi Shimbun*, 9 January 1979.) The following day, when Tanaka was departing for Bangkok, the next stop on his tour of five ASEAN countries, the Philippine government announced that President Marcos had given his consent to Kawasaki Steel's plan to construct the sinter plant. This approval came while the Board of Investment was still studying the desirability of having the plant in the Philippines. However, President Marcos claimed that the location of the plant would be his decision. At first, Kawasaki Steel was offered Tawi Tawi in the Sulu Archipelago as a site but it was turned down. Finally, on 10 January, the Mindanao site was offered. It is evident the Philippine government considered the project a countermeasure to the Muslim problem in Mindanao, where well-armed guerrillas scattered all over the island were rebelling against the government and conducting ambushes and harassment raids. Kawasaki Steel was fully aware of these problems. President Fujimoto stated that 'our project will contribute to the stabilization of the area by preventing Muslim guerillas from continuing their activities in southern Mindanao. Economic development will expand job opportunity, which will bring political stability. . . .' (Kaminogo Toshiaki, 1975: 101.) Kawasaki Steel accepted the proposed area, which faces the Macajalar Bay in Mindanao. The company was happy with the area, for, as another executive pointed out, '. . . the entire area is out of the typhoon belt. Limestone needed as catalyst for the sinter process is available from nearby Bohol Island. The site is very suitable as a transit base between Australia and Brazil, suppliers of iron ore, and Japan.' (*Kokusai Keizai*, July 1976: 107.) The site also could be amply supplied with electricity from Maria Christina Falls and with fresh cooling water from the Tagoloan River. The port can accommodate 250,000 d.w.t. ore carriers; the harbour will have a water depth of 25 m; and Kawasaki Steel plans to build a sea berth with modern loading and unloading equipment capable of handling 6 000 and 1 800 tonnes per hour respectively. The approximately 40 000 kWh electric power demand will be tapped from the National Power Corporation. This amount is more than that consumed daily by the entire population of Cagayan de Oro City.

About 4.42 million tonnes a year of required sinter feed is supplied from Australia and Brazil. About 350 000 tonnes a year of coke freeze is also imported from Japan. To obtain around

900 000 tonnes of limestone a year from Bohol, Kawasaki Steel founded a mining company called Consuelo Mining Company headed by a Filipino, as foreigners are prohibited by law from freely disposing of natural resources. Furthermore, the Japan–Philippine Treaty enabled Japanese vessels to transport the limestone through the inland sea. This agreement was necessary because '. . . the waters, around, between and connecting the islands of the archipelago, irrespective of their breadth and dimensions, form part of the internal waters of the Philippines'.

Although the *Asahi Shimbun* (15 January 1974) lauded the start of the project as 'the first concrete achievement of the consensus between the two countries for mutual economic development negotiated at the Tanaka–Marcos Talks', *Bulletin Today* in Manila wrote, 'This is a case of a "dirty" industry that can no longer be located in Japan because of pollution concerns. But the Philippine authorities have no objection to its installation in the underpolluted southern island.'

Meanwhile, some Filipino people began to raise their voices against bringing the 'dirty' plant into their living area. The news that 'pollution is coming' spread rapidly, and in response, Kawasaki Steel initiated a 'clean industry' campaign in Misamis Oriental. When local officials opposed the sinter plant project because of fear of pollution, Kawasaki Steel's management maintained that pollution would be minimal and would involve mainly the discharge of small amounts of sulphur into the air. Water pollution would be nil, as the water cooling system would be closed and waste water would not be discharged into the bay or river. To allay the fears of local officials, Kawasaki took ten of them on a tour of Taiwan and Japan, after which no further complaints were heard from them.

The pamphlet Kawasaki prepared for the campaign stated that (1) waste resulting from the production of iron sinter includes dust and waste gas but no waste water; (2) dust collection system consisting of a blower, a cyclone-type dust collector, and collecting fans will be installed at several locations in the sinter plant to control dust and waste gas; (3) the Philippine Sinter Corporation will use iron ore with very low sulphur content, and thus sulphur discharge would be minimal; and (4) the calculated quantities of effluents in the waste gas from the sinter plant are far below the limits set by the National Pollution Commission and are even lower than the very strict limits set in Japan.

However, in Japan, Kawasaki Steel has to allocate more than 25 per cent of the total construction cost for pollution-prevention facilities, whereas in Mindanao the ratio is far less than 10 per cent. Based on the original project cost, 4.5 billion yen was allocated for pollution-prevention measures out of a total cost of 52 billion yen. It was thus doubtful that Kawasaki Steel would comply with Japanese standards.

In November 1975, Kawasaki Steel invited the Governor of Misamis Oriental to Japan. After an observation trip to Chiba, he stated at a press conference that 'reports from the Philippines regarding opposition in Japan to Kawasaki Steel's project are not true at all. All the residents there are welcoming realization of the project and the state government is also giving strong support to it.' (*Nikkei Sangyo Shimbun*, 22 November 1975.) Kawasaki Steel exploited this statement in a pamphlet entitled 'Clean Industry', which was distributed in Chiba and stated: 'The sinter plant, which is the major source of nitrogen oxides and sulphur oxides, will not be built. The sintered ore required for the No. 6 blast furnace will be imported from the sinter plant in Mindanao and the authorities of the province and the city have shown their full support and understanding for our project....' More than 100,000 copies were distributed throughout the area. Kawasaki Steel even blatantly stated they did not intend to take measures to counter pollution in Mindanao. As one executive put it: 'When we talk about pollution, it is not suitable to apply the consciousness about pollution in Japan to Mindanao. The sinter plant was [*sic*] located far away from the city, and there is no residential area or factories. Every evening a strong wind blows the polluted air away.... Only a little dust will be produced since the process is just to mix powdered iron ore and burn it into sintered ore.... In principle, we have to take every measure to prevent pollution, but that depends on the location and surrounding[s] of the plant. It is ridiculous to bring the pollution-prevention facilities of Chiba to Mindanao as they are. First of all, people in the Philippines don't know anything about pollution ... I have never heard of their complaining about a pollution problem. The people there go barefoot; shouldn't that be called pollution?' (*Kokusai Keizai*, July 1976: 108.)

The Costs of the Kawasaki Project

But a sinter plant produces more than just 'a little dust'. The sintering process produces sulphur oxides, nitrogen oxides, arsenic, cadmium, zinc, and lead, in addition to dust containing poisonous metals emanating from the raw-material stockpile. The nitrogen oxides produced by a sinter plant accounts for about half of the total nitrogen oxides produced in an integrated steel mill; that is why Kawasaki Steel asked the local authorities to move people more than 8 km away from the site.

Because the Philippine Sinter Corporation is 100 per cent foreign-owned, it is not allowed to own land. Former Executive Secretary Alejandro Melchor found a way around this obstacle by assigning the Philippine Veterans Investment Development Corporation (PHIVIDEC) the task of acquiring 138 ha of land so that Kawasaki Steel could then lease it. PHIVIDEC was created soon after the country was placed under martial law by Presidential Decree 243 in 1972. By establishing PHIVIDEC, President Marcos may have intended to give his patronage to retired military personnel and to prevent a *coup d'etat* by keeping on good terms with this group, which formerly had been largely excluded from domestic economic activities.

An area encompassing the flatland of Tagoloan and Villanueva in Misamis Oriental was designated for the plant site, and the people living there were threatened with expropriation unless they sold their land to PHIVIDEC. Although PHIVIDEC was a quasi-governmental agency, it was specifically given the authority of eminent domain and probably could have expropriated the land. However, the appearance of legality is an important feature of Philippine martial law. Thus the PHIVIDEC Industrial Estate Authority (PIEA) was created by PD No. 538 on 13 August 1974 as a 'subsidiary Agency of PHIVIDEC', possessing both governmental and proprietary functions. It was then announced that a 3 000-ha industrial estate would be created in the area with Philippine Sinter as its first occupant.

Kawasaki Steel did not have to deal directly with the people in the affected area, except for the workers in the actual sinter project. After the land was acquired, the future of the people of the former barrio was handled by the Inter-Agency Task Force (IATF) created by Melchor and administered directly under the office of the President. Melchor created the Andam Mouswag project, which was to be carried out by IATF. Approximately 20 government departments and agencies were involved in the IATF, ranging from the Department of Public Highways for road building to the Public Housing and Homesite Corporation for architectural and construction expertise to the Bureau of Plant Industries for teaching agriculture, together forming a conglomeration of bureaucrats and technicians.

Those technocrats laboured hard and finally chose barrio Kalingagan. The selection was purportedly based, among other factors, upon the majority's preference. Kalingagan is located 7 km from the highway and rises 500 m above sea-level. It is a rolling rocky plateau, home to 14 farm families. Because the land was characterized as being agriculturally sub-marginal, the national government bought up 100 ha in 1975 at ₱0.30 per sq. m or ₱3,000 per ha. It has been renamed 'Andam Mouswag', which means 'Ready to Progress'. What alternatives did the displaced people have? A few families chose to relocate by their own efforts, but the majority favoured the proposed housing at the relocation site. In the meantime, work had to proceed on the sinter plant, notwithstanding that the proposed housing was still in the blueprint stage.

The Benefits of the Kawasaki Project

What was the dominant motive behind the Philippine government's decision to invite Philippine Sinter? Aside from the attempt to maintain political stability in Mindanao, the Philippine government had a strong desire for its own integrated steel mill. Kawasaki Steel explained, 'As our project is in line with the Philippines' national strategy to build an integrated steel mill of its own, we were able to get every kind of preference, taxes are exempted, a basic survey of the sea and port was conducted by the Philippine Navy, eviction and land exploitation were carried out by the Philippine government and 100% investment was specially granted.' (Kaminogo Toshiaki, 1975.)

According to the prospectus prepared by Kawasaki Steel, the project was expected to make a substantial contribution to the economic development of the Philippines, particularly in the integration plan of the local steel industry. The prospectus proclaimed that:

1. Since the plant is in Misamis Oriental, it would immensely

boost the Philippine government's plan to develop northern Mindanao through large investments in infrastructure and plant facilities. The company intended to make its port and material handling facilities available to the government-proposed integrated steel mill in the area.

2. Iron sinter would become a major dollar earner in the years to come. The project was expected to generate some US$280 million in net foreign exchange during the first ten years of operation.

3. The project would directly employ some 600 workers with an initial annual payroll of about ₱7 million. In addition, over 2,000 workers were to be employed in the construction.

4. During the first ten years of operation, the government stood to collect about ₱362 million in taxes.

5. Although the product of the proposed sinter plant was primarily geared to the Japanese market, the company was ready to service the raw material requirements of the government-proposed integrated steel mill in the area.

6. The experience to be derived from the construction and operation of a sintering plant and equipment capable of handling modern material would contribute to the advancement of local expertise in steel-related technology.

7. The project was also expected to give an added boost to the already burgeoning mining industry, considering that the plant would require substantial amounts of limestone and iron sand.

Will the Objectives be Realized?

At the ASEAN Economic Ministers' meeting in February 1976 in Bali, Indonesia, Philippine delegates presented the ambitious iron and steel plant in Mindanao as a regional ASEAN project. According to their proposal, the plant project envisages an investment of US$1.661 billion to produce 2.5–3 million tonnes a year of slabs, blooms, billets, and plates. They claimed the northern Mindanao plant would meet between 15 and 25 per cent of the five ASEAN countries' steel demand in 1985 (*Far Eastern Economic Review*, 26 March 1976: 50).

The Philippines is not the only ASEAN country attempting to promote industrialization by building an integrated steel mill—Indonesia and Malaysia have the same goal. Although the proposal was not approved at the meeting, the Philippine government still has a strong desire to establish a state-owned integrated steel plant. None the less, neither the Japanese government nor

Kawasaki Steel, nor any other steel company, is necessarily ready to co-operate with steel plant projects in ASEAN countries. 'The problem is that their expectation lacks reality since they give consideration to national prestige before thinking about social and industrial foundations' (*Kokusai Keizai*, July 1976: 106).

According to the report of the Japan International Cooperation Agency, the Philippine government's integrated steel mill project may be premature. The report points out that basic study or policy-making should be completed first to thoroughly examine the potential problems. Domestic raw material supply may be inadequate. Raw materials available domestically comprise only iron sand and iron ore; other major raw materials would have to be imported. Infrastructure—electricity in particular—is weak, and electricity-consuming industries need to be supported by favourable electric rates. Related industries should also be developed and fostered.

Although Kawasaki Steel promised to contribute to the advancement of local expertise in steel-related industries, it showed no interest in the steel plant project in Mindanao proposed by the Philippine government. The company's major overseas project is the Tubarao mill in Brazil. The Mindanao plant is only a transit base for Kawasaki Steel, which was deliberately selling an illusion to the people of the Philippines. This lack of understanding may one day cause conflict.

Conclusion: The Comprehensive Security System— What Price?

During the 1980s, the Japanese government began to talk about the establishment of a 'Comprehensive Security System'. Because of the collapse of Pax-Americana, the Japan–US Security System backed by the American nuclear umbrella has become inadequate for Japanese defence purposes, and it has become necessary to establish an enhanced economic security system based on strengthening Japan's military capabilities. The economic security system is in fact a strategy to secure stable supplies of industrial raw materials, as specified in the Pacific Basin Cooperation concept, to which energy resources and food have been added as strategic items. How does Japan intend to secure a stable supply of food and energy resources from abroad?

Securing Energy and Food Supplies

The Japanese government argues that the existence of OPEC, the powerful producers' cartel, not only results in higher oil prices but also limits supply. It stresses that since Japan depends almost entirely on oil as its primary energy source, and since 70 per cent of all crude oil is imported from the Gulf area, Japan's oil supply is very vulnerable to changes in the world political situation. In the petrochemical sector, a series of overseas investment projects are now underway; and in the electric-power industry, the largest oil-consuming sector, the government is encouraging a switch from oil to alternative energy resources such as nuclear power, coal, and LNG. According to the government plan, nuclear power generation will account for 35 per cent of the total primary energy supply in the 1990s; LNG will be used to fuel thermal power stations in place of oil; and the 'develop-and-import' formula for energy resources will serve Japanese energy needs into the 1990s.

Japan has been almost completely dependent on imports from the United States for wheat, soybean, and maize—staple foods for the Japanese people and fodder for their livestock. Japan is currently making an effort to switch the source of these foods from the United States to Japanese-controlled develop-and-import projects in Brazil, Indonesia, and other developing countries. For example, a Japanese consortium has launched a one million ha fodder plantation project at Cerrado in Minas Gerais state, Brazil, under the develop-and-import programme. In connection with the Cerrado project, an ambitious infrastructural development programme has been planned, which includes developing a grain export corridor linking the inland Minas Gerais to a port of shipment on the Atlantic coast via a trunk road; constructing grain elevators with silos and harbour facilities, and developing an 'Asian Port', which will store fodder from Brazil temporarily or be used for livestock-raising in a bonded area of the port. The ultimate country of destination for these products is, of course, Japan.

The 'comprehensive security system' is comprehensive because it combines Japanese military strength with an economic security system designed to secure a stable supply of industrial raw materials, energy resources, and food. The present security system also aims at achieving its objective by integrating the overseas investment structure of Japanese enterprises into a totally Japan-centred system. However, this strategy will inevitably make Japan richer and drive poor Asian nations further into poverty and marginalization, reintegrating them as dependent economies into 'Japan, Inc.'.

Clearly, Japan's much-vaunted 'stable growth' is maintained only through the export of stagnant industries to the Third World and a tightening grip on raw material resources abroad. Its reckless export drives cause increasing friction with other advanced industrial countries, and it seems that 'stable growth' is also to be achieved on the backs of the Japanese people. Thus, Japan seems headed towards crisis.

References

Asahi Shimbun, 9 January 1974 and 15 January 1974.

Far Eastern Economic Review, 4 March 1974, 14 January 1975, and 26 March 1976.

Kaminogo Toshiaki (1975), *Why Do We Go Abroad?*, Diamondsha.

Kido Junko (1977), 'Kawasaki Steel Corporation's Sinter Plant in Mindanao', *AMPO-Free Trade Zones and Industrialization of Asia*, Special Issue, Vol. 8, No. 4; Vol. 9, Nos. 1–2.

Kokusai Keizai, Vol. 13, No. 8, July 1976.

Mainichi Shimbun, 12 June 1976, 4 July 1976.

Monthly Bulletin of Keidanren, Tokyo: Keidanren, September 1975.

Nihon Keizai Shimbun, 12 June 1976.

Nikkei Sangyo Shimbun, 23 July 1975 and 22 November 1975.

Pacific Basin Report, Vol. 5, No. 8, August 1974.

Sangyo Kozo Shingikai (1974), *A Long Term Vision of Japan's Industrial Structure*, MITI, September.

The Aluminium Industry and What Its Policy Ought to Be, The Aluminium Section of the Industrial Structure Council, 12 August 1975.

Toyo Keizai, 8 November 1972 and 28 June 1975.

4

International Conflict over Marine Resources in South-East Asia: Trends in Politicization and Militarization

Mark J. Valencia

Since the late 1960s, marine awareness of nations has been enhanced by technological advances in marine use and resource exploitation capabilities, increased expectations of benefits from potential ocean resources, and perceptions that the 'freedom of the high seas' was advantageous to those countries with the knowledge, capital, and technology to harvest ocean resources. This enhanced marine awareness has resulted in widespread unilateral extensions of national jurisdiction over ocean resources out to 200 nmi or more from shore. All the coastal countries in South-East Asia have extended their maritime jurisdictions, leaving areal winners and losers, and many areas where claims overlap. The coastal states of South-East Asia are now engaged in efforts to identify and pursue their national development interests in the ocean arena. The superimposition of a mosaic of national policies on transnational resources and activities multiplies the possibilities for international competition and conflict. The interest of the developed world in the new resources gained—particularly oil and sea lanes—may exacerbate intraregional conflicts. Extension of jurisdiction may thus have opened a Pandora's box of continued uneven growth; volatile mixtures of competition, nationalism, and militarization; superpower involvement; environmental degradation; and increased technological and market dependence on the developed world.

Present and Future Conflict over Marine Resources

The Setting: Comparative Advantage and Disadvantage

The geography of political entities in the region is remarkably maritime. With extension of jurisdiction, this geography presupposes there will be areal conflicts and possibly explosive resource inequities. Several countries in the region have gained enormous marine areas with extended jurisdiction (Figure 4.1). The largest of these gains were made by Indonesia, the Philippines, China, and Vietnam; others, such as shelf-locked Kampuchea, Brunei, Singapore, and Thailand and land-locked Laos, were much less fortunate. Malaysia, although gaining considerable area, has been divided by Indonesia's Natuna salient.

Area gained is not by itself a measure of resource wealth. Water depth is a factor in hydrocarbon exploitation, mineral dredging, biological productivity, and bottom fish catch. In South-East Asia, the continental shelves are underlain by thick Tertiary sedimentary basins and thus contain possible petroleum deposits. Their shallow depth also offers the possibility of mining for detrital minerals and trawling for demersal fish. Continental shelf underlies the small areas gained by Kampuchea and Singapore and 80 per cent of that gained by Malaysia and Thailand, but only 10 per cent of that gained by the Philippines. Countries with approximately equal areas of shelf and deeper water are Brunei, Burma, Indonesia, and Vietnam.

Countries claiming geographic disadvantage due to extended jurisdiction include Laos, Kampuchea, Thailand, and Singapore. Laos is land-locked and desires guaranteed marine access as well as compensatory access to neighbouring countries' marine resources. Kampuchea is shelf-locked and has a restricted coastline, and Brunei is nearly shelf-locked; both are zone-locked and have marine access only on a semi-enclosed sea. Thailand is both shelf-locked and zone-locked in the South China Sea. Moreover, the Thai distant-water fishing grounds in the South China Sea have come under Malaysian, Kampuchean, Vietnamese, and Indonesian jurisdiction (Valencia, 1981: 302–55).

Singapore lacks an Exclusive Economic Zone (EEZ), a 200-nmi expanse from shore over which the coastal state has exclusive resource jurisdiction. It has little continental shelf, and its minuscule maritime territory is surrounded by that of other states. Nevertheless, its geographic position makes it the linchpin of the Indian Ocean–Strait of Malacca–South China Sea–Pacific Ocean

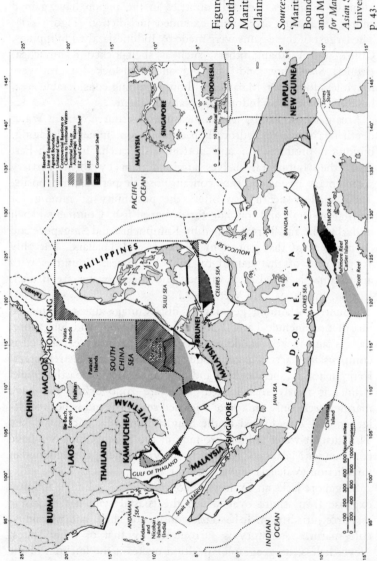

Figure 4.1
South-East Asia: Extended
Maritime Jurisdiction and
Claim Overlaps.

Source: J. R. V. Prescott (1983),
'Maritime Jurisdiction and
Boundaries', in J. R. Morgan
and M. J. Valencia, eds., *Atlas
for Marine Policy in Southeast
Asian Seas*, Berkeley:
University of California Press,
p. 43.

trade route. Singapore's economy depends more on the sea and on seafaring than does that of any other state in the region, and its influence on maritime affairs in the region is second to none because of its position as one of the world's foremost ports. As the maritime centre of ASEAN and as a centre for warehousing and pre- and post-marine exploitation services, Singapore may actually benefit from the extended maritime jurisdiction of its neighbours. However, if its neighbours become hostile and competitive in the marine sphere, Singapore could have serious economic and political problems.

Conflicts over Oil and Gas

Extended maritime jurisdiction encompasses many sedimentary basins having hydrocarbon potential (Figure 4.2). Much of the resource is speculative and will not be proven until it is drilled and discovered. For many countries, the potential is worth several times their annual GNPs (Table 4.1).

Consequently, for South-East Asian countries, increasing energy demands, decreasing energy supplies, and a greater reliance on foreign oil are spurring offshore exploration for new sources of production (Valencia, 1985a). Also, the expanded use of natural gas and its more realistic pricing as a premium fuel are factors encouraging companies and governments to explore for additional gas reserves (Gaffney et al., 1982). In 1975, 20 per cent of crude oil in the region was produced from offshore; by 1980, the proportion had risen to about 50 per cent. Brunei, Indonesia, Malaysia, Thailand, and the Philippines are the only countries with established offshore hydrocarbon potential. China's Mainland Shelf has become a major focus of exploration activity. Vietnam is being assisted in its offshore search by the Soviet Union, as is Burma by Japan.

Potential hydrocarbon-bearing areas with multiple claimants (Figure 4.2) include the northern Andaman Sea (India and Burma); the eastern Gulf of Thailand (Vietnam, Thailand, and Kampuchea); the south-western Gulf of Thailand (Malaysia, Thailand, and Vietnam); the area north, west, and east of Natuna (Vietnam, Indonesia, Malaysia, and China); offshore Brunei (Brunei, Malaysia, China, and Vietnam); the Gulf of Tonkin (China and Vietnam); the Dangerous Ground (Malaysia, Vietnam, the Philippines, and China); and the north-eastern South China Sea (China and Taiwan).

TABLE 4.1

Rough Gross Value of Oil and Gas Resources Gained by Extended Jurisdiction

Country	Shelf Area[1] (to 200-m isobath) '000 sq. km ('000 sq. nmi)	Ultimately Recoverable Offshore Resources[2]		Value[3] (US$ billion)		Total Value (US$ billion)	1980 GNP (US$ billion)[4]
		Oil (billion bbl)	Gas (TCF)	Oil	Gas		
Brunei	9.6 (2.8)	1–10	0.1–1.0	15–150	0.25–2.5	15.25–152.5	0.46 (1975)
Burma	229.5 (66.9)	1–10	10–100	15–150	25–250	40–400	5.0 (GDP)
China (South China Sea)		1–10	10–100	15–150	25–250	40–400	552 (+32 for Taiwan in 1979)
Indonesia	2 777 (809.6)	10–100	10–100	150–1,500	25–250	175–1,750	67.0
Kampuchea	55.6 (16.2)	1–10	1–10	15–150	2.5–25	17.5–175	0.5

Malaysia	373.5 (108.9)	10–100	10–100	150–1,500	25–250	175–1,750	21.6
Philippines	178.4 (52.0)	1–10	10–100	15–150	25–250	40–400	35.1
Singapore	0.3 (0.1)	n.a.	n.a.	n.a.	n.a.	n.a.	10.5 (GDP)
Thailand	257.6 (75.1)	1–10	10–100	15–150	25–250	40–400	32
Vietnam	404 (117.8)	1–10	1–10	15–150	2.5–25	17.5–175	4.9
Total	4,285.5 (1,249.4)	26–260	61.1–611	405–3,750	155.25–1,552.5	560–5,602	761.06 (209.06 without PRC)

Source: Valencia and Marsh (1986).

n.a. = not available.

[1] P. Tangsubkul (1982), *ASEAN and the Law of the Sea*, Singapore: Institute of Southeast Asian Studies.

[2] J. P. Albers, et al. (1973). *Summary Petroleum and Selected Mineral Statistics for 120 Countries Including Offshore Areas*, United States Geological Survey Paper 817, Washington, DC: US Government Printing Office.

[3] Using US$15.00/bbl of oil and US$2.50/1,000 cu. ft of gas.

[4] Central Intelligence Agency (1982), *The World Factbook*, Washington, DC: US Government Printing Office.

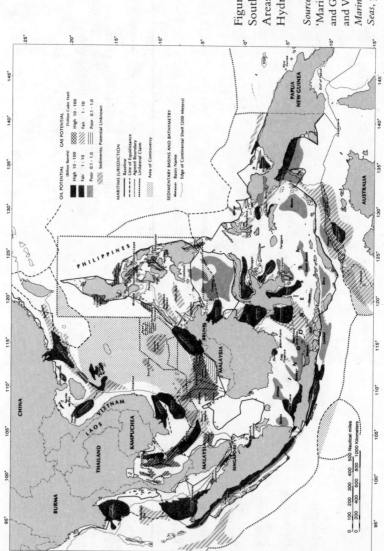

Figure 4.2
South-East Asia: Potential
Areas of Conflict over
Hydrocarbons.

Source: M.J. Valencia (1983),
'Maritime Jurisdiction and Oil
and Gas Potential', in Morgan
and Valencia, eds., *Atlas for
Marine Policy in Southeast Asian
Seas,* p. 132.

TABLE 4.2

Rough Gross Value of Oil and Gas in Overlapping Claim Areas

Area	Amount[1]		Value[2]		Total (US$ billion)
	Oil (billion bbl)	Gas (trillion cu. ft)	Oil (US$ billion)	Gas (US$ billion)	
Gulf of Tonkin	1–10	n.a.	15–150	n.a.	15–150
Dangerous Ground	?	0.1–1.0	?	0.25–2.5	0.25–2.5
Natuna	?	1–10	?	25–250	25–250
Eastern Gulf of Thailand	1–10	1–10	15–150	25–250	40–400
Offshore Brunei	1–10	10–100	15–150	250–2,500	265–2,650
Arafura Sea	10–100	?	150–1,500	?	150–1,500

Source: Valencia and Marsh (1986), Table 1.
? = unknown.
n.a. = not available.

[1] Albers et al. (1973), Summary Petroleum and Selected Mineral Statistics for 120 Countries Including Offshore Areas, Table 1.
[2] At US$15.00/bbl of oil and US$2.50/1,000 cu. ft of gas.

The disputed area offshore from Brunei and that in the Arafura Sea may contain up to US$2.65 trillion and US$1.5 trillion worth of oil and gas respectively (Table 4.2). The disputed basins in the eastern Gulf of Thailand may contain US$40 billion to US$400 billion worth of oil and gas. And the Natuna area may contain from US$25 billion to US$250 billion worth of gas and oil. It is small wonder the various countries are adamant about their claims to and interests in these areas.

Trouble Spots

TIMOR SEA, SULAWESI SEA, EASTERN GULF OF THAILAND

In the Timor Sea, Australia and Indonesia have negotiated a joint development agreement to resolve a dispute that began in February 1979. In the Sulawesi Sea, Malaysian and Indonesian differences over Pulau Sipadan continue to surface, intensified by possible hydrocarbon potential in the channel where the island is situated. In the eastern Gulf of Thailand, Kampuchea has protested Thailand's· renewal of a concession to Amoco, which it asserts encroaches on Kampuchea's claimed continental shelf, and similarly, Vietnam has warned Thailand not to allow international companies to explore for oil in areas claimed by Vietnam or Kampuchea. The warning followed the Thai renewal of concessions to Union and to a Japanese company (*Business Day*, 1983). In July 1982, Vietnam and Heng Samrin Kampuchea settled their boundary dispute and agreed on joint historical internal waters where petroleum and fisheries will be developed by 'common agreement'. However, the clandestine Voice of Democratic Kampuchea denounced this agreement as null and void and rejected the 12 November 1982 Vietnamese declaration of baselines for territorial waters that incorporated areas claimed by Kampuchea (*PN*, September 1982; *FBIS*, 1983).

NATUNA SEA

In the Natuna area, Indonesia believes Vietnam keeps the overlap area in dispute to prevent Indonesia from developing petroleum there. Indonesia included the area in its contract block system and has given approval to several American contract holders to proceed with exploration. On 29 November 1979, the Vietnamese Foreign Ministry issued a statement regretting Pertamina's 20 March 1979 invitation for exploration bids in Natuna Blocks A, B, C, and D-1 to D-6 in the disputed area and stated that 'foreign companies should pay attention to this matter and should not conduct survey and exploration operations in the disputed area without Vietnam's consent'. About this time, an Indonesian naval patrol intercepted 'foreign armed vessels believed to be Vietnamese' near the Natuna Islands (van der Kroef, 1982). Indonesia has promised military assistance to the American oil companies if they are bothered by Vietnam, and in 1981 Indonesia undertook a massive military exercise in the area to defend against a mock attack from the north. The possibility of a South China Sea conflict with Vietnam was an important stimulus to the purchase of military hardware from the United States (Crouch, 1985). Three American oil companies—Amoseas, Gulf, and Marathon—continue to explore in the disputed area under production-sharing contracts with Pertamina, despite the warnings by Vietnam.

SPRATLY AREA

The Spratly Islands have long borne the seeds of international conflict. They are claimed and now occupied in varying degrees by forces of China, Taiwan, Malaysia, the Philippines, and Vietnam (Figure 4.3). On 14 March 1988, the dispute over ownership of the islands and the resources in their attendant 200-nmi EEZs erupted into violence when Chinese and Vietnamese troops and ships exchanged fire on and near Sinh Cow island. The Philippines subsequently reinforced its garrisons on eight islands, and renewed its claim to most of the island group. Then in April 1988, the Malaysian Navy seized three Philippine fishing vessels near Rizal Reef and detained their 49-member crew for fishing without a permit. They were subsequently released only after an appeal by President Corazon Aquino to Prime Minister Mahathir Mohamad.

Many nations have been involved in offshore projects in the Spratly area, including China, the Philippine National Oil Company, and US companies. However, oil is only one factor in the milieu of international tensions focusing on the Spratly area. The Spratly Islands are strategic as bases for sea-lane defence, interdiction, and surveillance and possibly for launching of land attacks. The security interests of outside powers—Japan, the United States, and the Soviet Union—are involved (Nielsen, 1982: 70).

The dispute between Vietnam and China over the Spratlys is of

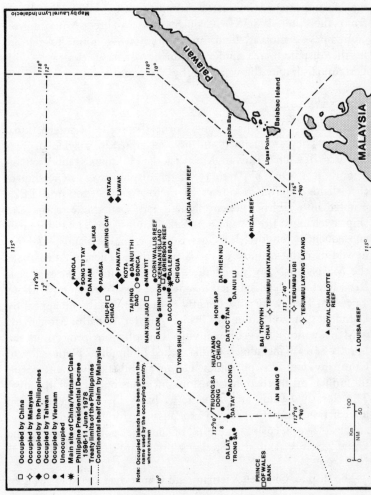

Figure 4.3
Dangerous Ground: Claims
and Occupations.

Sources: Updated from
J. R. V. Prescott (1981),
*Maritime Jurisdiction in Southeast
Asia: A Commentary and Map*,
East–West Environment and
Policy Institute Research
Report No. 2; 'Another
Spratlys Spat', *Asiaweek*,
20 May 1988, pp. 26–7;
Mark J. Valencia, 'All-for-
everyone Solution', *Far Eastern
Economic Review*, 30 March
1989, pp. 20–1.

particular interest to the Soviet Union, both as an ally and a supporter of Vietnam on this issue and as an enemy of China, because the controller of those islands could dominate the major sea lanes of communication. Vietnam believes China's objectives are to seize sole control of the sea, master this international lifeline, replace the US Navy in the region, hinder the Soviet Navy's navigation, apply political pressure on South-East Asian countries, build a military springboard in the region, seize territory, and exploit and plunder maritime resources.

The Soviet Union would consider its naval mobility and capacity for stealth threatened by Chinese control of the islands. Similarly, the United States has a national security interest in unimpeded and occasionally undetected transit by vessels of the Seventh Fleet through the South China Sea. Finally, all concerned are aware the Japanese used Itu Aba as a submarine base and jumping-off point for its invasion of the Philippines in the Second World War (*FBIS*, 21 February 1984: K-3; del Mundo, 1982: A-11).

China considers the islands to be a means of countering the growing Soviet presence in the area as well as of monitoring Soviet naval movements (Nielsen, 1982: 68). Recently China reasserted its claim as its blue-water navy made its first ever sortie through the area shortly before the ASEAN foreign ministers held their annual meeting in Singapore (Stockwin, 1987). Apparently China's military forces have now occupied about six features in the area. Vietnam has warned that China will 'face all the consequences' if it does not remove them (Wedel, 1988). China does believe there is oil in the area and it may have been trying to settle the dispute to bolster investment and development of Hainan, which would serve as a base for Spratly oil exploration. Of course, China may also have been serving notice to Vietnam that China has the confidence and military clout to back up its claims there. In making far-reaching boundary claims, China is not necessarily serving notice that it actually intends to undertake oil development within the entire area claimed, but it may be motivated by a desire to corner oil development rights as a bargaining chip in dealing with littoral states.

In the Philippines, then President Marcos pledged to defend oil concessions located up to 200 nmi offshore, including those already granted. Manila considers the islands vital to the defence of its western perimeter. Sino–Soviet rivalry may explain the increased Philippine reliance on the United States to support its claims to the area. The Philippines, and perhaps the United States, sees its efforts to consolidate and strengthen its military presence in the Spratlys as one way to prevent Vietnamese (and thus Soviet) control from spreading over the area (Valencia, 1981: 330).

Vietnam has consistently voiced its intention to maintain sovereignty over the entire Spratly archipelago. Vietnamese forces now occupy about 20 features in the area. Vietnam's main garrison, Song Tu Tay, is about 25 nmi north-west of the Philippines' main garrison, Pagasa, and is fortified with heavy coastal artillery and anti-aircraft guns (Park, 1978). And Taiwan has occupied the largest island in the Spratly group, Tai Ping Dao, since 1956, and a force of 600 troops is maintained on the island (Cooper, 1981: BRU-2).

In June 1983 Malaysia landed troops on Terumbu Layang-Layang (Da Hoa Lau), 64 km south-east of An Bang (Ambon), and accommodation modules were ordered for the atoll. Just after the occupation, three F5E fighters were moved to Labuan to provide cover for the occupying troops. Malaysia is developing a naval base at Sungai Aute in Sibu, Sarawak, for missile-armed patrol craft operating in the South China Sea. The occupation was justified by indications that Vietnam intended to occupy the atoll. Malaysian forces have since occupied two more features in the area. Brunei, with its almost total economic dependence on petroleum, may make a claim to part of the area as well.

THE GULF OF TONKIN

China, in granting contracts to US oil companies for exploration in the areas bordering the disputed area in the Gulf of Tonkin, has effectively merged US and Chinese interests in the event of a flare-up and has also pre-empted Hanoi's hope of wooing US oil companies. Also, US support for the Chinese position could be bolstered by the prospect of increased Chinese oil exports to ASEAN and Japan, and thus integration of China into a pattern of stable commercial relations with Japan, the United States, and ASEAN. Chinese troops continue to occupy scores of small but strategic positions on the mountainous border with Vietnam, not only for strategic reasons, but also for their use as bargaining chips in an overall settlement of the territorial dispute with Vietnam over the Gulf of Tonkin and the Spratly and Paracel Islands. At least half of the 600 vessels in China's South Sea fleet have been assigned to protection of the offshore oilfields and Chinese waters (Samuels, 1982: 139). Vietnam sees this as an attempt by China in collusion with the United States to eventually blockade Vietnam by controlling the sea lanes (Samuels, 1982: 139). Meanwhile, there are at least 10 Soviet vessels in the South China Sea at any time and at least 20 Soviet long-range surveillance flights per year originating or ending in Vietnam. China proved the seriousness of its island and maritime claims in 1974 when it forcefully expelled South Vietnamese troops from the Paracel Islands. The current Sino-Vietnamese conflict has sharply increased the strategic importance of the islands. Thus, the Soviet Union, now searching for oil on behalf of its ally Vietnam, and the United States, on behalf of its oil companies, may be brought face to face in an area disputed by two ancient and bitter enemies.

THE TAIWAN STRAIT

The EEZ claimed by Taiwan encompasses areas in the Taiwan Strait offered for bidding by China, including discoveries in the Pearl River Basin (*PN*, August 1983; *Honolulu Advertiser*, 24 August 1983). The waters in the Taiwan Strait represent a particularly sensitive area in the geopolitics of East–West relations. China–Taiwan relations are likely to continue to be tense and stalemated for some time to come. Indeed, Taiwan fears that China may eventually be tempted to launch a full-scale attack or throw a naval blockade around the island. Such a blockade could severely damage Taiwan's oil-import-dependent and export-oriented economy. Conflict over jurisdictional boundaries and oil resources in the Taiwan Strait could fuel China–Taiwan animosity and involve American oil companies and the US government as well.

Environmental Aspects

Exploration in deeper waters further offshore will have an environmental cost. Indonesia, the region's leading producer, is projected to experience two accidents every one and a half years. The region as a whole is expected to experience 1.4 accidents per year resulting in spillage of 52 million tons of crude oil (Hann *et al.*, 1981). Some of these spills could easily cross claimed national boundaries, e.g. between China and Vietnam or between Malaysia and Vietnam, and could exacerbate political tensions.

Common Threads in the Pattern of Conflict

Overriding security concerns involving East–West tensions can hinder or help peaceful resolution of these disputes (Østreng, 1985). Competition between the Soviet Union and the United States for influence in the region, and consequently the Kampuchea issue and the Soviet–United States–China triangular relationship, affect the disputes in South-East Asia. Vietnam is an actor in all of the multiple claim areas in the South China Sea. The Soviet Union is an ally of Vietnam and has signed an agreement establishing a joint venture for exploration and exploitation of hydrocarbons from the continental shelf of southern Vietnam (*Oil and Gas Journal*, 2 August 1982: 84). The United States is an ally of the Philippines and Thailand and a good friend of the remaining ASEAN countries and, until recently, of China. American oil companies hold concessions in all of the multiple claim areas except the Spratlys. Some of these areas are becoming increasingly militarized. All states in the region need to develop the resources to fuel their development drives through foreign exchange earnings. Thus, competition between regional states backed by their respective allies may exacerbate the militarization process.

Fisheries Disputes

CONFLICTING GOALS

Fisheries contribute only a few per cent or less of GNP of the ASEAN countries, but about 65 per cent of the animal protein consumed in Indonesia, Malaysia, and the Philippines; and more than 2 million persons are employed in fisheries (excluding secondary employment). Further, ASEAN countries exported nearly US$1 billion worth of fish in 1980 (Table 4.3) and have an annual potential product of over US$5 billion. Most important, rural coastal peoples in South-East Asia depend on fish for nutrition, employment, and their way of life. Yet the resource is in danger of destruction brought about by overfishing and fishing with destructive methods like explosives, poisons, and very fine mesh nets, pollution, and destruction of coastal breeding areas (*Asian Action*, March/April 1978: 1).

TABLE 4.3

Socio-economic Contributions of the Marine Fishing Sector in ASEAN Countries, 1980

Country	Marine Catch[1]		Fishery Exports		Percentage of Protein from Fish[5]	Labour Force in Marine Fishing[6] ('000 people)
	Value (US$ million)	Percentage of GNP[2]	Value[3] (US$ million)	As Percentage of Total Exports[4]		
Indonesia	964	1.4	226	1.0	65	1,650
Malaysia	644	2.7	135	1.1	65	109
Philippines	1,135	3.2	138	3.0	62	315
Singapore	45	nil	707	0.3	35	2
Thailand	382	1.1	354	5.3	n.a.	68
Total ASEAN	3,170	1.7	923	1.4	n.a.	2,144
Total SEA	6,615				n.a.	4,467[8]
% ASEAN/SEA	47.9				n.a.	n.a.

n.a. = not available.

[1] From Table 5 in E. Samson (1984), 'Marine Resources and Development', unpublished manuscript, Environment and Policy Institute, Honolulu: East–West Center.

[2] GNP data from *Far Eastern Economic Review, Asia Yearbook 1983*.

[3] From J. M. Floyd (1984), *International Fish Trade of Southeast Asian Nations*, East–West Environment and Policy Institute Research Report, Honolulu: East–West Center.

[4] Merchandise exports data from *Far Eastern Economic Review, Asia Yearbook 1983*.

[5] From E. Samson (1985), 'Fisheries', in G. Kent and M.J. Valencia, eds., *Marine Policy in Southeast Asia*, Berkeley: University of California Press.

[6] Computed from data in Samson (1985).

[7] Including re-exports.

[8] Extrapolated from percentage of ASEAN production to SEA production (48 per cent).

Extended jurisdiction offers the possibility of enhanced offshore potential. However, the valuable species such as tuna and mackerel are already fished by distant-water fishing countries, and some national development policies view joint ventures with foreign companies as vehicles for the technically modern exploitation, processing, and marketing of these resources. Thus high-value fish are exported out of the region to developed countries while intraregional offshore and artisanal fishermen compete with each other for dwindling coastal resources, sometimes violently.

The rapid introduction of sophisticated fishing technology by private or state-controlled companies has seriously disrupted the traditional organization of small-scale fishermen. The construction of small trawlers has intensified the pressure on coastal stocks, and small-scale fishing has been neglected in development plans which focus on full-time fishermen. Although policy-makers in these countries are beginning to become more sensitive to the plight of small-scale fishermen, laws prohibiting the use of trawlers close to the coast have not been effectively enforced, and over-exploitation of stocks threatens job opportunities for fishermen.

For the distant-water fishing countries, the negotiation of fishing agreements and joint ventures is often the only way both to use the overcapitalized fleets and to continue to control the importation of fish products. In 1982, Japanese large-scale deep-sea fishing enterprises participated in 184 joint ventures in 44 foreign countries. Not coincidentally, Japan supplies more than half of the bilateral fisheries aid given to the countries in the region (Josupeit, 1983). Denmark, Norway, and the Netherlands have also supplied European fishing boats and research boats.

Aquaculture is often seen as a panacea for diminished stocks, lost access to fisheries, and the resultant loss of food and cheap animal protein. However, it would be premature to present aquaculture as a remedy to the problems of maritime fishing. Many of the development programmes for aquaculture have been disappointing. Further, most aquaculture enterprises to date focus largely on high-value species, e.g. shrimp for export to the developed world. Aquaculture requires a relatively high capital investment, and potential mariculturists are often reluctant to invest because of the uncertainty of ownership laws. Pollution is also a deterrent. Thus the anticipated benefits have not materialized, and the potential of aquaculture remains largely unrealized.

FISHERIES POTENTIAL

Extended maritime jurisdictional claims are shown superimposed on total present marine catch in Figure 4.4, giving a rough picture of the amount being caught in each country's claim area, although not necessarily by the country itself. Several areas of overlapping claims may harbour fisheries potential of significant gross value. For example, the Dangerous Ground (US$8.4 million/yr), the Miangas area (as much as US$7.4 million/yr), and the eastern Gulf of Thailand (about US$7.3 million/yr) are especially promising (Table 4.4).

Potential fish product quantities and values (Table 4.4) range from negative for the Philippines and Thailand to a factor of three for Malaysia. However, these optimistic projections must be tempered by realistic cost estimates as well as the elasticity of demand for fish. Rapid expansion towards the potential goal could depress prices and result in negative returns. Diseconomies of scale can be anticipated in relation to vessel efficiency. Moreover, good port space is a scarce resource, subject to rising marginal costs. Finally, expansion of the fisheries would draw labour and other resources from other sectors of the economies. It is thus uncertain if the resulting social opportunity costs for any nation would be offset by the increased value of product.

EFFORTS TO PROTECT FISHERIES RESOURCES

The search for fish for export and domestic use by distant-water fishers produces conflict with states trying to protect their newly gained resources. Numerous enforcement actions have resulted in the seizure of fishing vessels, and many of these incidents have been accompanied by gunfire. Thailand's concern is directed toward protecting and regulating its own fishing fleet which has been exposed to armed attack and seizure by Kampuchea, Vietnam, Burma, and now Malaysia (McDorman and Tasneeyanond, 1987). The incidents of gunfire almost all involved Thai fishing vessels as targets of Vietnamese and Kampuchean patrol boats. Exclusion of foreign fishing vessels is clearly the policy of Kampuchea; naval units routinely patrol the Kampuchean EEZ, and apparently surveillance duties are also assigned to civilian observers. In nearly all cases involving Thai fishing boats, there was no reported protest by the government of Thailand, suggesting that the boats were in fact fishing illegally.

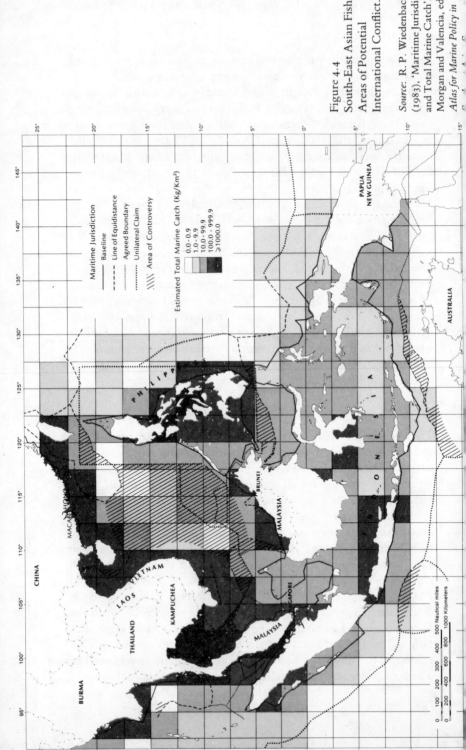

Figure 4.4
South-East Asian Fisheries:
Areas of Potential
International Conflict.

Source: R. P. Wiedenbach
(1983), 'Maritime Jurisdiction
and Total Marine Catch', in
Morgan and Valencia, eds.,
Atlas for Marine Policy in

TABLE 4.4

Rough Approximation of Total Catch and Gross Annual Value in Areas of Overlapping Claims[1]

Countries	Area of Overlap sq. km (sq. nmi)	Present Average Fishing Intensity (kg/sq. km)	Total Present Catch (tonnes)	Main Species[2]	Total Annual Gross Value[3] (US$ million)
Taiwan/Philippines	49 392 (14,440)	36.8	1 818		1.40
Taiwan/Philippines	13 274 (3,870)	4.5	60	Small pelagics,[4] skipjack, squid, demersal species	0.46
Japan/Philippines	2 058	4.5	9		0.10
Philippines/China/Taiwan/ Malaysia/Indonesia	240 615 (70,150)	45.5	10 950	Tuna, small pelagics[4]	8.40
Vietnam/Indonesia	38 656	220	8 504		3.00
Kampuchea/Thailand	19 887 (5,798)	> 1 000	> 19 887		> 4.40
Thailand/Vietnam	799 (233)	> 1 000	> 799	Demersal species, small pelagics[4]	> 0.20
Thailand/Vietnam/Kampuchea	12 382 (3,610)	> 1 000	> 12 382		> 2.70

(continued)

TABLE 4.4 (continued)

Countries	Area of Overlap sq. km (sq. nmi)	Present Average Fishing Intensity (kg/sq. km)	Total Present Catch (tonnes)	Main Species[2]	Total Annual Gross Value[3] (US$ million)
Philippines/Indonesia	14 749 (4,300)	450	6 637	Tuna, small pelagics[4]	5.10
Philippines/Indonesia	21 266 (6,200)	450	9 570		7.40
Malaysia/Philippines	8 301 (2,420)	4.5	37		0.03
Indonesia/Australia	41 160 (12,000)	1.6	66		0.02
Indonesia/Australia	74 088 (21,600)	1.5	111		0.04
Total	536 627	n.a.	70 830		> 48.11

Source: Valencia and Marsh (1986), Table 2.

n.a. = not available.

[1]This catch is included in the total catch for each country's claimed area. Rough approximations from Ronald Weidenbach (1983). 'Fisheries', in J.R. Morgan and M.J. Valencia, eds., *Atlas for Marine Policy in Southeast Asian Seas*, Berkeley: University of California Press, pp. 56–79.

[2]Expansion possible.

[3]Values calculated following method in Table 4.5. Of two or more countries, the higher price is used.

[4]Mackerels, roundscads, sardines.

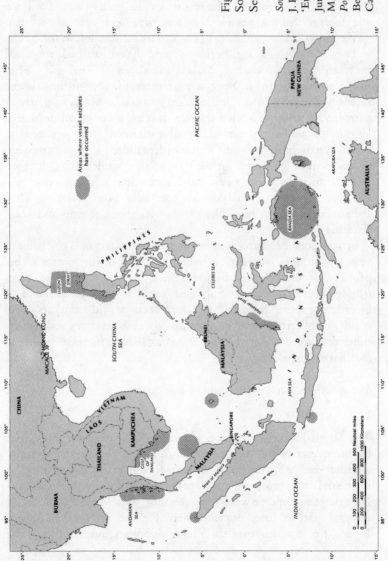

Figure 4.5
South-East Asia: Vessel Seizures.

Source: H. F. Olson and J. R. Morgan (1985), 'Enforcement of Maritime Jurisdiction', in G. Kent and M. J. Valencia, eds., *Marine Policy in Southeast Asia*, Berkeley: University of California Press.

Figure 4.5 shows the regions where vessel seizures have taken place. The Tenasserim coast of Burma, the Gulf of Thailand, the Gulf of Tonkin, and the Luzon Strait have been the principal areas. Indonesia seized at least 77 foreign fishing vessels between 1974 and 1980 (Olson and Morgan, 1985). Burma has been pursuing an active campaign against foreign fishing vessels within its EEZ, including those that may only be in transit to destinations beyond Burmese waters. The seizure by the Philippines of at least 162 foreign fishing vessels between 1972 and 1980 show that government's determination to enforce its jurisdiction in the EEZ.

The Malaysia/Thai fisheries dispute has disturbed relations between the two countries. Malaysia declared its EEZ and a new Fisheries Act in 1985. Malaysian seizures of Thai fishing boats intensified in mid-1986. One incident involved a Malaysian coastal patrol craft firing at a Thai trawler, leaving a crewman dead and another wounded. Some 824 Thai fishermen were arrested in 1986. Thai protesters in Pattani demanded the government despatch navy gunboats for their protection while fishing lobbies in Peninsular Malaysia's east coast states demanded more arrests of Thai fishermen. Malaysia has not only been arresting Thai fishermen caught fishing illegally but has been seizing and confiscating their vessels and equipment as well.

In addition, Malaysia has insisted that passage of Thai fishing vessels through its EEZ is conditional on prior notice. The problem is unlikely to disappear in the long term. The Thai fishing fleet has the sixth largest catch in the world, and a lucrative export industry to developed world markets. To maintain this, it must at least transit Malaysian waters and fish in other countries' waters because it has exhausted its own resources (Sricharatcharya, 1987).

Use of Ocean Space: Straits and Sea-lane Access

THE SETTING

The South-East Asian region is a nexus of maritime routes used by the navies of the superpowers and their allies. Strategic straits abound, and with extension of jurisdiction many fall within the territorial or archipelagic waters of the region's states. Competition between the superpowers for access to these straits will be an integral part of the *realpolitik* here for the foreseeable future. Figure 4.6 superimposes the major shipping routes through the

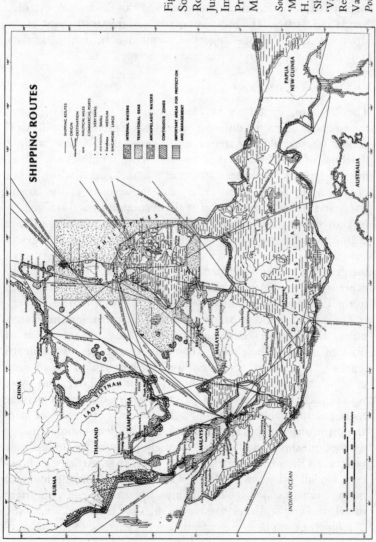

Figure 4.6
South-East Asia: Shipping
Routes, Maritime
Jurisdictional Zones, and
Important Areas for
Protection and
Management.

Source: J. R. V. Prescott (1983),
'Maritime Jurisdictions',
H. F. Olson and J. R. Morgan,
'Shipping', and A. White,
'Valuable and Vulnerable
Resources', all in Morgan and
Valencia, eds., *Atlas for Marine
Policy in Southeast Asian Seas.*

region over extended maritime jurisdiction zones and highlights critical straits and sea lanes encompassed by the claims of the Philippines and Indonesia. The following straits in the region are strategic because they all serve as entrances to and exits from South-East Asian seas and are choke points where naval forces could interfere with enemy shipping with relative ease: Malacca–Singapore, Lombok, Makassar, Taiwan, Luzon (including the Bashi, Balintang, and Babuyan channels), Ombai, Wetar, San Bernardino, Verde Island Passage, and, of lesser importance, Sunda and Torres. The most important and frequently used of the straits is the Malacca–Singapore combination, which funnels traffic from the Indian Ocean into the South China Sea.

THE LEGAL CONTEXT

The UN Convention on the Law of the Sea (UNCLOS) defines the rights of aliens for different activities in different jurisdictional zones. Internal waters are of two types—those inside straight baselines of normal coastal states, and those within closing baselines of archipelagic states. 'Innocent passage' is that which is not prejudicial to peace, good order, and the security of the coastal state, and it can be suspended if these conditions are violated. A foreign ship is considered to have violated the innocent passage regime of a coastal state if within its territorial sea it engages in any threat or use of force against the sovereignty, territorial integrity, or political independence of the coastal state, or in any other manner violates the principles of international law embodied in the Charter of the United Nations (UN, 1982: Article 19).

There is no innocent passage regime for normal internal waters unless those waters have been delimited by new methods of drawing straight baselines. There are two types of territorial seas—those territorial waters not used for international navigation, in which the regime of innocent passage is applicable, and those waters used for international passage, where the transit passage regime is applicable. An archipelagic state may designate sea lanes and air routes suitable for the continuous and expeditious passage of foreign ships and aircraft through or over its archipelagic waters and the adjacent territorial sea (UN, 1982: Article 53); however, in all other archipelagic waters, the regime of innocent passage remains applicable. All ships and aircraft enjoy the right of archipelagic sea lanes passage in such sea lanes and air routes. 'Archipelagic sea lanes passage' means the exercise of the rights of navigation and overflight in the normal mode. The archipelagic state is also obligated to promote the adoption of routeing systems designed to minimize the threat of accidents that might cause pollution of the marine environment, including the coastline, and pollution damage to the related interests of coastal states (UN, 1982: Article 211).

POINTS OF LEGAL CONTENTION

The UNCLOS text adopts most of the views promoted by the maritime powers, clarifying the right of innocent passage, codifying the rights of transit passage through international straits and of archipelagic sea lanes passage, and protecting navigational rights in the EEZ. However, the United States has refused to sign or ratify the UNCLOS. Although UNCLOS is specific about navigational rights and responsibilities, several states in the region have practices or positions on navigation that are not covered by or are counter to UNCLOS provisions. For example, there are no provisions in the UNCLOS or other treaties for air defence and military warning zones. Yet Burma, Thailand, Indonesia, and Taiwan have extensive air defence zones. Burma, India, and Vietnam have also established military warning zones 24 nmi wide, and Kampuchea has declared such zones 12 nmi wide. Alien warships and military aircraft are prohibited from these waters; in the Vietnamese zone, other vessels also must secure permission to traverse these waters (Prescott, 1983: 45), and Vietnam also restricts the access of foreign warships in a 24-nmi-wide contiguous zone (Dzurek, 1985). China also disputes the right of innocent passage through its 12-nmi territorial sea, and after 1997 it will require permission for foreign warships to enter Hong Kong waters (*Far Eastern Economic Review*, 4 October 1984).

Although the Philippines and Indonesia have ratified UNCLOS, they assert that non-signatories of UNCLOS like the United States do not have the right of transit passage in straits and sea-lane passage in archipelagos. Meanwhile, the United States does not recognize territorial sea claims of other countries more than 3 nmi from shore and has stated it will challenge such claims with US Navy ships, including specifically the claims of Burma and the Philippines (Wilson, 1979: 17). The United States has repeatedly made good on its threat, most notably in the Gulf of Sidra, which is claimed as a historic Gulf by Libya. Thailand, Malaysia, and Indonesia claim 12-nmi territorial seas, which in some places encompass straits used for international navigation.

The Philippines' territorial sea claim reaches up to 284 nmi in width and includes all its critical straits. Although the Philippines ratified UNCLOS, it did so with reservations (Republic of the Philippines, 1982; Tolentino, 1982; Foz, 1983: 1, 14). The Philippines feels that sea lanes denigrate the integrity of the archipelagic concept and the unity of the nation. However, it has agreed to designate two sea lanes through the heart of the archipelago—one extending from the Sibutu passage through Mindoro Strait and the other from the Surigao Strait through the Balabac Strait (Figure 4.7). However, the United States wants a third sea lane, particularly for nuclear submarines—San Bernardino Strait through the Verde Island passage. The Philippines does not want the submarines and other warships passing close by Manila. It feels its case is different from that of Indonesia because it borders the Pacific and its straits are internal to the country and less than 12 nmi wide and so could be declared territorial waters.

It is not only the indigenous and maritime powers that face conflict over the use of sea lanes. The declaration of the archipelagic principle by Indonesia has implications for most of its neighbours. In particular, Peninsular Malaysia is separated from Sarawak and Sabah by Indonesia's baselines enclosing the Natuna Islands. Malaysia and Indonesia have concluded a treaty providing Malaysia with, among others, the right of access and communication for Malaysian ships and aircraft in and over designated sea lanes and traditional fishing rights. However, the treaty provides Indonesia with the right, in the interest of its security, to suspend temporarily the exercise of the right of access by Malaysian ships (Hamzah, 1984).

Environmental Aspects

Environmental degradation and conflicts over diminishing shares of renewable natural resources are now an important cause of violent human conflicts both within and between states (*Honolulu Advertiser*, 29 November 1984: B1). In South-East Asia, oil is a major pollutant, and the major at-sea source is tankers traversing the region. Eastbound tankers proceeding along the Malacca–Singapore straits–South China Sea route are for the most part loaded with crude petroleum from the Arabian Gulf area bound for East Asia, with some originating in Malaysian west coast ports or Indonesian ports on the north-east coast of Sumatra. South-

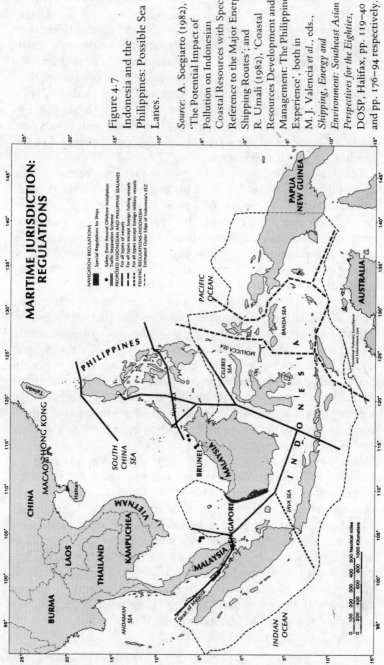

Figure 4.7
Indonesia and the
Philippines: Possible Sea
Lanes.

Source: A. Soegiarto (1982),
'The Potential Impact of
Pollution on Indonesian
Coastal Resources with Special
Reference to the Major Energy
Shipping Routes'; and
R. Umali (1982), 'Coastal
Resources Development and
Management: The Philippine
Experience', both in
M.J. Valencia *et al.*, eds.,
*Shipping, Energy and
Environment: Southeast Asian
Perspectives for the Eighties*,
DOSP, Halifax, pp. 119–40
and pp. 176–94 respectively.

MARITIME JURISDICTION: REGULATIONS

NAVIGATION REGULATIONS
● Safety Zone Around Offshore Installation
Special Regulations for Ships
Traffic Separation Scheme
PROPOSED INDONESIAN AND PHILIPPINE SEALANES
For all types of vessels
For all types except foreign fishing vessels
For all types except foreign military vessels
FISHING REGULATIONS-INDONESIA
Estimated Outer Edge of Indonesia's EEZ

and west-bound traffic either carries refined products or is in ballast.

The physical restrictions imposed by channel depths of less than 23 m (75 ft) in the straits, and the safety limitation of a 3.5-m under-keel clearance added by the three coastal states, effectively preclude the use of this route by fully laden tankers of more than 200,000 d.w.t. which commonly have a draft of 19 m (62 ft) or more. The alternative route for these Very Large Crude Carriers (VLCCs) is through the deep (150 m) and wide (12.5 nmi minimum) waters of the Lombok and Makassar straits and the Celebes Sea south of Mindanao.

The Malacca–Singapore straits, greatly preferred because of the shorter distance involved, is used by 72 per cent of the eastbound, loaded tankers; the Lombok–Makassar straits by only 28 per cent. At any one time, there would be approximately 51 loaded or returning VLCCs in the region (Olson and Morgan, 1984). This creates a likelihood of 24.5 spills per year averaging 1 000 tonnes each within 50 miles of land and 5.6 spills per year averaging 3 338 tonnes each outside of 50 miles (Hann et al., 1981).

Between 0.35 and 0.50 per cent of a tanker's cargo settles to the bottom of the tank during long sea voyages, and unscrupulous operators discharge this residue into the sea. Approximately 1,000 tons or 300,000 gallons on a single voyage of a 200,000-ton tanker could be discharged into the sea with tank wash water. In South-East Asia this phenomenon results in major concentrations of ballast discharge at each end of the Malacca Strait, in the western Java Sea, west of Madura, off Balikpapan, and off Brunei and Sabah. Also, plumes of tank washings are generated along the two major tanker routes (Figure 4.8).

World-wide between 1978 and 1983, there were 473 reported marine accidents. Of this total, liquefied propane gas (LPG) ships accounted for 224 of the accidents, and specialized tankers accounted for 242 accidents. The accidents involving LPG carriers have been useful in designing better ships, but LNG carriers are still an unknown quantity. Even less is known about nuclear waste carriers, which carry spent nuclear fuel in steel flasks. The major hazard these ships pose is that, in the event of a loss of cooling water, the flasks would heat up and eventually breach the container. If this were to happen in a confined waterway, the ecological results could be catastrophic (Lauriat, 1985).

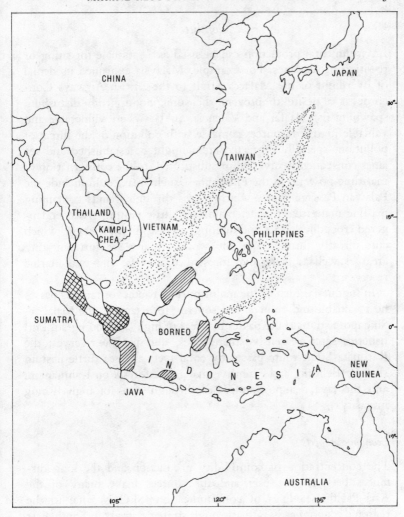

Figure 4.8
South-East Asia: Ballast
and Tank Washings.

Source: R. W. Hann, Jr. *et al.*
(1981), 'The Status of Oil
Pollution and Oil Pollution
Control in the Southeast Asian
Region', Texas A&M
University, April, p. 182
(Figure 5–25).

 BALLAST DISCHARGE PRIOR
TO TRANSITING STRAITS

 BALLAST DISCHARGE PRIOR
TO LOADING

 TANK WASHINGS

Conflict

Environmental protection can be used as a rationale for siting or re-siting of sea lanes. For example, Malaysia explained its denial of overflight of the Malacca Strait to the British Airways Concorde as a desire to prevent the sonic boom from disturbing spawning fish (Jaafar and Valencia, 1985). Where vulnerable and valuable marine resources coincide with pollution or the threat of pollution, specially protected areas might be established and sea lanes consequently diverted or substituted, to the consternation of maritime powers. In the Philippines, such areas could include the Palawan Passage route, which passes through islands containing pristine mangrove forests, major sea turtle nesting areas, endangered crocodile species and dugong, and the Sibitu Passage, which cuts directly through one the world's major sea turtle nesting areas as well as mangrove forests, coral reefs, and two marine reserves.

In Indonesia, each of the major normal routes for tankers passes near valuable and vulnerable resources; for example, the Malacca–Singapore straits route passes by areas of high (>1 000 kg/sq. km) fisheries catch, extensive mangroves, and marine reserves; the Karimata Strait route passes by coral reefs and sea turtle nesting sites on Belitung and extensive mangrove forests on Kalimantan; and the Java Sea portion passes through areas of high fishing intensity.

Economic Aspects

The concentration of commodity production and the long distances between the user and the sources make many of the Asia–Pacific sea lines of communication (SLOCs) vital to the region's economies. Traffic through strategic straits in South-East Asia could be interrupted by mines or obstacles to navigation placed within them. Sea lanes in South-East Asia are especially important because they serve as potential choke points for a significant share of world trade in this region. For example, much of Indonesian oil production from Sumatra is fed into refineries and tanker ports on the Malacca Strait. If the Strait were interdicted, much of Indonesia's export earnings would be lost, and Japan would lose 16 per cent of its oil supply and a significant share of its LNG imports. The cutoff of oil to Japan would have a

TABLE 4.5

Effects of Sea-lane Blockage[1,2]

To San Francisco	via Malacca/ Singapore Strait	Outside 200-nmi Regime	Difference
Per Barrel Cost (US$)	1.13	1.48	0.35
Total Annual Costs[3] (US$ million)	206	270	64
Non-discounted Costs 1976–2000 (US$ million)	5,510	6,750	1,240

From South-East Asia to Japan, the United States, and Europe
(For Oil from Indonesia/Singapore to the Rest of the World)[4]

Trading Partners	Percentage Drop in Real GDP			Secondary Impacts on Other Major Trading Partners
	1983	1984	1985	
United States	0.4 (0.6)	0.8 (1.1)	1.0 (0.3)	Minimal
Japan	1.6 (4.9)	6.5 (4.9)	7.1 (2.4)	Varying—severe to minimal
Belgium	1.6 (0.7)	2.5 (1.4)	2.5 (1.3)	Minimal

[1]Assuming all trips are made in 250,000-d.w.t. tankers at 1973 charter hire rates and bunker fuel is priced at US$70/ton.
[2]From D. B. Johnson and D. E. Logue (1976), 'U.S. Economic Interests in Law of the Sea Issues', in R. C. Amachen and R. J. Sweeney (eds.), The Law of the Sea: U.S. Interests and Alternatives, Washington, DC: American Enterprise Institute for Public Policy Research.
[3]Assuming 2.0 million bbl/day to Atlantic and 0.5 million bbl/day to the Pacific coast.
[4]From R. C. Fabrie (1983), 'SLOC Security–Economic Impact', paper presented at the 1983 Pacific Symposium, Washington, DC, National Defense University.

secondary economic impact on its major trading partners, including Indonesia and the United States. Singapore's economy would be virtually shut down. Singapore, with its oil refineries and tanker ports, serves as an outlet for some Malaysian oil exports, and thus interdiction of the Malacca Strait would severely impact Malaysia's economy as well. As for secondary effects (Table 4.5), interdiction of sea oil movements between Indonesia and Singapore and other ports world-wide could reduce Australia's GDP by 8.1 per cent in the third year and Japan's GDP by about 5 per cent in the first two years with severe secondary impact for Australia (Fabrie, 1983).

Even the re-routeing of maritime traffic, particularly oil tankers, can be expensive. For example, the diversion from the Malacca to the Lombok Strait of all tankers on the Middle East–Japan route could cost importers over US$100 million per year (Das, 18 March 1977: 82–3). In addition, such diversions could affect the location of ship repair, refining, and finance industries, and could, in this specific example, seriously adversely affect Singapore's economy and possibly benefit that of other countries bordering the new route. An alternative to re-routeing might be the up-grading of tankers, which is equally expensive.

Strategic Considerations

A major ASEAN initiative for peace, freedom, and neutrality may be in the works, incidentally affecting the use of the strategic straits and sea lanes for nuclear-armed submarines and aircraft (Valencia, 1985b). In 1976 ASEAN declared its intention to make the region a zone of peace, freedom, and neutrality (ZOPFAN). As a start for ZOPFAN, an ASEAN standing committee endorsed a nuclear weapon-free zone in the area controlled by ASEAN's six members (*Far Eastern Economic Review*, 27 September 1984: 13).

A nuclear-free zone in South-East Asia could in theory ban nuclear weapon-bearing US and Soviet surface vessels, submarines, and aircraft from the strategic straits in the region. This possibility places ZOPFAN and policies on sea-lane siting and strait access at the top of the *realpolitik* agenda. Even advance notice or monitoring of such traffic would erode the strength of the US nuclear deterrent. Much to the dismay of the United States, Indonesia temporarily closed the Sunda and Lombok straits in late September 1988 for what it said was live firing exercises.

Nuclear-armed and -powered submarines, aircraft carrying nuclear bombs, and nuclear missiles comprise the triad of US and USSR nuclear strike capability. In order to attack or defend against a nuclear submarine, its location must of course be known. Indeed, the United States maintains that the vulnerability of its nuclear missile-armed submarines (the Poseidon/Trident fleet) and hence their indispensable role in a second-strike depends on their ability to pass through straits and sea lanes submerged, unannounced and undetected. Four of 16 strategic straits in the world which are important to the mobility of the US fleet to reach target areas are in South-East Asia—Malacca, Lombok, Sunda, and Ombai–Wetar. But only the Indonesian straits of Ombai–Wetar and Lombok are physically and politically usable by submerged submarines.

The United States currently has an advantage because the important straits states are friendly to the United States, and because most Soviet submarines leaving port must pass through the Straits of Japan or between Iceland and Norway where they are detected and targeted. Effective denial of military overflight over key straits and sea lanes would seriously impair the utility of the US strategic bombing force as a deterrent. Also, in a war between the Soviet Union and China, the Soviet Union would have to resupply its Far Eastern front by sea through the South-East Asian region on a time-critical basis. Extension of jurisdiction over straits thus gives a small group of straits states considerable strategic significance and the opportunity to exercise enhanced political leverage (Valencia and Marsh, 1985: 543).

However, US deployment of naval and air forces in ocean space will not ultimately depend on the agreed or claimed territorial sea boundaries of coastal states or on the national positions and international laws and treaties governing passage through or over international straits. The imposition of restrictions on straits by littoral states is apt to be a far more important impediment to surface naval mobility and the shipping of oil and other resources than to the US underwater strategic nuclear force.

Superpower Militarization in the Marine Region

During the post-Vietnam era, the United States withdrew from the Asian land mass and consolidated its defence positions off-shore on the Pacific rim. The US forward deployment network now stretches from Japan to Clark Air Force Base and Subic Naval Station in the Philippines, to Diego Garcia, and thence to East Africa and the Middle East. The US Pacific Fleets (the Third and Seventh) have 87 warships, 6 carriers, 44 attack submarines, and 10 strategic missile submarines. There has been a corresponding build-up of Soviet military power in the Pacific and Indian oceans: the Soviet Pacific Fleet has 87 warships, 1 carrier, 80 attack submarines, and 30 strategic missile submarines. In each of 1981 and 1982 an average of three Soviet warships, including nuclear-powered submarines, passed through the Strait of Malacca to the Indian Ocean. Only one US submarine used the strait in the same period, but an average of 7 to 8 US warships per month did so, for a total of 87 (including 11 carriers) compared to 42 for the USSR.

Vietnam provides the Soviet Union with a strong defence outpost to support Soviet naval operations in the Indian Ocean. Being a forward base, Cam Ranh Bay's value to the Soviet navy lies primarily in its proximity to several economic and political–military centres of consequence—China, Subic Bay, the ASEAN states, the Indian Ocean, and the Malacca and Indonesian straits (Martin da Cunha, 1986). The Soviets have taken to showing the flag in the region for political effect. A four-ship flotilla appeared in the Gulf of Thailand in November 1980, and a lone cruiser appeared off the Singapore waterfront in February 1983. The Soviet naval presence exhibits its solidarity with Vietnam and challenges ASEAN (Martin da Cunha, 1986). This increases the importance of military alliances to the United States, because the US Seventh Fleet is effective between Japan and the Persian Gulf only through its network of defence treaties and alliances in the region. Yet, the physical surveillance and protection of the sea lanes are beyond the present capability of regional states. The United States is pressuring Japan to shoulder responsibility for defending shipping lanes up to 1,000 nmi from Tokyo so that the United States can focus its attention on other areas. Although ASEAN countries have increased their defence allocations, this only allows limited local patrolling. For these reasons, the United States has been strengthening its military co-operation with the ASEAN nations, and attempting to organize a *de facto* combined fleet so that the annual pan-Pacific combined exercise by the United States, Japan, Canada, and Australia will gradually expand US military strength in the area. For example, the loss of Subic and Clark bases in the Philippines would greatly increase the strategic value of the South-East Asian straits for projection of US military power into the Gulf. China is also expanding its naval activities in the South China Sea and beyond, and has undertaken a 'passing exercise' there with the US Navy (Intelligence, *Far Eastern Economic Review*, 16 January 1986).

The Military Role of Marine Scientific Research

Submerged-launch ballistic missile (SLBM) submarines are of extreme strategic importance in the Soviet–US arms race, and thus control of the deep waters through seabed detection and possibly attack devices could become the crucial factor in a great-power conflict. This control will be achieved through marine scientific research. The information gathered by research vessels in coastal states' EEZs may be used to their detriment, or the research activity may be a subterfuge to mask the acquisition of military or resource information.

According to UNCLOS, marine scientific research is supposed to be conducted exclusively for peaceful purposes (UN, 1982: Article 240) and, in the EEZ and on the continental shelf, only with the consent of the coastal state (UN, 1982: Article 246). Although in normal circumstances, coastal states are supposed to grant their consent for marine scientific research projects by other states or competent international organizations in their EEZ or on their continental shelf, they can withhold their consent if that project is of direct significance to the exploration and exploitation of living or non-living natural resources or if it is for non-peaceful purposes.

Western and Soviet efforts have dominated oceanographic research in South-East Asia (Valencia and Evering, 1983). Notwithstanding the consent regime, it is likely that Western efforts will continue to dominate marine science exploration in South-East Asia, although now under the guise of international institutions and 'cooperation' with or 'assistance' to indigenous institutions. This subterfuge is assisted by the fact that the numerous international organizations with marine science interests operating in the region are not indigenously derived, developed, funded, or directed and comprise both extra-ASEAN and extra-South China Sea states. These organizations include the Indo-Pacific Fisheries Council of the Food and Agriculture Organization; the Southeast Asia Fisheries Development Center (SEAFDEC); the International Center for Living Aquatic Resources Management (ICLARM); the UNDP Project on Regional Offshore Prospecting in East Asia; and a new Intergovernmental Oceanographic Commission (IOC)-sponsored body, the Programme Group for the Western Pacific (WESTPAC), which includes the South China Sea within its geographical terms of reference. In addition, several specialized

UN agencies whose terms of reference include marine scientific problems have offices in the region—for example, the UNESCO Regional Office for Science and Technology for Southeast Asia in Jakarta, the UN Environment Programme Regional Office in Bangkok, and the relevant divisions of ESCAP (e.g. Natural Resources).

Regional Militarization of Ocean Space

Extended jurisdiction and expectations of resources and territory to be protected arouses among these newly independent countries emotions of nationalism, which, in combination with alliances with superpowers, leads to militarization. Figure 4.9 schematically summarizes the areas of enforcement concern, geographically and by activity (Olson and Morgan, 1985). Prime fishing areas requiring protection are found in Philippine, Indonesian, Thai, and Malaysian waters. 'Smuggling' is significant in the Gulf of Thailand, the Andaman Sea, the Natuna area, Sabah waters, the Celebes and Sulu seas, western Philippine waters, the Bashi channel, and the Arafura Sea. The Strait of Malacca has high pollution potential from shipping. Major oil exploration and production areas requiring protection are found off North-west Palawan; off Sabah, Brunei, and Sarawak; in the Natuna area; off the east coast of the Malay Peninsula; and in the Gulf of Thailand. Refugees fleeing Vietnam are also an enforcement concern for littoral states. Piracy is endemic in the region and has been undergoing a resurgence in the Malacca and Singapore straits, the Bangka Strait, and in the Sulu and Sulawesi seas. Some pirates view their booty as tolls (*Asiaweek*, 27 May 1988: 26–9). These enforcement functions are additional to the classic naval missions of protecting national territory against enemies and keeping critical sea lanes open and, in South-East Asia, controlling piracy, smuggling, and rebellion.

Table 4.6 summarizes the capabilities of the South-East Asian navies and the fleets of China and Taiwan (Morgan, 1983). China's navy is the world's largest if measured in terms of the number of ships, but it is mostly composed of small vessels. Chinese naval strategy is primarily defensive, designed to protect the mainland from attack by an aggressor. The Taiwanese forces have as their primary mission protection of the island against attack from the Chinese mainland.

Brunei's small but powerful fleet protects its ports and oil

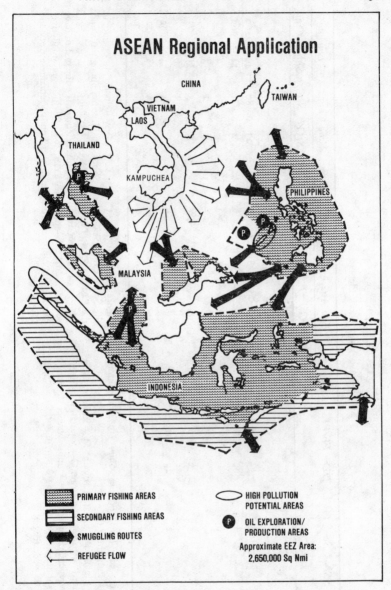

Figure 4.9
South-East Asia: Areas of Concern in Enforcement.

Source: Boeing Commercial Airplane Company (1982), EEZ Management and Control, November, Seattle, ASEAN Regional Application.

TABLE 4.6
South-East Asian Navy Fleets

	SSN	SS	CVL	DD	FF/PF	Escorts	Fast Attack			Patrol Craft				Mine Craft		Landing	
							M	G	T	P	L	C	R	S(O)	S(C)	Ships	Craft
Brunei							3					3	3				2
Burma					1	4				30	3	6	41				
China[1]		102		12	16		207	372	255	28	21	7	110	23	80	40	469
Indonesia		4			10		4	6	2		15	8		4	1	14	62
Kampuchea												15	25				
Malaysia					2		8	6			25				2	3	
Philippines					7	10	6				15	59				31	71
Singapore							6	6							2	6	
Taiwan		2		23	10	3	2		9			10			14	4	22
Thailand					6		6				21	21	40		14	28	22
Vietnam[2]					6	2	8		9		6	3		1		7	

Source: J. E. Moore, ed., *Janes' Fighting Ships* (1982–3 edition), New York: Janes' Publishing Co.

Legend: FF = fast frigate. PF = patrol frigate. M = missile. G = gun. T = torpedo. P = patrol. L = large. C = coastal. R = river. S(O) = minesweeper (ocean). S(C) = minesweeper (coastal). SS = diesel submarine. SSN = nuclear submarine. CVL = light aircraft carrier. DD = destroyer.

[1] Figures represent entire Chinese fleet. Many units do not operate in the South China Sea, but the South Sea Fleet has about 300 ships, the East Sea Fleet (Taiwan Strait) about 600 ships.

[2] Figures are for operational units only. Vietnam is estimated to have 866 additional non-operational craft, 560 of which are small river patrol boats captured from the former South Vietnamese navy and US forces.

resources. Burma has a fleet designed primarily to protect its fisheries. Indonesia's present navy could prevent enemy ships from interfering with its trade routes; moreover, the country's aerial marine reconnaissance capability is considerable and growing.

Kampuchea's navy consists of 40 patrol craft, all of small to moderate size and limited capabilities; most are not operational. The Malaysian navy must maintain lines of communication between Peninsular Malaysia and Sabah/Sarawak, prevent a foreign power from closing the Malacca Strait or interfering with shipping through it, and protect offshore oil terminals like Pulai and its claimed and occupied islands, e.g. Terumbu Layang-Layang, in the South China Sea.

The age of its fleet, its disrepair, and the small size and light armament of most of the vessels make the Philippine navy the least effective of the ASEAN member navies. However, the United States, with its important naval base at Subic Bay and air base at Clark, has an equal need to keep sea lanes in the archipelago open; thus some Philippine navy functions are being carried out by the United States. The Singapore fleet is small but powerful for its size and capable of keeping the sea lanes in its vicinity open.

Thailand has coastlines and claimed waters in both the Andaman Sea and the Gulf of Thailand, and therefore needs a large patrol force to maintain adequate surveillance. Although the navy is designed primarily for patrol duties, the fleet is numerically inadequate for its tasks. Vietnam's present active navy numbers 48 ships, but since the country has a long coastline and claims an EEZ second only in size to Indonesia's and the Philippines', the size of the Vietnamese navy appears inadequate to patrol its marine area effectively, let alone conduct any offensive operations against other countries in the region. However, it is being improved with assistance from the Soviet Union. The Soviet Union maintains a naval presence at Cam Ranh Bay, Vietnam, and Kompong Som, Kampuchea, and air bases at Da Nang, Vietnam, and Xieng Khoung, Laos.

Figure 4.10 shows the locations of naval and air bases in the region. Most bases are occupied by the forces of the host nation. Most of the Indonesian navy is based at Surabaya, with additional bases at Belawan, Medan, Renai, Tanjungpinang, and Ambon. Except for the small base at Ambon, all of eastern Indonesia is without support facilities for its naval fleet. Similarly, the Philip-

134

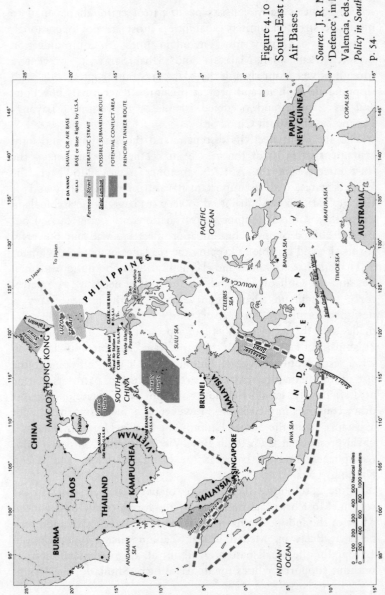

Figure 4.10
South-East Asia: Naval and
Air Bases.

Source: J. R. Morgan (1983),
'Defence', in Morgan and
Valencia, eds., *Atlas for Marine
Policy in Southeast Asian Seas,*
p. 54.

pines bases most of its naval units at Langley Point, and only Zamboanga is used to support ships operating in the southern islands. Burma, with its small fleet, has naval bases at Sittwe, Bassein, Moulmein, and Mergui, spaced roughly evenly along the long coastline. Thailand's bases at Bangkok and Songkhla and the partially operational Andaman Sea base at Ban Thap Lamu are poorly equipped to support the fleet. Malaysia needs additional base facilities, since the two naval bases at Pasir Gudang and Labuan are widely separated. China, with six bases on the South China Sea coast, has good facilities to support the hundreds of small ships in its navy. Bases at Tsoying, Kaohsiung, and in the Pescadores are likewise adequate for the naval units of Taiwan.

There has been an impressive array of bilateral defence exercises among ASEAN members, and although ASEAN members have never considered the organization to be a defence alliance, there have been intermittent pressures to turn ASEAN into a military pact. In addition to, or perhaps in response to US preferences, Singapore has called for greater ASEAN military co-operation to meet the threat of the Soviet Union in the region (*Far Eastern Economic Review*, 6 September 1984: 11) and the United Kingdom has called for increased military co-operation with ASEAN. Further, Singapore has recently offered military facilities to the United States.

New Directions for Co-operation

Numerous constraints must be overcome to reduce the potential for international conflict and move toward increased co-operation on marine resource issues in South-East Asia (Valencia, 1980: 16–38). In the wake of the successful Indo-Chinese revolution, the United States, the Soviet Union, and China are vying for areas of influence within the region, thus fostering instability. With the exception of Thailand, all of the countries in and around the region have achieved independence or have experienced society-transforming movements within the past quarter century. Many are still struggling with the basic problems of nationhood, thus bringing a nationalistic fervour into regional affairs. Within ASEAN itself, relations are cordial but competitive and perhaps unstable in the long term. The ASEAN countries produce many of the same raw materials, and the resulting direct competition for credit, investment markets, and development assistance may increase with advancing economic development. South-East Asian countries only now are beginning to perceive clearly their own national marine interests and how these differ from those of neighbouring states or outside maritime powers. At this juncture, commonalities are neglected and differences tend to be emphasized.

National marine resource management policies will also both influence and be influenced by maritime powers from outside the region and by nations with adjacent jurisdictional zones. Maritime powers may choose to exploit policy diversities by shifting activities (e.g. shipping of oil, fishing) towards areas of least resistance. Regardless of national agreement with international treaties, legal precedents, and provisions of the UNCLOS, there will remain problems of national and regional implementation of management designs. Marine policy in the South-East Asian seas will be shaped by the exigencies of both national development and international relations. Policies will be largely unilateral; occasionally bilateral where necessitated by the UNCLOS and practicality; and, rarely, multilateral. These and related policy problems will dominate marine affairs in the region during the remainder of the twentieth century.

What is needed is an ethic of co-operation *centred* on the community, *implemented* through participatory democracy, and *based* on the common needs of self-protection and sustained development. The ZOPFAN and its implementation through a nuclear weapon-free zone in South-East Asia would be a first critical step in the process of achieving real economic and political freedom for the people of South-East Asia. An initial step in this direction could be the demilitarization of the Spratly region and establishment of a zone of peace there. The most important application of this concept would be the removal of critical straits, sea lanes, and air routes in the region from the naval and air, nuclear defensive and offensive strategies of the superpowers. This in turn would remove an important plank from the superpower *realpolitik* that is enveloping and threatening to consume South-East Asia.

In the case of oil, resolution or muting of boundary disputes may be a prerequisite for development of any hydrocarbon resources in areas of unresolved boundaries, regardless of potential (Valencia, 1985). Since oil and gas discovery and development is a common high priority among the South-East Asian nations, overlapping claims to areas with hydrocarbon potential provide an opportunity for separating sovereignty from function by setting aside the question of the actual boundary and providing for joint exploration and exploitation of hydrocarbons in an agreed area of overlap. Joint development could diffuse tensions between claimants and detach these disputes from the matrix of super-power machinations. The Thai–Malaysian joint development agreement is the prime example in South-East Asia. In the eastern Gulf of Thailand, joint development might be feasible between Vietnam and Kampuchea.

Major areas for possible co-operation in fisheries include informa-tion exchange, research and training, access arrangements, surveillance and enforcement, conservation, production, pro-cessing, and marketing (Valencia and Kent, 1985). One form of access arrangement is the single merged zone, with a single licence providing equal access to all waters. Alternatively, there could be co-ordinated licensing arrangements, in which fishing vessels could move with relative ease from one nation's jurisdiction to another. Or transit arrangements could be liberal, with fees and royalties paid to the country in whose jurisdiction fishing was undertaken. The nations of South-East Asia have to date shown little receptivity to simple licensing arrangements, however, or to access by each other, preferring to engage in joint-venture opera-tions with outside countries.

The more ambitious ideas for regional co-operation in fisheries surveillance and enforcement contemplate jointly operated, high-technology schemes such as satellites or high-altitude aircraft systems, possibly combined with a joint coast guard. As an example, in the South Pacific, vessels convicted of poaching in the fishing zone of any member of the Nauru Agreement may be deprived of access to the waters of any other member nation. Members have also agreed to a vessel registration system, in which only vessels registered with the Forum Fisheries Agency are allowed to fish for tuna in any member's EEZ.

Joint fisheries production and management might be considered for shared or migratory stocks. A single corporate structure could manage particular fisheries, with the corporation under the joint control of representatives of several nations, perhaps operating a single regional fleet of fishing vessels. It also may be possible to undertake co-operative efforts in processing or marketing or in some integrated combination of production, processing, and marketing. In South-East Asia, regional joint ventures in pro-cessing might be considered for foreign markets (e.g. tuna canning), for import-substitution in regional markets (e.g. to re-place canned mackerel presently imported from Japan), or for spe-cialty products for local markets (e.g. fish pastes or snacks). Port infrastructure might be created on a regional basis and to accom-modate several enterprises of each member nation. The nations of South-East Asia could also work together to increase trade in fishery products among themselves and with countries outside the region. For example, it might be possible to create a regional marketing board that would actively promote legal barter trade, with a central agency to serve as a clearing house (Samson, 1985).

Politically, ventures between countries in South-East Asia could be concrete manifestations of co-operation and unity, particularly in a subregional organization such as ASEAN. They could provide co-operating nations with greater leverage for marketing, for the acquisition of capital, and for seeking external development assist-ance, and they could lead to other forms of co-operation on marine matters. Joint ventures could also eliminate or reduce the motivations for poaching. Capital could come from regional development institutions. Regional development organizations could more rationally allocate their funds and efforts if assistance were directed at common marine resources, since duplication of aid on a per-country basis would be avoided. The major advantage of increasing trade with nations outside the region would be increased foreign exchange earnings; the major advantage of increased intraregional trade would be promotion of intraregional self-reliance and food security.

In marine conservation lie possibilities of joint development of a network of community-based reserves and of common criteria for their designation. Trans-frontier co-operation could involve shared marine reserves, a regional task force on marine conserva-tion, and possibly harmonization of laws and regulations (White, 1983).

Dispute management is a marine policy issue in which countries outside the South-East Asian region also have great interest. Mechanisms for dispute avoidance or settlement, so vital for the orderly implementation of the new ocean regime, might be regionalized or subregionalized to conform to regional or local cultural systems.

Finally, an *ASEAN* (or eventually South-East Asian) *Institute for Marine Resources Management (ASIMARE)* (or SEASIMARE) could be established to undertake research and education and training *in* the ASEAN (South-East Asian) region, *for* ASEAN (South-East Asian) nations, and as far as is feasible, *by* ASEAN nationals. The institute should not be narrowly and esoterically individualistic and scientific, but should focus international, inter-disciplinary teams on resource exploration, assessment, sustained development and management in support of ASEAN goals. These teams could provide technical support to formal and informal ASEAN committees and respond to *ad hoc* ASEAN requests for resource management studies. Highest priority should be on truly shared resource management problems that can only be solved by gathering data from several countries' areas. Second priority should be given to issues held in common but not transnational in themselves. Research to only one nation's benefit should be of lowest priority and on a rotating basis. The institute would serve as a node and clearing house for requests for scientific research by foreign nations and international organizations, and offers of, and requests for, technical assistance. Such research and technical assistance would have to fit the institute's existing research agenda. The institute would also be a central data bank, and a co-ordinator and implementor of human resource development for marine resource management.

Most marine science data in the region has been and is still collected and analysed by scientists of countries external to the region; ASIMARE could be a focal point for a massive marine science knowledge and technology transfer to the region. The need for indigenous regional co-operation is accentuated by the inadequate trained personnel resources, facilities, and funds required to undertake major resource exploration and develop-ment programmes in each of the ASEAN countries. ASIMARE could be a regional focal point in which knowledge and personnel would be pooled to carry out research and development on problems of common interest (UN, 1982: Article 276). Since ma-rine resources research is generally costly, regional co-operation could also help ease the financial burden for each member country. Regional co-operation in marine resource studies could also produce synoptic coverage over a longer time period and wider area.

The research agenda for ASIMARE should include as over-arching themes the present and potential economic costs and benefits of exploration and exploitation of the resources known or expected in the new jurisdictional space; the present and projected role of marine resources in development; multinational sea use planning and management; the role of new national marine resources such as oil, minerals, and navigational space in the implementation of global concepts such as the New International Economic Order or a Pacific Community; and identification and evaluation of possible consortia of developed and ASEAN countries to harvest these new resources.

At present, co-operation on marine issues is incipient at best. However, political relationships change over time, and the underlying economic potential of the marine resources of the region remains more or less as a constant—part of the geography of the region. Under changed political conditions, an increasing share of this potential might become available to be tapped by co-operative efforts.

Progressive Management Concepts

The extension of jurisdictions creates a wide and varied spectrum of opportunities for reconsidering the principles on which resources might be managed and exploited on a national, subregional, or regional basis. The options finally chosen could be piecemeal, non-innovative, responding to immediate symptoms—this oil spill, that failed fishery—or they could respond more deeply by bringing about national and international co-operation instead of conflict and by ensuring that resources are used to alleviate some of the fundamental problems causing national and regional social instability.

A general principle that could be applied to resource exploitation, management, and conservation is a national, subregional, or regional application of the common heritage concept. The idea that all marine resources beyond national jurisdiction be administered by an international organization for the benefit of all—but particularly the developing countries—received widespread and ardent support from Third World nations, including those in South-East Asia. The common heritage principle is reflected in the terms and substance of the UNCLOS.

Another concept that may be directly applicable is compensation to those segments of society that are displaced, marginalized, or otherwise injured by marine or marine-related developments. Thus when a combination of industrial pollution, habitat destruction, and destructive foreign and domestic trawling deprive small-scale fishermen of their livelihood, they should be compensated from the profits of the industrialists, land developers, and trawler fishermen. Such compensation should include education about the causes and consequences of their dilemma and help in making necessary adjustments. Similarly, developers of coastal land for tourism should directly compensate displaced villagers with acceptable new land and a long-term percentage of the profits from the tourism development.

Urgently needed is an analysis of the myriad rights, claims, and practices that presently govern the use of contested marine resources, and the changes required to achieve equitable and sustainable development. Not only should processes be researched, but the institutions for implementing progressive management options at national and international levels should also be closely examined. Conclusions should be based on careful case studies of who might pay how much to whom. Now is the time to depart from business as usual; the peoples of South-East Asia must seize the opportunity.

References

Asiaweek, 'A Tide of Pirates', 27 May 1988, pp. 26–9.

Asian Action, March/April 1978, Bangkok: Asian Cultural Forum on Development.

Business Day (Kuala Lumpur), 'Viets Warn Thais on Oil Drilling in Disputed Area', 10 January 1983, p. 11.

Cooper, B., ed. (1981), *Far East Oil and Energy Survey, 1981*, Geneva and Dublin: Petroleum Economists and Petroconsultants.

Crouch, H. (1985), 'No Enemy in Sight', *Far Eastern Economic Review*, pp. 82–3.

Das, K. (1977), 'Tankers Face Strict Rules in Straits', *Far Eastern Economic Review*, 18 March, pp. 82–3.

del Mundo, F. (1982), 'Will Spratlys Become Another Falklands?', *Honolulu Advertiser*, 28 April, p. A–11.

Dzurek, D. (1985), 'Boundary and Resource Disputes in the South China Sea', in E. M. Borgese and N. Ginsburg, eds., *Ocean Yearbook 5*, Chicago: The University of Chicago Press, pp. 254–84.

Fabrie, R. C. (1983), 'SLOC Security–Economic Impact', paper presented at 1983 Pacific Symposium, Washington, DC: National Defense University.

Far Eastern Economic Review, 6 September 1984, pp. 10, 11; 27 September 1984, p. 13; 4 October 1984; 16 January 1986, p. 23.

Foreign Broadcast Information Service (FBIS), 'Asia and the Pacific', 21 February 1984, p. K–3; 14 January 1983.

Foz, V. B. (1983), 'U.S. "Assailed" over Law of the Sea Provisions', *Bulletin Today*, 27 March, pp. 1, 14.

Gaffney, P. D., Moyes, C. P., and Archer, J. D. (1982), 'Southeast Asia Looks to 1990', paper presented at Offshore Southeast Asia 82 Conference, 9–12 February, Singapore.

Hamzah, B. A. (1984), 'Indonesia's Archipelagic Regime: Implications for Malaysia', *Marine Policy*, January, pp. 30–43.

Hann, R. W. Jr., *et al.* (1981), 'The Status of Oil Pollution and Oil Pollution Control in the Southeast Asia Region', mimeograph, Texas A & M University.

Honolulu Advertiser, 24 August 1983; 29 November 1984, p. B–1.

Jaafar, Abu Bakar and Valencia, M. J. (1985), 'Management of the Malacca/Singapore Straits: Some Issues, Options and Probable Responses', *Akademica*, No. 26, January, pp. 93–117.

Josupeit, H. (1983), 'External Assistance to the Fisheries Sector of Developing Countries in Asia and the Pacific', *Infofish Marketing Digest*, No. 3.

Lauriat, G. (1985), 'Shipping', in G. Kent and M. J. Valencia, eds., *Marine Policy in Southeast Asia*, Berkeley: University of California Press.

Martin da Cunha, Derek (1986), 'A Moscow Naval Cordon around the "Yellow Peril"', *Far Eastern Economic Review*, 4 September, pp. 28–9.

McDorman, Ted L. and Panat Tasneeyanond (1987), 'Increasing Problems for Thailand's Fisheries', *Marine Policy*, July, pp. 205–16.

Morgan, J. R. (1983), 'Defense', in J. R. Morgan and M. J. Valencia, eds., *Atlas for Marine Policy in Southeast Asian Seas*, Berkeley: University of California Press, pp. 53–4.

Nielsen, A. (1982), 'Territorial Disputes in the South China Sea: Managing Conflicts through International Law', MA thesis, Department of Political Science, University of Hawaii.

Oil and Gas Journal, 2 August 1982.

Olson, H. F. and Morgan, J. R. (1985), 'Shipping', in J. R. Morgan and M. J. Valencia, eds., *Atlas for Marine Policy in Southeast Asian Seas*, Berkeley: University of California Press, pp. 80–97.

Østreng, W. (1985), 'Reaching Agreement on International Exploitation of Ocean Mineral Resources', in M. J. Valencia, ed., *Geology and Hydrocarbon Potential of the South China Sea and Possibilities of Joint Development*, New York: Pergamon Press, pp. 555–71.

Park, C. H. (1978), 'The South China Sea Disputes: Who Owns the Islands and the Natural Resources?', *Ocean Development and International Law Journal*, Vol. 5, No. 1, p. 49.

Petroleum News, August 1983; September 1982.

Prescott, J. R. V. (1983), 'Maritime Jurisdiction and Boundaries', in J. R. Morgan and M. J. Valencia, eds., *Atlas for Marine Policy in Southeast Asian Seas*, Berkeley: University of California Press, p. 45.

Republic of the Philippines (1982), Declaration on the signing of the Convention on the Law of the Sea, 10 December.

Samson, E. (1985), 'Fisheries', in G. Kent and M. J. Valencia, eds., *Marine Policy in Southeast Asia*, Berkeley: University of California Press, pp. 101–52.

Samuels, M. (1982), *Contest for the South China Sea*, New York: Methuen.

Sricharatcharya, Paisal (1987), 'Fishing Boat Friction', *Far Eastern Economic Review*, 16 April, p. 23.

Stockwin, Harvey (1987), 'China Stakes Its Claim Quietly', *South China Morning Post*, 29 July.

Tolentino, A. (1982), Statement at the signing of the Convention on the Law of the Sea, 10 December.

United Nations (1982), Convention on the Law of the Sea, 7 October.

Valencia, M. J. (1980), 'South China Sea: Constraints to Marine Regionalism', *Indonesian Quarterly*, Vol. VIII, April, pp. 16–38.

_____ (1981), 'National Marine Interests, Transnational Issues, and Marine Regionalism', in Chia Lin Sien and C. MacAndrews, eds., *Southeast Asian Seas: Frontiers for Development*, Singapore: McGraw-Hill, pp. 302–55.

_____ (1985a), *Southeast Asian Seas: Oil under Troubled Waters*, Kuala Lumpur: Oxford University Press.

_____ (1985b), 'ZOPFAN and Navigation Rights: Stormy Seas Ahead?', *Far Eastern Economic Review*, March, pp. 38–9.

_____ (1988), 'The Spratly Islands: Dangerous Ground in the South China Sea', *Pacific Review*, Vol. 1, No. 4, pp. 438–43.

Valencia, M. J. and Evering, G. (1983), 'South China Sea: Marine

Scientific Research Accomplishments, Capabilities, and Co-operation', East–West Environment and Policy Institute Working Paper, Honolulu: East–West Center.

Valencia, M. J. and Kent, G. (1985), 'Opportunities, Problems, and Prospects for Cooperation', in G. Kent and M. J. Valencia, eds., *Marine Policy in Southeast Asia*, Berkeley: University of California Press, pp. 365–82.

Valencia, M. J. and Marsh, J. B. (1985), 'Access to Straits and Sealanes in Southeast Asian Seas: Legal, Economic, and Strategic Considerations', *Journal of Maritime Law and Commerce*, Vol. 16, No. 4, pp. 513–51.

—— (1986), 'Southeast Asia: Marine Resources, Extended Maritime Jurisdiction and Development', *Marine Resource Economics*.

van der Kroef, J. M. (1982), 'The South China Sea: Competing Claims and Strategic Conflicts', *International Security Review*, Fall, p. 322.

Wedel, Paul (1988), 'Leave Disputed Islands, Vietnam Warns Chinese', *Honolulu Advertiser and Star Bulletin*, 28 February, p. A-11.

White, A. T. (1983), 'Priority Areas for Marine Resource Management', in J. R. Morgan and M. J. Valencia, eds., *Atlas for Marine Policy in Southeast Asian Seas*, Berkeley: University of California Press, p. 141.

Wilson, G. (1979), 'Government Sails Different Courses on Offshore Limits', *Washington Post*, 14 August.

5
Conflict over Natural Resources in Malaysia: The Struggle of Small-scale Fishermen

Lim Teck Ghee

Introduction

ROUGHLY 40 per cent of the world's total fish production comes from Asia and for many years, the great proportion of this catch came from the vast number of small-scale or artisanal fishermen who live by the coastal water. The contribution of these fishermen, estimated in 1982 in the ASEAN countries alone to number 2 million (or 10 million including their dependants), to their national economies and the protein food needs of their countrymen has been enormous. In 1982, for example, it was estimated that the fisheries contribution to the economies of Philippines, Indonesia, Singapore, and Thailand was US$3.2 billion. Nevertheless, the economic positions of small-scale fishermen have never been stable. The low productivity of traditional fishing gear, the control of the market by middlemen, the seasonal nature of their income, their chronic indebtedness; all these problems have plagued small-scale fishermen for a long time and prevented them from reaping the full rewards of their labour.

In recent years, their precarious economic positions have worsened as a result of new threats and today there is a real danger that unless strong policies and measures are undertaken to counter the new and old threats, small-scale fishermen will be left out of the mainstream of economic and social development, and reduced to being the poorest of the poor in their countries. The new threats to small-scale fishermen, most visible in the ASEAN countries, are due in large part to the adoption of the policy of export-led growth through increasing foreign and local capitalist investment by the governments of the region in the 1970s and 1980s.

In the larger national economy, the export-led growth strategy of ASEAN governments has resulted in misguided infrastructural development, the clearing of swamps, and the establishment of industrial areas close to traditional fishing grounds, thereby destroying fish spawning areas and denying fishing communities easy access to the rivers and seas. The depletion of fish stock available to small-scale fishermen has been further aggravated by the consequences of other types of economic expansion. As an example, the Sungai Skudai in Johore, Malaysia, is so heavily polluted by the untreated discharge from 30 factories that hardly any aquatic life forms can live or propagate for a distance of more than 6 miles upstream. Water pollution all over the ASEAN countries is also being caused by the excessive use of fertilizers, insecticides, and weedicides.

Within the fishing industry itself, the rapid development of heavily capitalized, export-oriented large-scale fishing operations has had adverse consequences on the well-being of small-scale producers. Invariably, the large trawler fleets of this 'modern' fishing sector have competed directly for the fish resources of the coastal waters worked by small-scale fishermen, to the detriment of the latter. As a result, a clear pattern has emerged of diminishing catches by small-scale fishermen. In the Philippines, it is estimated today that 98 per cent of the fishermen produce 50 per cent of the total catch whilst 2 per cent of fishermen engaged in large-scale industrial-type fisheries net the other 50 per cent. In Thailand, large capitalist enterprise fisheries now produce 65 per cent of the total catch while small-scale fishermen net only 35 per cent.

Although the fact of marginalization of small-scale fishermen throughout the Asia–Pacific region has become quite indisputable, it is still important to know how exactly this process has taken place so that the lessons learnt can be applied to help traditional communities dependent on other types of natural resources avoid the same fate. What are the forces at work that have undermined the interests of traditional producers? What has been the role of government in the transformation of the fisheries industry from one based on small-scale producers to large-scale ones? How has fisheries as a natural resource been affected by the transformation taking place within the industry? This case study will answer these questions through the use of a historical approach so as to show how conflict over a crucial natural resource has been generated over a long period of time and the impact of the conflict on the interests of various parties. By focusing on a single country—Malaysia—and examining the role of government through a study of administrative policies towards the fisheries sector, it is also hoped that a clearer understanding would emerge of the reasons why national governments behave as they do towards natural resources and the communities that exploit them.

The 1950s: Early Developments in the Malayan Fisheries Industry

Our review of fisheries in Malaysia begins with the immediate post-war period when the colonial government began reconstruction of the country's battered economy, and concern for the proper development of the fishing industry was expressed by the authorities due to the urgent problem of adequate food supplies for a population much ravaged by the war. At that time, too, the colonial authorities had recognized that important changes were beginning to take place in the traditional fishing industry, mainly as a result of the impact of modern technology. The High Commissioner, in a foreword to a publication by one of his officers, had sounded the warning that when 'fishing areas receive the full impact of modern technology the resources must not be permitted to diminish' (Kesteven, 1949: 1). He also commented that the question of marine resources was 'a problem on which scientific investigation and wise administration' must be turned to since 'unlike the land, the sea has no barrier'. These words were to prove prophetic as the issue of technological change in the industry and its impact on fishermen who could not participate in the change was to become a recurrent problem over the next four decades until the present, when it is still largely unresolved.

Despite the acute perceptivity with which some officials in the colonial administration viewed the problems of development in the fishing industry, the colonial government appears to have done little for the fishing industry in the short interregnum between the war's end and the passing of authority over to an independent government. Rehabilitation of the industry following the gear losses and depreciation brought about by the war was largely due to the initiative of individuals within the fishing community. Similarly, the use of artificial fibre nets and the mechanization of boats came about less through the efforts of the Fisheries Department than the private sector's own interests in improving the industry's efficency and profitability. Preoccupied with a prolonged guerrilla war waged by the Malayan Communist Party and more important political developments, it was not until the eve of independence that the authorities began to initiate a closer scrutiny of the fishing industry. In September 1955, largely at the urging of the local representatives in the Legislative Council, the colonial government established a committee to investigate the fishing industry in view of the fact that 'the occupation of fishing is one of the lowest rewarded in the country' and to suggest 'ways to improve the economic condition of the local fishing population' (Anonymous, 1956: 1). Unlike other committees appointed by the colonial government, the committee was not dominated by government representatives who might have minimized the seriousness of the fishing community's problems in defence of colonial economic policies. Ten of its eleven members were Malayans and the strength of local representation appears to be largely responsible for the unambiguous character of its output and the candid recommendations made. The committee's report produced in 1956 warrants discussion as it was in many ways a landmark study that can be used to evaluate the shortcomings of government policy towards the small-scale fishing community during the following years.

The committee prefaced its report by noting that although it was able to provide recommendations in some detail for the improvement of the equipment and operations of fishermen, it did not feel sufficiently confident to provide more than a limited and superficial survey of the marketing and distribution side of fishing, which were extremely complex activities related to the capital structure of the industry. Nevertheless, its main recommendations were directly connected to the question of changing the prevailing ownership and control patterns in the industry. Principally, the committee found that the industry's main problem arose from the dependence of fishermen on financing, and through the loan of boats, gear, and nets, by capitalists who rarely went to sea themselves and exploited the former group by offering them low prices for their catches and charging high prices for the equipment or goods sold. To free fishermen from this exploitative capital structure, the committee proposed that provision be made for financial assistance in the form of boats and gear to selected groups of fishermen. Specifically, the government was advised to encourage fishermen to form themselves into co-operatives or associations which would receive loans in the form of credit for the purchase of equipment, repayable over a certain period with nominal interest and including a non-repayable subsidy of one-third the amount of the loan. To administer the co-operatives, the committee recommended the establishment of a Fisheries Board which was set up as a statutory body with an initial capital of M\$3 million. Recognizing the difficulty of administering a loan scheme successfully from previous government experience with loan defaults, it emphasized that the Board should be provided with adequate advisory and supervisory staff. Other major recommendations of the committee were directed towards overcoming the 'utter dependence of fishermen upon the sea for a livelihood and upon the almost complete lack of alternative employment' and the inadequacy of amenities and social services for fishing communities. To overcome these problems, it put forward a wide range of recommendations requesting that the government give special consideration to providing land for fishermen, the introduction of cottage industry and agriculture, the construction or improvement of fishing harbours, jetties, and roads, the expansion of training for fishermen, and control over the price of ice.

Clearly, the committee had performed well its task of identifying 'the relevant problems connected with the fishing industry' and recommending 'ways to improve the economic condition of the local fishing population'. Besides meeting with representatives from all sectors of the industry, its members had also visited fishing villages to study at first-hand the opinions of fishermen and the fishing communities. The resultant report was a comprehensive yet thoughtful document which could have been the basis of a long-term programme to bring about the upliftment of the fishing community. However, this did not happen. Although it was a government-appointed committee and despite the presence of three senior members of the Alliance party who were later to reach the ministerial ranks,[1] it failed to make an impact on the incoming government's policies. Except for an attempt at establishing fishing co-operatives and providing them with credit, little was done to implement the other recommendations and the urgency which had prompted the committee's investigation of the poverty-stricken fishing community was quickly lost. Why this

1. These were Abdul Aziz bin Ishak, Mohamed Khir bin Johari, and Abdul Ghafar bin Baba. Aziz Ishak became the first Minister of Agriculture.

happened is not clear. It could be that the recommendations were unworkable or that they became a casualty of the political differences between rival factions of the post-independent government. Whatever the reason, it was to weigh heavily on fisheries development during the next decade.

The Experience with Fishing Co-operatives, 1957–1965

The general failure of the newly independent government to implement smoothly the committee's recommendations is clear when government policy towards the industry and small-scale fishermen during the next ten years is examined. The decade from 1956 to 1965 saw the implementation by the new government of two national Five-year Plans. These Plans could have provided for the advancement of the fishing community through the correction of the adverse consequences that neglect by the colonial government had produced (and which were identified so clearly by the 1955 fishing committee). But little progress was achieved. No doubt, the Plans included public expenditure allocations for fisheries development and had ambitious schemes to extend fishing co-operatives throughout the East and West Coasts, provide facilities such as jetties, fishing gear, and ice stores, and accelerate the mechanization of fishing boats to enable fishermen to operate in deeper waters. However, the sums set aside were wholly inadequate for the purpose. Amounting to M$2.4 million for the first development plan for Malaya and M$7.2 million for the second, these sums amounted to 0.24 and 0.33 per cent of the total public expenditure budgets respectively,[2] and the public funds committed hardly lent credence to the professed aim of the country's development plans to accord the 'highest priority' to improving the livelihood of peasant fishermen (amongst other peasant groups) by raising output and diversifying and intensifying production. The inadequate allocation of funds was one problem but more important was the absence of a clear-cut policy of fisheries development aimed at the small fishermen community and the lack of an effective administrative structure to supervise ongoing projects.

2. For details of the First Five-year Plan budget, see 'Memorandum by the Economic Adviser in a Development Plan for Malaya, 1956–1960' (unpublished). The Malaya Plans should not be confused with the Malaysia Plans which began in 1966.

Some indication of the government's failings in these two key areas can be obtained from an analysis of its policy in the area of co-operatives. The history of the government's attempts to establish fishermen co-operatives which had been suggested by the committee as a means of enabling fishermen to purchase their own equipment and free themselves from the clutches of middlemen–financiers has been examined by various scholars (see, for example, Fredericks, 1973; Gibbons, 1976). Their findings indicate that the experiment with co-operatives was a failure. In the East Coast of Peninsular Malaysia between 1957 and 1963, a total of M$1.4 million was loaned by the government to a marketing and transport union formed by 43 fishing co-operatives which supervised its disbursement to fishermen to enable them to buy equipment. An estimated 16 per cent of the 21,000 fishermen in the East Coast were said to have participated in the scheme but only a negligible amount of the loans was repaid and the extent of operations of the unions was short-lived, with the scheme coming to a virtual standstill by 1962.[3] The loan-scheme did result in some diffusion of improved technology and provided an alternative source of credit but it generally failed to make much inroad into the entrenched capitalization patterns which were disadvantageous to fishermen and did not bring about significant improvement in the income levels of fishermen. This was the first major attempt made by the government to benefit fishermen through their own organizations and its failure demonstrated the ill-preparedness of the government.

In the West Coast, a redesigned co-operatives scheme was introduced between 1961 and 1966 but just as little success was achieved as with the earlier effort in the East Coast. Of a total of M$841,000 loaned by government to seven fishing co-operative establishments, only 13 per cent was repaid. Three co-operatives had completely collapsed within a few years and few benefits of a lasting nature had been provided to the small number of fishermen who managed to participate in the schemes (Gibbons, 1976: 97).

Why did these attempts at fisheries co-operatives fail when they had so much potential to benefit fishermen? In 1968 a paper by the Malaysian authorities reviewing fisheries development since

---

3. According to Fredericks (1973: 125), attempts to reorganize the scheme after 1962 proved to be abortive.

independence attributed the failure of its attempts to organize fishermen into co-operatives to an 'apparent lack of leadership' among fishermen and their low level of education (Anonymous, 1968: 229). 'Good and able leaders are few and far between and in turn when they lack organization and co-operation amongst themselves they can easily fall prey to any unscrupulous middlemen or profiteers,' argued the paper. It was no doubt true that the fishing industry was not served by good leaders, but the critical lack of leadership was more within the bureaucracy than with fishermen. According to Fredericks (1973: 123–4), the Co-operatives Department, in explaining the failure of the East Coast scheme, admitted in a departmental document that there was inadequate staff for administrative and supervisory work, share capital requirements were unrealistically high, there was divided administrative responsibilities and authority, and a lack of co-ordination between the Departments of Fisheries and Co-operatives.

The government also could not claim that the problem of infiltration of co-operatives by influential and opportunistic individuals or interests was unexpected. In many other parts of the world, the history of co-operatives is littered with failures chiefly due to poor management, incompetence, and dishonesty, and a pattern of individuals or groups not representative of the target community's interests gaining control of the co-operative management and monopolizing the activities. The 1955 committee investigating the fishing industry had anticipated these same problems in Malaya and cautioned that the government should ensure 'the provision of adequate advisory and supervisory staff whether under the Department of Co-operative Development or otherwise, since these Associations will for the most part lack that degree of satisfactory leadership without which they cannot hope to survive' (Anonymous, 1956: 5). Neither was the government unaware of the inherent difficulties in trying to organize often dispersed groups of individualistic fishermen to whom the advantages of co-operative production or marketing were not easily discernible. In more congenial conditions in rural and urban Malaya, co-operatives had failed time and again, thus putting the onus on the government to approach the subject with caution.[4]

4. In the pre-war period, according to Fredericks (1973: 190–1), the economic impact of credit co-operatives was extremely limited in the smallholding sector, although they were more successful among Indian estate workers. With the

The key to the co-operative experiment is the attitude and response of the participants and their perception of the benefits likely to be attained. Without genuine participation by its members, no co-operative venture could hope for success. This was known to the government. At the same time, a selective programme of co-operative establishment with sufficiently trained and motivated government personnel supervising activities, together with stringently administered financial procedures, could have prevented many of the subsequent problems of mismanagement, abuse, and dishonesty which plagued co-operatives and reduced their effectiveness in assuming a leading role in the development of small-scale fishermen.

The immediate result of the unhappy experience with co-operatives was to deter the authorities from supporting their expansion. The defaults on loans were viewed with much concern by the financial authorities and the regulations for credit procurement were stiffened with fishermen being called upon to provide as much as 70 per cent of the capital cost of new projects. Although this large proportion of initial càpital investment was later relaxed, the lower requirement was still beyond the resources of most fishermen. One effect was to restrict the opportunities available to fishermen to adopt more productive gear through loans obtained from the public sector which could lessen their dependency on middlemen–financiers. Another effect was to discourage co-operatives from embarking on projects which could bring benefits to members. In the light of this, it is not surprising that even functioning co-operatives failed to provide much benefit to their members and there were few, if any, examples of successful small-scale fisherman collective activity that the authorities responsible for fisheries could point to, so as to justify an increased financial and institutional commitment from the government. It was a vicious circle of failure breeding neglect and inadequate support, which in turn created more failures.

The lack of success of fisheries co-operatives sounded the warning that there were important inadequacies in government

---

exception of these two functional types, co-operation was virtually non-existent in the agricultural sector, save for some socially oriented societies. After the war, initially the colonial government, and then the post-colonial government, attempted to provide co-operatives with a central role in rural development policy. However, the various co-operative schemes that were implemented were generally unsuccessful, and failed to provide sufficient resources for the requirements of the smallholding sector.

policy and the implementational capacity of the administrative machinery entrusted with the task of protecting the interests of small-scale fishermen and developing the industry. However, it failed to lead to any serious review of the problems faced by small-scale fishermen and the fishing industry. Within the Department of Co-operatives, it appears that an investigation was conducted on the reasons for the failure of the East Coast co-operatives scheme but it was mainly an internal exercise, confined to the department and inaccessible to other interested parties. Thus, valuable experience which could have been the basis for improved policy and effective administration was quickly forgotten and lost. That the government's inability to objectively carry out a self-examination of its weaknesses and initiate the necessary policy changes weighed heavily on fisheries development can be gauged from the fact that when co-operative development in fisheries was encouraged again in the 1970s, the same problems which had dogged the earlier efforts at co-operative establishment were treated by the authorities as if they were entirely new ones.

A Decade of Trawling Development, 1960–1970

The next critical development in the fisheries industry was to expose more glaringly the shortcomings in government policy towards the sector of small-scale traditional fisheries. During the 1950s and 1960s, despite the absence of a leadership role by the fisheries department, the fishing industry had seen much technological change. These changes centred on the increased use of powered craft, synthetic fibre nets, and more efficient gear and had important results on the structure of the industry. Some indication of the impact can be inferred from Table 5.1, which shows that although the number of craft in the peninsula declined by 15 per cent between 1957 and 1967, the quantity of fish landed increased to almost three times.

The story of how the increased production was achieved is more complicated than the statistics suggest. Prior to the 1950s, although the fishing industry was characterized by a diversity of gear and craft, the greater proportion of landings had come from the traditional small-scale sector of labour-intensive fisheries which mainly relied on unpowered craft with limited fishing range and simple gear. In the 1950s and early 1960s, increasing

TABLE 5.1

Number of Powered and Unpowered Boats and Catch by All Boats
in Peninsular Malaysia, 1957–1967

Year	Number of Powered Boats	Number of Unpowered Boats	Total Boats	Total Landings (tonnes)
1957	6,283	17,541	23,824	110 863
1958	7,296	17,752	25,048	112 104
1959	7,884	14,379	22,263	118 622
1960	8,940	14,608	23,548	139 469
1961	9,665	13,293	22,958	150 650
1962	9,772	12,338	22,110	170 207
1963	10,483	12,262	22,745	183 636
1964	10,727	10,903	21,630	192 158
1965	12,183	10,281	22,464	198 377
1966	12,535	8,371	20,906	236 607
1967	13,032	7,204	20,236	301 856

Source: Anonymous (1968), pp. 215–16.

numbers of fishermen in the traditional sector, many with credit obtained from financier–traders, began to invest in powered craft and synthetic nets which helped raise their productivity. In so far as this development represented an upgrading of the technological levels of small producers, it was certainly to be welcomed as it resulted in greater efficiency, higher productivity, and an increase in income trends. A properly organized government programme providing deserving fishermen with ready access to new but more expensive inputs could have ensured that the distributive effects of the new technology would be more widespread. However, as pointed out earlier, the failure of co-operatives which the authorities had intended to use as focal points for the distribution of government assistance prevented this from happening, so that most of the financing for the new technology came from the ubiquitous financier–traders, who extracted a high price for it.

The absence of government assistance would not have had such adverse effects on traditional fishermen had not trawler fishing been introduced at this crucial period. Introduced from Southern Thailand into Malayan waters in 1959/60 (there is some dispute as to whether it was first introduced into the East or West Coast), trawler fishing was a major technological advance over all previous fishing methods found in the country.[5] Carried out by dragging large, machine-winched trawl nets along the seabed, the method required heavy capital investment in bigger boats, larger-capacity engines, and expensive nets but it justified its high capital costs by proving highly efficient and productive in comparison with the passive traditional methods of fishing which mainly relied on stationary gear. Trawling quickly established itself as the most lucrative fishing method and attracted the attention of a large number of capitalists who were lured by the prospect of quick profits.[6] According to one report, about 400 trawlers were operating mainly in Perak, Selangor, and Johore by 1965[7] but another source estimates that there were as many as 200 large trawlers and 700 small ones operating by 1963.[8] The example above of conflicting information about how many trawlers were found in the peninsula and where they were operating points to the failure of the authorities to mount a close watch on the industry during the early period of its development and monitor its scale of operations and impact on fish resources, which could indicate more precisely the economic and social benefits and disadvantages of the new technology.

Despite the absence of information on the early development of the trawler industry in the country, there is much evidence to show that its impact on traditional fisherman interests was immediate and adverse. Although fisheries in Malaysia, as elsewhere, are a common property resource in the sense that there is open access to it, there has arisen over time some notion of fishing boundaries and prior rights over fishing areas among the various traditional fishing communities.[9] Few serious conflicts seem to have arisen in the past on the crucial matter of rights over fishing

5. Trawler fishing and its impact on employment, resource-use and small fisheries, and government policy towards it have been examined in a number of studies. See, for example, Yap (1977 and 1980), Munro and Chee (1978), and Gibbons (1976).

6. The authors of a study of trawler fishing in Penang have estimated the average capital return in the industry to be 37 per cent over a four-year period between 1966 and 1969. See Munro and Chee (1978).

7. Figures obtained from Table V(i) in Kementerian Perpaduan Negara, July 1972.

8. Jahara Yahaya (undated), p. 4.

9. These rights obviously could not be defined so clearly as land rights but nevertheless there was a sense of usufructuary priority amongst fishermen from different fishing areas, especially when set entrapment gears were used.

areas partly because of the small size and limited power of traditional boats which restricted their range of operation, so that communities were mainly confined to working the waters closest to them. The advent of powerful boats with longer fishing range and with crews drawn largely from outside the traditional fishing industry who had no knowledge of or respect for long-established rights of fishing villages quickly upset the previous stability. Although equipped with more powerful engines which could have enabled the boats to operate much further offshore, trawler fishermen preferred to work within the inshore waters where the more profitable demersal fish resources and prawns were located. This often meant intruding into the established grounds of fishing villages in pursuit of profitable shoals and damaging the nets and other gear of traditional fishermen when these came in their way. Less immediately provocative but also a cause of concern to traditional fishermen was the resource-damaging nature of trawler operations, in which small-mesh nets were dragged along the sea-bed, damaging breeding grounds and sweeping up young fish, prawns, and other marine life before they were commercially valuable.

It was inevitable that bad feelings between trawler fishermen and traditional small-scale and inshore fishing communities should grow and take a violent turn. By the early 1960s relations between the two fishing groups had worsened and bloody conflicts began taking place regularly. Between 1964 and 1976, a total of 113 incidents involving 437 trawlers and 187 inshore vessels were reported, mainly along the West Coast, with 'considerable loss of property and life'[10] (Goh, 1976: 19). These figures are official estimates and probably represent only a small part of the total number of clashes, with many clashes either going unreported or failing to make their way into the official records. Besides the threat to law and order, there were other good reasons why strong government intervention in regulating relationships between inshore small-scale and trawler fishermen was required. Almost all the trawlers were owned by non-fishing capitalists who recruited largely Chinese crews comprising mainly unemployed urban youths. Many inshore fishing villages, on the other hand, contained predominantly ethnic Malay populations,

10. Forty-five vessels were reported to have been destroyed, 62 sunk, and 34 lives lost.

TABLE 5.2

Estimated Landings per Trawler Unit,
Peninsular Malaysia, 1966–1972

Year	Estimated Trawlers in Operation	Landings by Trawlers (tonnes)	Landings per Trawler (tonnes)
1966	425	24 500	57.6
1967	1,099	58 100	52.9
1968	1,305	64 800	49.7
1969	2,056	56 400	27.4
1970	3,548	84 700	23.9
1971	4,272	112 200	26.3
1972	5,378	109 900	20.4

Source: Jahara Yahaya (undated), p. 7, Table 1.

although there was a fair sprinkling of mixed communities. In the clashes between the trawler and inshore fishermen, there was a potential danger of ethnic conflict which could affect the wider society.[11]

Another compelling reason for government action was the danger to fish resources that unregulated trawler operations posed. Although no accurate statistical data is obtainable, it is now generally agreed that the rapid build-up in trawler numbers and the expansion in their operations have been the main factors contributing to the present situation of overfishing, which faces some species in the inshore waters of the West Coast. By 'overfishing' is meant that catches were exceeding the maximum sustainable yield of species, thus bringing about the depletion of the resource. The problem of overfishing was not only an outcome of the increase in the number of trawler boats and their operation in inshore waters but it was due also to the illegal use of small-mesh nets which resulted in a high proportion of the juvenile marine-life being caught in the nets. Some indication of the overfishing can be deduced from Table 5.2, which shows the declining productivity of trawlers as measured in landings per unit, between

11. Intra-ethnic confrontations between Chinese inshore fishing communities and trawlers also occurred in the 1960s but many Chinese inshore fishermen were able to obtain capital to operate trawler boats, unlike their Malay counterparts.

1966 and 1972. At the same time, the proportion of 'trash' fish[12] (which includes juvenile fish and prawns) increased considerably. For example, Yap (1980: 29) estimated trash fish to comprise 60 per cent of the total increase of trawler landings between 1973 and 1974. In Perak, which had the largest increase in trawlers, increases in trawler fish landings accounted for 99.5 per cent of the total increase in fish landings.

As a result of the depletion in fish resources, trawler fishermen have had to increase their catch effort to maintain a level of production that ensures profitability.[13] More seriously affected were the inshore fishermen, who were caught in a vicious spiral of smaller catches which reduced their incomes and inadequate capital to increase their catch effort or purchase bigger boats and engines. By the mid-1970s, the outlook for small fishermen was gloomy, with 'unemployment and underemployment in the fishing village' being 'grim, daily realities' (Goh, 1976: 22).

The government's response to this crisis, which mainly affected fishing along the West Coast, has been studied by other scholars and what is provided here is a summary of some of the main findings (Gibbons, 1976; Yahaya, undated; and Yap, 1977 and 1980). The initial government response to the introduction of the new technology in gear and engines had been to welcome it. This can be seen from the thrust of policy objectives in the First Malaysia Plan which was towards greater productivity in fishing. By 1965, the country had transformed itself from a net importer of fish to a net exporter for the first time since it obtained independence, and the authorities were optimistic of greater returns from further development.

The Fisheries Division's programme of activities strongly

12. The term 'trash fish' is applied to immature fish which cannot be sold in the market and is used as feedmeal for animals instead. The practice of feeding animals with fish meal is extremely wasteful from an economic point of view since much more fish protein is required to produce its equivalent in the form of animal protein. However, the practice is acceptable to animal rearers so long as cheap supplies of trash fish are readily available.

13. According to the Deputy Director of Fisheries, trawl landings were responsible for 57 per cent of trash fish landings in 1976, a high figure which he attributed mainly to the trawlers' use of small-mesh nets to fish for prawns. See his paper on 'The Status of the Malaysian Fisheries—Management and Development Aspects' in Consumers Association of Penang (1980). However, the fact that many trawlers fished illegally close to the shore could have contributed to the unsatisfactory state of affairs.

reflected the production-oriented approach of the First Plan. Among the priorities were the training of fishermen to man larger, more powerful, and more sophisticated vessels, the provision of financial assistance to the industry to modernize, and the expansion of research and fisheries extension services to support the development. Although it had no firm data as to the size of fisheries resources in the country, there was a strong belief amongst fisheries officials that the country's waters were underfished and trawler fishing was assigned a major role in fisheries development since it was regarded as the most productive method and had the greatest potential for expansion. In 1968, a report produced by the Division of Fisheries on the position of the fishing industry declared that it was the policy of the government 'to encourage trawling' and 'steps had been taken to encourage this objective' (Anonymous, 1968: 221).

These steps consisted in part of the government's resistance to the strong pressure exerted by inshore fishermen on the authorities to ban trawler fishing. In 1964 a ban on trawler fishing was imposed by the government in response to the escalating violence between the two fishing groups but this ban was short-lived. In 1965 the government reversed its decision[14] and agreed instead to give out trawler licences through co-operatives, subject to various regulating conditions such as minimum mesh size, fishing hours, specific landing centres, and a prohibition on fishing inside the 12-nmi zone. In 1967, the regulations were relaxed to permit smaller trawler boats to participate and to expand the areas officially permitted for trawler fishing. On the surface, it appeared that government policy had taken a correct position by curbing the activity of individual trawler entrepreneurs and by paving the way for the poorer small-scale fishermen who were to be organized into co-operative societies to participate in the more lucrative fishing method. Also, restricting trawler fishing to beyond the inshore waters and during daytime would ensure that trawler boats did not intrude into the traditional grounds of the inshore

14. It has been suggested that this decision was taken after trial fishing expeditions off Pulau Langkawi in 1964 had established the economic viability of trawler fishing in offshore waters but it is unlikely that this was the only reason behind the government's change of mind. Pressure from commercial interests and the hope of the government that Malay and non-Malay fishing interests could be accommodated by policy stimuli were probably stronger factors.

group or operate undetected. In this way, both production and social objectives would be attained.

However, the limitations of these policy decisions were quickly exposed. There was an almost immediate increase in the number of trawling co-operatives and the granting of a large number of trawler licences with the liberalization of the previous restrictions.[15] But, contrary to expectations, inshore fishermen continued to be largely excluded from the industry. Findings from Gibbons' study investigating the impact of public policy on fishing development in Penang and Kedah reveal that the trawler co-operatives were dominated by non-fishermen entrepreneurs who joined the co-operatives solely to obtain its substantial financial and preferential benefits, a development which should not have been surprising to the authorities since co-operatives were the only means through which licences for trawling were given. These entrepreneurs who provided the boats and working capital worked closely with the local-level élites and state- and federal-level politicians who facilitated their obtaining the trawler licences and membership in the co-operatives. Not only did genuine fisherman participation in trawler co-operatives fail to materialize, the great mass of inshore fishermen also failed to obtain substantial employment benefits from the development of the trawling industry, contrary to the hopes of the Fisheries Department. This was because most of the trawling positions were taken up by new entrants to the industry. Also, trawlers generally require less labour per unit of catch

15. In Perak and Penang alone, the number of licensed trawlers increased from 31 in 1966 to 1,862 in 1972. The steady increase in licensed trawlers between 1966 and 1970 and then its spectacular increase in Perak after 1970 can be seen in the table below:

Number of Licensed Trawlers, Penang and Perak, 1966–1972

Year	Penang	Perak	Year	Penang	Perak
1966	21	10	1970	212	53
1967	48	15	1971	250	1,713
1968	89	21	1972	280	1,582
1969	159	23			

Source: Goh (1973), p. 19.

The number of licensed trawler fishermen in Peninsular Malaysia also increased sharply from 80 in 1965 to 1,312 in 1968, 5,396 in 1970, and 15,892 in 1972. See Table 10 in Gibbons (1976: 105).

compared to traditional gear and did not create as many employment opportunities as their numbers would lead one to expect.

Clearly, the decisions taken by the government in 1965 and 1967 to permit trawler development were short-sighted, especially given the inadequate resources it could muster to ensure that the regulations on trawling were properly observed[16] and its inability to ensure that large numbers of small-scale fishermen could share substantially in the benefits arising from the relaxation in anti-trawling policy. What is surprising is why the situation was permitted to continue unremedied for so many years and why the government tolerated the political interference which permitted a small group to reap substantial benefits to the detriment of the larger inshore fisherman interests. One would have expected that the loss of political credibility, if not damage to national interests, would have produced pressure for decisive remedial action from the more responsible ranks of the government, but this did not happen. As one puzzled high-ranking government member (who was not yet in power when the policies were formulated) puts it: 'By the 1960's, it was already known that the inshore waters of the West Coast were being over-fished and the marine resources were being fast depleted. Yet the situation was allowed to drag on and grow worse for another decade until the mid 1970's ...' (Goh, 1976: 23). It was not until 1975 that the government arrived at the decisions not to issue new trawler licences for boats of below 25 gross tons except in the East Coast, to ban night fishing by small trawlers, and to renew only licences which had no previous record of violation of regulations. These decisions restricting entry into the industry left it too late to alter the pattern of ownership and control in the trawler industry or to arrest the declining productivity of the West Coast waters, especially since the new rules were not accompanied by any great increase in the government's enforcement capacity. Moreover, a new generation of illegal mini-trawlers have managed to evade the efforts of the Marine Police and Fisheries Department at implementing the new regulations. Various estimates put the annual landings of demersal finfish for the West Coast at 125 000–178 000 tonnes for 1973–80

16. The Fisheries Department had no independent regulating capacity but was dependent on the Marine Police and Royal Malaysian Navy which provided patrols of trawler grounds. The latter two departments, however, had other priorities and were themselves short of fast, shallow-draught patrol boats for their own work.

with a substantial proportion coming from the trawler landings. The estimated maximum sustainable yield, however, is estimated at about 110 000 tonnes per annum, leaving a tonnage of overfishing of between 15 000 and 68 000 tonnes annually. In fact, demersal fish landings had peaked by 1977–8 and begun to decline thereafter. Other evidence of overfishing include the increasing incidence of trash fish in the demersal landing and the decline in the value of catch per unit effort. In the coming years, the full impact of the substantial overfishing of the 1970s was to be felt more severely.

The Poverty Eradication Programme of the 1970s: New Deal for Small-scale Fishermen?

The adverse impact that major policy decisions in the 1960s regarding trawling development had on small-scale fisherman interests could have been cushioned by other policy initiatives in the transformed political context of the 1970s. This was because in the aftermath of the May 1969 violence in the nation's capital, the government decided on a new economic policy (commonly referred to as the NEP) to eliminate what it regarded as the major factors underlying racial conflict in the country. There are two prongs of the NEP: one aimed at restructuring the economy such that Malay participation in the modern sectors would be greatly increased and the perceived identification of race with economic functions would be removed, while the other seeks to eradicate poverty through a variety of development programmes aimed at the poorer groups. Since the fishing community contains a high proportion of poor as well as Malay households, the implementation of the NEP held much hope that the fishing community's long-standing grievances would finally receive the attention they deserved.

In fact, a promising start was made with the establishment of a new public authority, Majuikan (Fisheries Development Authority of Malaysia), in 1971 as a parastatal corporation under the Ministry of Agriculture and Rural Development to take charge of fisheries programmes. The establishment of Majuikan, to a great extent, mirrored the government's disappointment with the Fisheries Division and its inability to provide institutional support for the development of the fishing community. It also represented an effort by the government, through a separate public body, to participate in such aspects of the fishing industry as production, processing, and marketing, which the Fisheries Division was not equipped to do. This aim of the government can be deduced from Majuikan's objectives, which include developing and exploiting fisheries resources in accordance with sound fisheries management practice, generating employment opportunities in the fisheries sector by expanding and modernizing fish production and related secondary industries, and supervising, promoting, and undertaking the economic and social development of Fishermen Associations. Thus two broad roles were defined for the new body: on the one hand, fostering the social development of artisanal fishermen and, on the other, engaging in commercial operation in competition with the private sector.

To build up Majuikan and finance its activities, the government allocated large amounts of public funds to it. This can be seen from a comparison of the allocations to fisheries in the four Malaysia Plans up to 1985. In the First Plan period, fisheries was allocated M$22 million. The Second Plan saw the allocation to fisheries almost doubled to M$42 million but since the total public expenditure budget was also substantially increased, fisheries' share of total public expenditure in fact dropped to 0.41 per cent compared with 0.49 per cent in the earlier Plan. With the Third Plan came a dramatic increase in the allocation to fisheries to the sum of M$323 million or almost eight times the previous Plan allocation. This amount, about 1.0 per cent of the total public expenditure budget for the period, was a formidable injection of public funds and a considerable portion was set aside for Majuikan's development and its programmes. The Fourth Plan (1981–5) further increased public expenditure allocation to fisheries to M$434 million or about 1.1 per cent of total public expenditure.

Unfortunately, no detailed accounting of how the organization has spent the money is available but the indications from public statements are that the thrust of Majuikan's expenditure has been towards commercial operations. The major investment of Majuikan has been in a programme to develop trawler fishing in the East Coast with M$24 million being spent to construct a large number of trawler vessels of 40 tonnes and above to exploit the South China Sea offshore resources.[17] During 1971–80, a total of

17. Although the main fish markets are found in the urban centres of the West Coast, the decision to invest in the East Coast was made because of the greater

152 boats were launched under the programme, whose expressed purpose was to increase Malay fisherman participation in the modern sector with Majuikan initially acting as a caretaker to the trawlers until a fixed period of time had elapsed and ownership of the trawler boats could be transferred to the selected fisherman participants. According to the programme's publicity, a substantial number of fishermen would benefit if the scheme proved successful. This objective, however, was clearly unrealistic since the proposed beneficiaries (several hundred boat owners and fishermen involved in construction work) would comprise only a tiny minority of the East Coast fishermen estimated at 35,000. The fear that an élite class of fishermen was being created by Majuikan's programme has been compounded by evidence indicating that the authority's management of the new fleet has been an operational and financial disaster.

Trawling is only one of a wide range of ambitious projects being undertaken by Majuikan. Other projects include joint ventures with foreign capital on deep-sea fishing in the East Coast and Kuching, and the establishment of aquaculture farms, processing plants, ice factories, and marketing complexes in various ports. As with the trawler project, most of these other activities, designed with predominantly commercial objectives in mind, have had to rely on a considerable amount of government financial support. Concentrated in the main fishing ports, it is likely that the new facilities will mainly service the offshore industry, leaving the thousands of small fishermen scattered in the hundreds of small fishing villages still lacking in infrastructural support. It could be that such heavy investment is necessary as an inducement to the private sector to invest in commercial fishing and to enable Majuikan itself to engage in commercial development, but if so, the purpose must be clearly expressed and must not be confused with the needs of traditional fishing communities, which are of a different nature.

Little else is known about Majuikan's activities but from the above evidence, there is a need for the authorities to explain which Majuikan projects are intended to help traditional fishermen and

potential for fisheries development there compared to the West Coast, where fisheries resources have been rapidly depleted. Another reason was the strong competition that Majuikan boats would encounter from private-enterprise trawlers in the West Coast.

in what way, and which projects are commercial with little or no direct relation to improving the well-being and welfare of traditional fishermen. This distinction is necessary because, as one fisheries development expert correctly points out, '[T]he whole strategy of planning artisanal fisheries must be related to welfare criteria of assisting fishermen in a social as well as an economic context. This may be contrasted to the aims of modern commercial fishery, which are more concerned with increasing productivity' (Lawson, 1975: 10).

Apart from the question of the distribution of social and economic benefits which affects the fishing population's interests directly, other questions, such as the economic cost/benefits of the programme and the extent to which subsidization of a public organization having virtual monopoly powers is justifiable, must be answered by the authorities managing Majuikan.[18] This is especially so since the projects involve substantial amounts of public funds and it has been found by one consultant who had access to privileged data, that 'the commercial operations directly managed by Majuikan are incurring substantial and in some areas heavy losses' largely as a result of a lack of sufficient expertise over too many functions (Moore, 1976: 3).

The ambiguity that surrounds Majuikan's activities and its precise role in the socio-economic development of small-scale fisherman communities has clearly become one of the major obstacles standing in the way of a consistent government policy towards these communities. This ambiguity has troubled Majuikan ever since its establishment and is an issue addressed by a number of missions of international development agencies during the 1970s advising the Malaysian government on fisheries development (Crutchfield et al., 1975; Lawson, 1975; Moore, 1976). All these missions agree that there is a need for the authorities to clarify the responsibility and functions of Majuikan, especially in terms of its relationship to the Fisheries Division. As explained earlier, Majuikan had been set up mainly because of the dissatisfaction with the performance of the Fisheries Division and the

18. As with most other government and quasi-government bodies in the country, it is not easy to obtain detailed information on the activities carried out by Majuikan. The budget estimates of various ministries and departments published annually (*Anggaran-Anggaran Belanjawan Program dan Prestasi*) contains a listing of the projects carried out or planned by Majuikan but only the barest information is provided.

desire to create a more appropriate institutional framework for overall fisheries development. However, in doing so, the authorities have unwittingly created a vague division of responsibility between the two institutions which has been detrimental to the interests of fishermen.

A number of examples can be cited. Until Majuikan's formation, the development section of the Fisheries Division had been responsible for the drawing up of development programmes and the implementation of schemes, including subsidies, grants, and other assistance to fisherman organizations. When Majuikan was formed, it was entrusted with control of Fishermen Associations which were to be the main vehicle through which government assistance to traditional fishermen was to be channelled. The impact of this transfer of power from the Fisheries Division to Majuikan has been documented in the case of one Fishermen Association. In early 1973, the Geting Fishermen Association in Kelantan established an open auction scheme for its members. The scheme was a success and together with the sale of ice and fuel, brought in a monthly income of more than M$3,000 to the Association. In March 1974, a Majuikan commercial fisheries scheme was established in Geting. At about the same time, overall central control of Fishermen Associations was transferred to Majuikan while local supervision was in a transitional stage between Majuikan and the Fisheries Division. In September and October 1974, the Association found itself in financial difficulties and Majuikan Headquarters, despite opposition from the members of the local Association, transferred its marketing and input supply functions to Majuikan. As a result, the Association collapsed and ordinary fishermen were said to be boycotting the Majuikan marketing scheme because of the low priority given to them.[19]

Another example of traditional fishermen's interests being adversely affected by the lack of clear division between the two departments in their functions is the proposed programme for the integrated development of artisanal fishermen in the East Coast undertaken by the Fisheries Division. The basic purpose of the

19. The situation, according to Moore who studied it in some detail, has arisen because of the inherent conflict of interest existing in decision-making which, although not readily perceptible in the operations of the policy decision, is really the underlying reason deciding the issue without the conscious realization of the decision-maker.

programme is to improve income opportunities of fishing communities both within and outside the fisheries sector. To succeed, the programme requires strong and independent fisherman organizations that can function as pressure groups for community development. However, with management and policy control of these organizations located in a separate government body, it is difficult to envisage how the Division can carry out its work successfully. This is especially so since Majuikan also has interests in trawler development along the East Coast which obviously are contrary to the interests of the great majority of small-scale fishermen and which, if successful, could depress the standard of living of inshore fishermen through increased competition for limited stocks.[20]

To defuse the 'unhealthy rivalry' between the two institutions which could result in both failing to attain their basic goal, namely the development of fisheries in Malaysia, it would be better if Majuikan could take primary responsibility for commercial activities, that is, control over the operation of fishing fleets, joint ventures, processing plants, and commercial marketing, while the Fisheries Division handled socio-economic development, including financial support and subsidy programmes. This separation is required because there is no way in which Majuikan can presently meet both production targets for the nation's fisheries and economic and social development goals for the traditional fishermen without serious internal pressures on the organization and the need for compromises.

Even if the government does take decisive action in clarifying the allocation of functions between the two organizations responsible for fisheries development and the interrelationship between them and other departments engaged in activities which impinge on fish resources, it should be manifestly clear that its efforts would still come to nought if the organizations are not provided with competent and dedicated staff who will work for the interests of small-scale fishermen. Such staff must be willing at critical points to stand up against vested or opportunistic interests and exercise control and guidance which can assist the broad mass of small-scale fishermen and bring about their development in an orderly fashion. Otherwise, the outcome is an expansion of the

20. Although Majuikan vessels are licensed to operate only in waters beyond 7 nmi, several have been caught infringing into inshore waters.

bureaucracy and the drawing up of policies dictated by weightier economic and political interests.

Besides the establishment of Majuikan to improve government capacity to develop the fishing industry, the government has attempted to initiate changes at the level of fishermen co-operatives to enable them to participate in the new development programmes. Earlier we had seen how co-operatives, as an instrument to improve fishermen welfare, have been largely discredited by the experience of the 1950s and 1960s. Various studies which have looked closely at these experiences at the local level have identified, among other factors, bad management and inadequate supervision of schemes as being responsible for their failure.[21] In the early 1970s, the authorities decided on rebuilding fisherman organizations to act as conduits for the increased government assistance which was to flow into the sector and to enable the fishing community to participate in new economic and social activities. This was mainly done through the establishment of Fishermen Associations,[22] the transference of responsibility over the new Associations and existing Fishermen Co-operatives from the Departments of Fisheries and Co-operatives to Majuikan in 1974 and the amalgamation of the associations and co-operatives into a new organization called Koperasi Nelayan.

Two levels of the new organization have been established by Majuikan: one at local level, referred to as Koperasi Nelayan Kawasan, and the other at national level, Koperasi Nelayan Nasional, which is to engage in trading, fishing enterprises,

21. See, for example, the detailed unpublished study of Elliston (1978) of a M$578,000 development scheme established by the Federal Government in Kuala Linggi. Administered through a co-operative, it included a loan of M$300,000 for boats and fishing gear, M$93,000 for low-cost housing, and M$73,000 for landing and storage facilities. Six years after the scheme began, the co-operative society had repaid only M$70,000, accumulated new debts totalling M$80,000, and was M$8,000 in arrears in interest payment. Among the reasons identified by Elliston as responsible for the failure of the scheme were wrongly sited housing, poorly designed boats, wrong choice of engine, cumbersome and unreasonable repayment requirements, lack of technical training of co-operative members, and a wrongly conceived system of shared ownership.

22. The establishment of these associations was permitted under the Fishermen Association Act of September 1977 which replaced the Fisheries Co-operative Ordinance. Although its stated functions include social development ones, it proposed economic activities such as obtaining and administering capital subsidies and loans for distribution of members' produce and providing fishery equipment and other inputs which were more relevant to members' needs.

finance, credit and loan services, and education and training. Forty-two local-level Koperasi Nelayan had been established in Peninsular Malaysia and Sarawak by 1985. To ensure that the new organizations could carry out the planned activities, the government made available a grant of M$23.8 million during the Fourth Plan period to be used as a revolving fund for the association and co-operatives to finance their activities. Whilst these efforts at building local organizations of producers which can sell cheaper inputs, provide easier access to credit, and initiate schemes to improve the common welfare are to be lauded, the priority given to the establishment of a formidable organizational structure is premature. Even though the various government-sponsored fisherman organizations have a substantial number of members— it was estimated that by 1977 there were 40,000 fishermen enrolled as members of these organizations or 48 per cent of all fishermen in Peninsular Malaysia and Sarawak—there is little participation in their activities and the authorities have assessed that only 14 out of 98 of these organizations could be considered to be active. Until the local-level organizations can function effectively, there seems little use for the national organizational structures that are being created by the authorities.

One of the key problems in the development of Fishermen Associations has remained unchanged since the earliest attempts to build up fishermen co-operatives—the short supply of committed management staff who are sensitive to the aspirations of the fishing community and strong enough to withstand the pressures that will invariably be exerted.[23] Judging from past experience in fisheries and other sectors where active government intervention has taken place, it would require a new breed of managers from those presently available who can meet these exacting requirements and initiate the necessary projects which can enable the associations to function effectively. At the same time, caution must be taken against the opposite tendency of too much bureaucratic control of fisherman organizations. Since a co-operative or producers' organization is by definition a small-scale body comprising members from a specific area who share common benefits, its ideal form is where the community itself is involved in project

---

23. Besides the role played by the government, there are, of course, other important factors responsible for the success of fishermen's associations. They include leadership at the local level, the sense of urgency felt by the community, and the nature of economic activity pursued.

identification and solution-seeking. Overmanagement can lead not only to insensitivity to the community's needs and the setting up of priorities different from those that the fishermen desire, but can also stifle local initiative and result in a situation of dependency of the fishermen on bureaucrats. The means to establish the correct balance between a lack of management and overmanagement in such a way that local initiative and participation is stimulated rather than retarded unfortunately still eludes the government. Until this admittedly difficult pre-condition is obtained, co-operative organizations of fishermen or any other impoverished producer community will remain either dormant bodies unable to provide any meaningful service to its members or captive organizations of vested interest groups working for narrow ends.

We have outlined so far the delivery systems through which the authorities are attempting to implement the development programmes aimed at eradicating poverty among small-scale fishermen, an objective promised in the New Economic Policy. In doing this we have briefly considered the developmental activities of Majuikan, the new organization assigned to restructure the fishing industry and improve the livelihood of fishermen, and found it more oriented towards commercial ends than relieving the poverty of small-scale fishermen. At the same time, the various fishermen organizations through which the fishing community was to participate in the new programmes have also been found wanting.

In addition to these measures aimed at the fishing community as a whole, the government has attempted to provide direct assistance to individual small-scale fishermen through the granting of subsidies. The granting of subsidies is not a new idea for helping fishermen, having been used intermittently by the authorities in the past to fund inputs at below market rates and offer fishermen increased access to engines, boats, and nets. It was hoped that this form of direct assistance would increase the incidence of ownership of productive assets among fishermen and therefore their productive capacity. Since non-ownership of the necessary means of production is commonly held to be an important factor forcing the fishermen into a subordinate position with respect to the financier–traders and hence subjecting them to poverty, the subsidy programme was seen as playing a role in helping to free non-owning operators from their bondage to owners of the boats and gear.

The new schemes were initially introduced in 1972 to fishermen in the East Coast as a result of a M$1.5 million allocation under the Second Plan. Initially very generous to the favoured few recipients who received gear and engines on a full-grant basis, the level of subsidy was subsequently reduced in 1973 and 1974. As with other government subsidization schemes, the scheme quickly ran into problems of 'political interference and abuse'[24] (Lawson, 1975: 25). In late 1974 it was suspended with only one-half of the sum set aside having been put to use. However, it was restarted in 1976 with greatly increased funds made available under the Third Plan.[25] The new allocation of M$70 million reflected to some extent the country's extremely favourable fiscal position in the late 1970s which enabled the authorities to inject more money into the depressed peasant agricultural and fishing sectors. At the same time, it was a recognition that the small-scale fisherman community deserved a higher level of public assistance to subsidize their low incomes until such time as development plans for the community began to take effect.

The main application of the scheme has been in the East Coast where, according to government estimates, the distribution of M$142 million worth of subsidies has benefited thousands of fishermen and helped increase production considerably. Between 1976 and 1980, an estimated 15,000 fishermen received subsidies in the form of nets and other equipment whilst 1,846 were provided subsidized engines. The value of the scheme to recipients is undoubted but whether the subsidies have reached the really needy fishermen is open to question. According to its present regulations, the scheme is available only to *bona fide* fishermen with Fishermen Association members receiving first priority and members of Fishing Co-operatives, second priority. At the same time, participant fishermen must only operate unpowered fishing boats or boats powered with an engine of less than 45 hp. However, according to field interviews conducted with fishermen in five villages in North-east Malaysia,[26] it is mainly people of

24. Although Lawson mentioned these problems in her report, she unfortunately made no attempt to elaborate on them so that we have no idea how serious they are and whether they will invariably wreck all subsidy schemes. Lawson herself, however, tended to the more optimistic view that pre-investment study and inputs of training, extension advice and supervision, and marketing might result in more successful schemes.

25. Further details of the scheme are obtainable from Jahara (1976: 72–80).

26. Interviews conducted with fishermen in Sungai Semilang, Bukit Tambun, Datuk Keramat, and Kuala Juru.

influence (who have obtained membership in the various associations and co-operatives in one way or another) or well-to-do fishermen who do not deserve the assistance who are selected to receive the subsidies. As evidence that poor fishermen are not benefiting, it has been pointed out by respondents that according to existing policy, the grant of subsidies is being confined only to engine and boat owners.[27] This has resulted in the exclusion of the poorest fishermen who do not own their own boats or whose boats are in bad condition. The question posed by one boatless fisherman is apt. 'Siapa yang lebih miskin? Orang yang memiliki bot atau orang yang hanya ada tenaga—penjual tenaga? Bukankah ini satu skim untuk menolong orang yang lebih kaya?' (Who is poorer? Someone who owns a boat or someone who is merely a seller of his labour power? Isn't the scheme only to help people who are more well-to-do?) Another cause of complaint is the rule permitting people who work on the sea for only 90 days a year to qualify for subsidies. According to most interviewees, many part-time fishermen generally have other sources of livelihood such as padi land, *dusun* (fruitland), or petty businesses and therefore they should not be permitted to apply. One full-time fisherman exclaimed, 'Ninety days in a year is really not fair! They work only one quarter of a year on the sea. And yet they receive assistance.'

Even among the successful applicants interviewed, some dissatisfaction was expressed with regard to the working of the scheme. One common grouse was the length of time said to be required to process applications. Some applicants for prawn nets, for example, alleged that they received the nets only after the prawn season had passed, so that they had to wait for the next season before they could use the subsidized nets. Many instances of unsuitable gear and engines were also reported and some respondents said that the difficulty of getting replacements often compelled them either to underutilize the engines or to sell them off discreetly.

All these problems emphasize the need for the authorities to monitor more closely the progress and effectiveness of the subsidy scheme. However, whilst correction of administrative problems or the weak implementational capacity of the personnel managing

27. It is possible that government policy on subsidies for equipment has operated in this fashion because it requires evidence of a fisherman's commitment to fishing before granting assistance; thus a man who has built or bought a boat qualifies for engine assistance or vice versa. Such a policy, however, discriminates against poorer fishermen whose commitment to fishing might be even greater than that of their better-endowed counterparts.

the scheme is possible, the problem of preventing domination or monopolization of the scheme by better endowed fishermen with greater economic or political leverage is more difficult.[28] Given the existing unequal access at both local and national levels, it is difficult to be optimistic about the prospect of the subsidy scheme serving the interests of the great masses of poor fishermen. Beyond the question of the equity of subsidy distribution looms the larger one of the resource base which will surely be affected by a drastic increase in technological levels of a large body of fishermen. Thus, it is obvious that subsidies to artisanal fishermen working the inshore zone in the West Coast will result in overcapitalization and bring about a faster rate of diminution of already endangered stocks. In other words, subsidization, beyond a certain stage, is counter-productive and should be regulated not only with welfare considerations in mind but also within the larger matrix or market impact and the availability of fish resources or else it could create more difficulties than it resolves. Because of this, it is necessary that the concept and practice of subsidization should be linked closely to the question of surplus fishermen and its operation cover both retained and displaced fishermen.

Policy Developments in the 1980s

By the early 1980s, it had become clear to the government itself that much stronger measures were needed to overcome the problems of overcapitalization and over-exploitation which were affecting the well-being of small-scale fishermen as well as the fisheries resource base. A first step was the introduction of a zoning system in 1981 which reserved the first 5 nmi of inshore waters to traditional fishing gear and the 5–12-nmi zone to Malaysian owner-operated trawlers and purse-seiners below 40 gross tonnage. Boats exceeding 40 gross tonnage were permitted to fish only in the 12–30-nmi zone while all foreign and partially Malaysian-owned vessels were limited to waters beyond the thirtieth nautical mile. Besides the allocation of fishing grounds,

28. As with Lawson, a more optimistic view of the scheme is held by Jahara Yahaya (1976: 80), who maintains that although subsidies may aggravate rather than solve the problems of the artisanal or small-scale fishermen, 'the difficulties are not insurmountable provided attempts are made to avoid mistakes experienced in similar schemes to assist the fishermen sector'.

the regulation also increased the trawl mesh size from 25 mm to 40 mm at the cord end in an attempt to regulate and control the minimum size and weight of fish caught. A moratorium on licence issuance for small fishing boats operating in waters within the first 12 nmi was also imposed. Licences were to be issued only to larger boats capable of operating in waters outside this zone. To deter violation of regulations, the Fisheries Act was amended in 1984 to increase the penalties for illegal trawling in inshore waters (up to M$100,000 for Malaysian vessels and M$1 million for foreign vessels caught infringing the rule).

However, the impact of these new measures has not been entirely to the advantage of small-scale fishermen. The zoning system, for example, has had the effect of eliminating all non-owner–operator fishing units from inshore waters, thus discriminating against the poorest group of fishermen—those who do not own their own boats. The effect of the regulations on fishing conflict is also questionable. On the one hand, surveillance is grossly inadequate. With a coastline measuring some 2,899 nmi and a sea area covering 138 700 sq. km (inclusive of the Extended Economic Zone area) to look after, it is not surprising that the two bodies responsible for surveillance—the Department of Fisheries and Marine Police—have had little success. A further disadvantage is that both are poorly co-ordinated and suffer from a shortage of vessels, personnel, and equipment. The result has been blatant violations of the zoning regulation by the trawlers, especially in the stretch between Pangkor Island and Penang. This is also the area of greatest conflict between the trawling and the traditional fishermen. A recent case study of the Penang fishermen reveals that more than half (54 per cent) of them find the trawling ban to be ineffective while 5 per cent of them are not even aware of the ban. Another 21.6 per cent show ignorance of the regulation regarding the minimum mesh size of trawl net (Jahara Yahaya and Tadashi Yamamoto, 1988).

Lack of political support for the well-being of fisheries resources continues to be a major problem in the 1980s. There is little political awareness of the problem of depleting marine resources in the country. As such, legal proceedings against violators of the zoning regulations are often met with political interference, as is the implementation of the moratorium on fishing licence issuance and the regulation regarding minimum mesh size. The political reality of the country is such that politicians trade political favours for electoral support and such favours include assistance in obtaining fishing licences and protection against government actions for violations of what they consider to be 'unreasonable' regulations.

It is quite inconceivable that rapid depletion of the marine resources in inshore waters can be arrested through fishing policies alone. Seasonal fluctuations and migratory patterns of the fish stock make the zoning system quite impractical. Moreover, given the scanty information available on the marine resources and resource potential, it is difficult to assess exactly the rate of 'over-fishing' and to decide what is the optimal number of fishing licences to be issued; how these licences are to be distributed by types of fishery, gear, and area; or to suggest alternative fishing methods in areas where trawling has been banned.

Despite the new policies, the government is clearly caught in a bind. Its past weak and vacillating policies have permitted trawling together with purse-seining, the other large-scale and capital-intensive technique, to become firmly established as the most important fishing methods in the country. In 1985, the two methods accounted for 11 per cent of total estimated gear and 69 per cent of total fish landings. Despite some evidence of a decline in man/boat ratio over the last ten years and the failure of poorer inshore fishermen to participate, the labour-absorbing capacity of the two methods has been considerable and in 1986 they provided employment to about 20,179 fishermen or 37 per cent of the total labour force in fisheries in the peninsula. Whatever the merits of the claim of small-scale fishermen that their livelihoods have been adversely affected by trawler fishing, it has been argued that to ban trawling altogether would not serve the overall national interests. Too much capital, human resources and skills have been invested which, if ejected by a drastic policy reversal, would not only flood the labour market with a large number of unemployed young men but would also result in a substantial decline in production, affecting the poorest consumers in the country for whom fish is still the cheapest and main source of protein. However, to permit trawler fishing to continue in its present form and at the prevailing intensity of operations runs the risk of a more serious and rapid rundown in already depleted fish stocks, aggravating the economic plight of inshore fishermen and causing even more widespread social distress. The latter two considerations deserve as much attention as trawler fishing's contribution to production and steps should be taken to minimize the heavy social and ecological price that is being currently paid for its development. Measures such as quicker phasing out of licences, effective restriction of trawlers to certain waters, confiscation of offending trawler boats, increased charges on trawler gear and boats to discourage new entrants; all are immediately necessary but require a degree of administrative firmness and political will which the government has up to the late 1980s not shown itself capable of exerting.

Conclusion

What are the lessons to be learnt from the Malaysian experience with the development of the fisheries industry over the past 30 years? An obvious one is that the nature and dynamics of the environment and its resources (including aquatic) is a critical factor to take into consideration. Not only is the distribution and abundance of fish greatly controlled and affected by variations in the environment, but at the same time, the environment itself is affected by the type of exploitation carried out. Unfortunately, in most countries in the region, the present pool of knowledge with regard to the geographical, limnological, and oceanographic characteristics affecting water masses and aquatic resources, and fish resources themselves, continues to be extremely limited. No country in the region has, as yet, systematic information on the biological characteristics of even the most economically important species. Without such baseline data, it is difficult, if not impossible, to calculate potential yield or what are sustainable levels of fishing activity, and design policies which will ensure optimal returns to small-scale fishermen over a long-term period.

A policy recommendation flowing from this is that no government in the region should permit the introduction of new fishing technologies or expansion of new fishing fleets in its waters unless a data base exists showing conclusively a position of under-utilization of stocks. Meanwhile, policies preventing the further undermining of the bio-ecological basis of fish stocks by the imposition of strict environment standards on all existing and new land-based programmes should be immediately pursued. A start has been made in this by some countries in the region with the enactment of environment standards legislation, but there has been little or no implementation capacity so that the legislation have remained pieces of paper.

Since information on the sustainable exploitation of fish resources on an *ex-post-facto* basis is not very useful from the experiences of Malaysia and other countries, it is also proposed that an assessment of the demersal stocks fished by small-scale fishermen be immediately conducted and data on size, identity, growth-rate, etc., collected and evaluated to enable suitable policies and restrictions to be designed to limit over-fishing. At the same time, since present modern theories of fisheries management are based upon work carried out in high-latitude single-species fisheries, new conceptual tools to assess multi-species have to be quickly devised and policy decisions regarding level of exploitation, type of technology, and other crucial aspects of fisheries arrived at.

The difficulties in obtaining and interpreting the data on fish stocks, relating it to a wider environmental matrix and to current and future levels of exploitation by small-scale fishermen and arriving at policies which permit a long-term maximum sustained yield per small-scale fisherman unit must not be under-estimated. To achieve it requires much greater national and international effort in the scientific and technical spheres than has been obtainable and a co-ordinated link between research management, education, and training.

At a different level, the problems of small-scale fisherman communities relating to low income, adverse conditions of production, limited access to credit and marketing in Malaysia and many other countries of the region are relatively well served by a strong data base and the general directions of policy orientation required to resolve them are clear although they might vary in detail from country to country. In general, the problems of small-scale fishermen require an integrated bottom-up approach as opposed to the conventional approaches of development planning. Such an approach would entail, first, the direct involvement of small-scale fishermen in solution-seeking through field-level dialogues[29] and, secondly, the participation of small-scale fishermen themselves in project formulation and implementation. Placing small-scale fishermen at the centre of the policy will ensure not only participation but also permit the socio-economic

29. Such an attempt was made at a meeting held in Bangkok in July 1977 of small-scale fisherman leaders from Malaysia, the Philippines, Thailand, Indonesia, and Japan.

and cultural needs of the communities to be taken into account and their own sense of priorities respected.

In making these recommendations, two key assumptions have been made. One is that national objectives of maximizing protein yield, employment, and foreign currency can be achieved by a systematic programme of long-term improvement in the social and economic status of small-scale fishermen. In this respect, the courting of corporate-type fisheries development by the countries in the region through joint ventures with foreign companies must be condemned as short-sighted and injurious to small-scale fishermen and national interests. The second assumption is that small-scale fishermen can be presumed to act as rationally as other groups in society wanting to improve their lives. Thus, they will be ready to adopt or adapt new technologies which will improve their catches and incomes, but they will not support restrictions which seek to conserve and increase fish stocks and rehabilitate depleted fishing grounds if these restrictions are not understood by them, and they do not see how their interests are best served by such action.

Finally, it must be emphasized that the future development of the fishing community is to a great extent dependent on the availability of resources other than fisheries provided to it. Many small-scale fisherman groups are extremely mobile, moving from fisheries to agriculture and back, according to the season. This mobility can be used advantageously by policy-makers to widen the economic base of the fishing community through the establishment of supplementary means of livelihood based on agriculture and land-based projects.

References

Anonymous (1956), 'Report of the Committee to Investigate into the Fishing Industry', Kuala Lumpur, Government Press.

Anonymous (1968), 'Possibilities and Problems of Fisheries Development in Southeast Asia', unpublished paper, Food and Agriculture Organization.

Consumers Association of Penang (1980), *The Malaysian Fisheries, A Diminishing Resource*, Penang.

Crutchfield, J. A., *et al.* (1975), 'Malaysia Legal and Institutional Aspects of Fisheries Development', South China Sea Fisheries Development and Co-ordinating Programme (SCS) paper, Manila, July.

Elliston, G. (1978), 'A Critique of the Kuala Linggi Scheme', unpublished paper, Penang.

Fredericks, L. J. (1973), 'Cooperative Structure and Government Policy in Malaysia', Ph.D. thesis, University of Uppsala.

Gibbons, D. S. (1976), 'Public Policy towards Fisheries Development in Malaysia: A Critical Review Emphasising Penang and Kedah', *Kajian Ekonomi Malaysia*, Vol. XIII, Nos. 1 and 2.

Goh Cheng Teik (1976), 'The Fishing Conflict in Penang and Perak: Personal Memoir', *Kajian Ekonomi Malaysia*, Vol. XIII, Nos. 1 and 2.

Government of Malaya (1955), 'Memorandum by the Economic Adviser in a Development Plan for Malaya, 1956–1960', unpublished paper, Kuala Lumpur.

_____ (1956), *Report of the Committee to Investigate into the Fishing Industry*, Kuala Lumpur, Government Press.

Government of Malaysia (1971), *Second Malaysia Plan, 1971–75*, Kuala Lumpur: Government Printer.

_____ (1976), *Third Malaysia Plan, 1976–80*, Kuala Lumpur: Government Printer.

_____ (1981), *Fourth Malaysia Plan, 1981–85*, Kuala Lumpur: Government Printer.

Jahara Yahaya (undated), 'A Critical Review of Government Policy and Regulation towards the Development of the Trawler Industry in Peninsular Malaysia', unpublished paper.

_____ (1976), 'Some Implications of the Fishermen's Subsidy Scheme in Peninsular Malaysia', *Kajian Ekonomi Malaysia*, Vol. XIII, Nos. 1 and 2.

Jahara Yahaya and Yamamoto, Tadashi (1988), *A Socio-Economic Study of Fisheries Management and Conservation with Particular Reference to Two Artisanal Fishing Villages in Penang, Peninsular Malaysia*, Nihon University.

Kanniah, Rajeswari (1985), 'How Development Displaces the Poor', paper presented at Seminar on 'Problems and Prospects of Rural Malaysia', Consumers Association of Penang.

Kementerian Perpaduan Negara (1972), 'A Study of the Conflict between the Inshore-fishermen and the Trawler Fishermen in West Malaysia', unpublished paper, Kuala Lumpur, July.

Kestevan, G. L., ed. (1949), *Malayan Fisheries*, Singapore: Malaya Publishing House Ltd.

Lawson, R. M. (1975), 'Interim Report on Socio-economic Aspects of the Development of Artisanal Fisheries on the East Coast of Malaysia', SCS paper, July.

Moore, G. K. (1976), 'Malaysia—Legal and Institutional Aspects of Fisheries Development', SCS paper.

Munro, G. and Chee Kim Loy (1978), *The Economics of Fishing*, Penang: Universiti Sains Malaysia Press.

Ness, G. (1967), *Bureaucracy and Rural Development in Malaysia: A Study of Organizations in Stimulating Economic Development in New States*, Berkeley: University of California Press.

World Bank (1975), *Agricultural Credit: Sector Policy Paper*, Washington.

Yap, C. L. (1977), 'Trawling: Its Impact on Employment and Resource Use on the West Coast of Peninsular Malaysia', in B. Lockwood and K. Ruddle, eds., *Small-scale Fisheries Development: Social Science Contribution*, Honolulu, East–West Center.

—— (1980), 'A Socio-economic Analysis of the Problems of "Over Expansion" on the West Coast of Peninsular Malaysia', in Consumers Association of Penang, *The Malaysian Fisheries, A Diminishing Resource*, Penang.

6
Conflict over Natural Resources in the Pacific

James M. Anthony

THE history of the Pacific islands is in no small measure a history of conflict over natural resources. Before foreigners came to the Pacific in search of whales, gold, cheap labour, sandalwood, land in the sun, noble savages, and candidates for conversion to their religious beliefs, Pacific islanders themselves were engaged in contention over one natural resource that was sacred and scarce—land. With the arrival of foreigners, the islanders were pitted in long and often bitter disputes with the new arrivals and sometimes among themselves.

In the wake of European rediscovery of the Pacific and its peoples, an era of unsurpassed conflict over natural resources began. Land was at the core of these struggles. The more flagrant instances are well known—the Maoris of New Zealand were divested of 63 million of the 66 million acres once owned by them; the Kanaks of New Caledonia were deprived of ownership of all their lands when the French colonized them in 1853; by the early part of the twentieth century, the Hawaiians had lost almost all of the land once held under native customary tenure; in Fiji, shortly after that country had become a British Crown Colony in 1874, some of the best land was judged by a Land Claims Commission appointed by the newly established British colonial government to have been 'properly alienated' to a motley collection of itinerant foreigners. But the loss of as precious a resource as land was not the end of the story. In time, there was conflict over other natural resources as well. In each case the natives lost, perhaps not completely but substantially. Ownership and control of most natural resources passed into foreign hands.

The conflict over natural resources in the Pacific islands has so far largely been over those that are land based: minerals, people, sandalwood, lumber, and fresh water.[1] Largely ignored in the first two decades after the end of the Second World War, the Pacific is now being 're-rediscovered'. That in itself ought not to be considered too surprising. The Pacific, after all, is a huge body of water separating the United States from its largest trading partners—the countries of East Asia, and Japan in particular. Moreover, it is through the Pacific that an increasing volume of American, Soviet, and other maritime traffic, military as well as commercial, travels into East and South-East Asian ports, beyond them into the Indian Ocean, and from there to the Middle East. The United States claims that this is yet another area vital to its interests. And to lend legitimacy to that claim, the familiar spectre of the Soviet threat to this area has also been raised. The elements to make this a new theatre of the Cold War are present: strategic seabed mineral resources, petroleum and gas, marine space, and specks of land in a vast ocean that must not be allowed to fall into hostile hands, domestic or foreign. It is against this background of 'strategic denial' that the general subject of conflict over natural resources in the Pacific will be addressed.

Although it might be revealing to document, assess, and analyse the historical record of the various manifestations of conflict over natural resources in the Pacific, that is not the purpose of this essay. The concern here is with the 're-rediscovery' of the Pacific and its effect on the frontier resources of the ocean—fish, seabed minerals, marine ecosystems, hydrocarbons, and marine space—in the expanded ocean areas that now fall within the jurisdiction of island states.

Since the island states themselves are surrounded by metropolitan, industrialized states—North and South America to the east; the Soviet Union, South Korea, Japan, China, and parts of South-East Asia to the west, and Australia and New Zealand to the south-west—it will be necessary to examine to some extent the involvement of these metropolitan powers (as well as others such as France and West Germany) in the present and future exploitation of Pacific marine and related resources. In addition, it will be

1. In Hawaii, for example, large quantities of water were diverted—without any compensation to native and other owners—by foreign-owned sugar companies for their own use.

necessary to examine such actual and potential conflict as might exist within and between island states over questions like disputed ocean boundaries, rates and terms of resource exploitation, and protection of the marine environment.

Underlying the issues examined, the questions posed, and the trends identified is a narrow spectrum of complex, interrelated, and in some ways paradoxical concerns that are of fundamental importance to the future of this vast, now strategic region. Small in terms of population, smaller still in terms of land mass, this is a part of the world that lies in the centre of a vast ocean that covers a third of the earth's surface. Despite their physical location in the centre of the region, the islands have long been relegated to the periphery by some of the larger countries around the Pacific rim. This is nowhere more clear than in the volume of material on what has come to be known variously as the Pacific Community or the Pacific Basin Economic Community.

In the grand plans discussed in Tokyo, Washington, Canberra, and other distant capitals, the islands of the Pacific have for a long time been taken for granted. This was illustrated by Jiro Tokuyama, Dean of the Nomura School of Advanced Management and an adviser to the important Tokyo-based Nomura Research Institute, when he spoke on the subject of 'The Emerging Pacific Community' at a closed meeting in Honolulu in October 1984. Tokuyama, in a 21-page prepared address, had not one word to say about the Pacific islands. When questioned from the floor about this omission, he seemed perplexed at first, but then answered that the islands could, in the emergent twenty-first century economic order, be the playground for tired businessmen (and women) and others from the rim countries. It might be argued that being figurative 'hewers of wood and carriers of water' in a super twenty-first century hotel industry may not be the worst fate for Pacific islanders. What is intriguing in this scenario is the question of whether Pacific islanders will own the hotels or whether they will be owned and controlled by the transnational corporations that will have mined the ocean floor for minerals and reinvested the profits in a Pacific-wide island hotel boom.

If this scenario were to be realized—and it might be—it would be a repetition of history. The resources of the land made others rich the first time around. Now that the islanders have a rare second chance to play the resource exploitation game again—this time with their last resources on land and those of the ocean—how will the spoils be divided? Developed nations view the South Pacific as a place to freely fish for tuna, test their weapons and, possibly, store or dump their waste and mine the seabed minerals. The islanders are pitted again, albeit in different historical circumstances, against those who possess technological superiority and financial power. The issues for the island states, collectively and individually, coalesce around dependence, equity, lifestyle and survival. These issues lie at the heart of this struggle, and the consequences, if not approached with creativity, vision, and unusually enlightened political and intellectual leadership, may, in the emerging world division of labour, relegate all the inhabitants of the Pacific (barring a few local political and economic brokers) to permanent servitude. In this respect, Pacific islanders are in a position no different from that of other resource-rich Third World peoples. Their problems and opportunities are in microcosm the very same as those of others in the Third World.

The Region and Its Resources

The Pacific region contains some 10,000 islands having a total land area of 550 000 sq. km and a total population of approximately 5 million (Table 6.1; Figure 6.1). The total area claimed by the island states as part of their 200-nmi exclusive economic zones (EEZs) is about 30 000 000 sq. km in an ocean with an area of 165 000 000 sq. km.

The tropical islands of the Pacific are distributed both north and south of the equator roughly between 140° W and 130° E longitude (Figure 6.1). These are islands that have long stretches of white sandy beaches, palm trees, and summer all year long. Not all of them are low-lying coral atolls—some, such as Fiji, Vanuatu, New Caledonia, Papua New Guinea, and the Solomons, are 'high islands'. They are relatively rich in land-based natural resources including minerals such as gold, copper, and manganese.

Because of their geographical location, all of these islands have two resources that are particularly important—climate and marine space. Climatic and related conditions provide an environment that attracts increasingly large numbers of travellers, and the islands are becoming resort areas financed by international sources of capital. This development provides jobs for islanders, thus sustaining increasing appetites for foreign-produced goods and

TABLE 6.1

Population and Land and Sea Area of Countries in the
South Pacific Commission Area[1]

Country	Population (mid-1978)	Land Area (sq. km)	Sea Area (sq. km)	Sea Area / Land Area
American Samoa	31,500	197	390 000	1,980
Cook Islands	18,500	240	1 830 000	7,625
Fiji	607,000	18 272	1 290 000	71
French Polynesia	141,000	3 265	5 030 000	1,541
Guam	90,000	541	Included in TTPI	n.a.
Kiribati	56,000	684	3 550 000	5,190
Nauru	7,000	21	320 000	15,238
New Caledonia	138,000	19 103	1 740 000	91
New Hebrides	101,500	11 880	680 000	57
Niue	3,700	259	390 000	1,506
Norfolk Island	1,900	36	400 000	11,111
Papua New Guinea	2,990,000	462 243	3 120 000	7
Pitcairn Island	100	5	800 000	160,000
Solomon Islands	214,000	28 530	1 340 000	47
Tokelau	1,600	10	290 000	29,000
Tonga	93,000	699	700 000	1,001
Trust Territory of the Pacific Islands	133,000	1 832	6 200 000	3,384
Tuvalu	7,400	26	900 000	34,615
Wallis and Futuna	10,000	255	300 000	1,176
Western Samoa	153,000	2 935	120 000	41
Total	4,798,200	551 033	29 390 000	(Av.) 53

Source: Feleti Sevele and Alan Bollard (1979), South Pacific Economies: A Statistical Summary, Occasional Paper, v. 15, Noumea: South Pacific Commission.
n.a. = not available.
[1]Includes 200-nmi EEZs.

services. This is part of the vicious cycle of import dependence and adverse balance of trade that characterizes the islands' economies.

Conflicts over Marine Space

The fundamental resource is marine space itself. The Pacific Ocean has become more important than the Atlantic to both the

Figure 6.1
The South Pacific Region with
200-nmi Exclusive Economic
Zones.

Source: Based on B. Cicin-Sain and
R. W. Knetch (1989), 'The
Emergence of a Regional Ocean
Regime in the South Pacific',
East–West Environment and Policy
Institute, Working Paper No. 14,
January, Figure 1.

United States and the Soviet Union, and particularly the US
allies—Japan, South Korea, and Australia. The Pacific islands have
grown in strategic importance, as both superpowers deploy
increasing numbers of surface and subsurface vessels as part of an
unprecedented buildup of their nuclear-powered and nuclear
weapon-carrying fleets.

Despite withdrawing from the Asian land mass after its
Vietnam fiasco, the United States has continued to consolidate its
military positions on the Pacific rim and presently has a forward
deployment network stretching from its East and South-East
Asian bases in Japan and the Philippines to Diego Garcia in the
southern Indian Ocean. At the same time, there has been a
corresponding buildup of Soviet military power in the Pacific and
Indian oceans—the Soviet Pacific fleet of almost 200 warships,
carriers, attack submarines, and strategic missile submarines today
is probably as strong as, if not stronger than, the US Pacific fleet.

More ominous for peace and security in the region is the
deployment of a new generation of nuclear weapons on naval
vessels in the western Pacific—the Tomahawk cruise missile with
a 200-kiloton warhead more than nine times as powerful as the
bomb that devastated Nagasaki—highlights the spread of the
nuclear arms race into the Asia-Pacific region.

The United States claims that the Soviet Union already has
cruise missiles on its ships and submarines in the western Pacific.
The most significant development has been increased Soviet
access to military facilities in Vietnam's Cam Ranh Bay and
Danang airfield. About four 'Bear' long-range patrol aircraft
conduct maritime surveillance of submarine and surface shipping
in the South China Sea sea lanes from Bashi Channel to the
Natuna Islands and can probe radar and air defences of ASEAN
countries. There is also a constant presence in Vietnam of nine
'Badger' medium-range bombers, capable of attacking surface
shipping and submarines in the South China Sea, and 20 to 26
surface ships and 4 to 6 submarines in Cam Ranh Bay.

These powers recognize that marine space itself, aside from the
mineral and pelagic resources it contains, is a vital resource in its
own right. This resource has so far apparently been unrecognized
by islanders for its strategic importance, in terms of surface and
subsurface naval mobility, and surveillance and seabed weapon
systems. It could give the islanders a valuable bargaining chip in
dealings with both major and minor foreign powers.

UNCLOS is not yet in force and will not come into force until or unless it has been ratified by 60 signatories (Kimball, 1984). At present, only 41 states have ratified the Treaty (Coquia, 1989) and it may be years before the requisite 60 ratifications are in hand, if ever. Most states have signed the Convention and thus have an obligation not to defeat the object and purpose of the Treaty between signature and its entry into force. However, signatories could argue that only an action which would cause irreversible harm to the Treaty would be a violation of this obligation, and that there are relatively few actions that would do so. For example, a state claiming a 200-nmi territorial sea could argue that it was not incompatible with UNCLOS because the claim could be converted to a 200-nmi EEZ if and when the Convention enters into force (Gamble and Frankowska, 1984).

The United States, West Germany, and the United Kingdom have refused to sign the Treaty and have declared they will not ratify it. The refusal of these countries to sign the Law of the Sea Treaty may cause navigational difficulties for vessels flying their flag, particularly their warships. The Treaty elaborates the right of innocent passage in the territorial sea, formalizes the right of passage through straits used for international navigation and through archipelagic sea lanes, and protects navigational rights in exclusive economic zones. These rights include the submerged passage of submarines through straits and archipelagic waters over which countries claim sovereignty. These provisions were adopted after difficult negotiations over nearly 15 years and many important developing nations feel they gave up important security interests in agreeing to these provisions. Indeed, many nations feel that the United States negotiated in bad faith by refusing to sign the Treaty after inducing them to agree to many compromises over a long period of time regarding navigation rights. Some nations believe that non-signatories do not have these rights and a few of these may even try to prevent vessels of non-signatories from navigating in specific areas under their control (Kimball, 1984).

In this atmosphere of legal and political uncertainty, states could take one or more of several actions. States which ratify UNCLOS could deny to the United States, the United Kingdom, and West Germany passage and overflight along sea lanes in archipelagos and transit passage through straits within territorial seas, arguing that these rights are not customary law and do not accrue to non-signatories of UNCLOS. Whether or not such an interpretation is made will presumably depend on the overall quality of the state's relationship with the non-signatories. In and bordering the Pacific, Indonesia, the Philippines, Fiji, the Solomon Islands, and Vanuatu have claimed archipelagic status (Figure 6.1). New Caledonia could claim archipelagic status according to the Treaty provisions except Chesterfield and South Bellona reefs, and Hunter and Matthew islands (Prescott, 1983). The Philippines and Tonga claim as territorial waters the seas within their historic frame defined in 1898 and 1887 respectively (Figure 6.1) (Prescott, 1983: 496). El Salvador, Panama, Ecuador, and Peru claim territorial seas out to 200 nmi (Borgese and Ginsburg, 1982). Chile, Colombia, Ecuador, and Peru claim sovereignty within the 200-nmi limit (Juda, 1986). If a warship does not comply with the laws and regulations of the coastal state concerning passage through the territorial sea and disregards any request for compliance therewith, the coastal state may require it to leave its territorial sea immediately (United Nations, 1982). Some Eastern European countries even maintain that warships enjoy no right of innocent passage in the territorial sea (Lowe, 1986).

States could substitute the innocent passage regime for transit passage and sea-lane passage, especially for non-signatories. Innocent passage is that which is not prejudicial to the peace, good order, or security of the coastal state, and it can be suspended. Submarines must travel on the surface. Transit passage through straits must be a continuous and expeditious movement between high seas and exclusive economic zones and it cannot be impeded. The sea-lane passage regime is similar and cannot be obstructed (United Nations, 1982: Articles 17–22, 38, and 53).

If the party using innocent passage is not a party to UNCLOS or UNCLOS is not in force, the coastal state could argue that the 1958 Convention applies and that the coastal state can characterize passage as offensive or prejudicial to coastal state interests based on the simple presence of the vessel, including its cargo type (Jin, 1986; Burke, 1986). If the state is not a party to the 1958 Geneva Convention and has not signed UNCLOS, it becomes a question of whether the state has acceded to customary practice in this regard or whether it has, like China, declared that it is not bound by this Convention[2] (Jin, 1986). Even if the user is a party, the

2. None of the developing Pacific island countries were present at the 1958 Conference—indeed, few were independent nations. However, the metropolitan

coastal state could argue that an activity of the vessel not having a direct bearing on passage—perhaps the discharge of radioactive material—makes its passage non-innocent (United Nations, 1982: Article 19).

States could require prior notification and authorization for foreign warships to enter their territorial sea, or for that matter, their archipelagic waters, arguing that although the Convention is silent on this matter, under the Convention the coastal state does retain the right to adopt measures to safeguard its security interests (United Nations, 1982: Articles 19 and 25; Burke, 1986; Sohn, 1986; Anand, 1986). Some 38 states presently require prior notification and/or approval for foreign warships to enter their territorial sea, including China and Papua New Guinea. Indonesia requires such notification for innocent passage of warships unless the innocent passage is conducted through designated sea lanes (Noegroho, 1986). France has certainly broken new ground in the interpretation of non-innocent passage by denying the *Greenpeace* access to its harbour for repairs because, in the words of Bernard Gerard, the High Commissioner of French Polynesia, 'Greenpeace through its attitude, has violated the right of innocent passage in international waters' (*Honolulu Advertiser*, 9 October 1985). This could become a precedent for Pacific states to ban foreign warships. States could require foreign ships exercising the right of innocent passage through their territorial sea to use designated sea lanes and traffic separation schemes (United Nations, 1982: Article 22).

States could claim various limits and regimes on the basis of uniqueness and the fact that many other states have done so, including the maritime powers. Some fifteen states already claim territorial seas to 200 nmi; three others claim box-like territorial sea limits around island groups (Alexander, 1986). Over a dozen states have special security zones (Lowe, 1986: 181). Burma, India, and Vietnam prohibit alien warships and aircraft from military warning zones 24 nmi wide while Kampuchea and Indonesia have such zones 12 nmi wide (Prescott and Morgan, 1983). China has a military warning zone extending at some points to 50 nmi from the coast; North Korea has one out to

powers may argue that they represented their colonies and that their accession applies to the former colonies. Or some independent island nations may have acceded to the 1958 Treaty.

50 nmi; South Korea, a US ally, one extending 150 nmi in the Sea of Japan and 100 nmi in the Yellow Sea; and Nicaragua, one extending 25 nmi and requiring 15 days' advance notice by foreign warships and planes. At least two dozen water bodies have been claimed as historic, including Canada's Hudson Bay, the Soviet Union's Sea of Azov, Panama's Gulf of Panama, China's Bohai Bay, Burma's Gulf of Martaban, Thailand's Bight of Bangkok, and Vietnam's Gulf of Tonkin (Sohn, 1986; Alexander, 1986).

Restrictive regimes could be applied to aircraft overflying a state's land and marine airspace. In principle, there is no right of innocent passage for aircraft over land or territorial sea and states commonly require aircraft to identify themselves one hour's flying time outside national territory. Outside of UNCLOS, there are no general transit rights analogous to the concept of straits used for international navigation. State aircraft, defined as aircraft used in military, police, and customs services, are excluded from the scope of the Convention on International Civil Aviation and are therefore mainly subject to national regulation. With regard to rights of overflight for foreign military aircraft, states are generally reluctant to incur far-reaching obligations. On the whole, freedom of overflight is granted only in particular situations and with the proviso of revocability[3] (Christol, 1978; Hailbronnery 1983).

States might even claim the space above their maritime jurisdictional zones as a national resource. In 1976 eight equatorial countries claimed segments of the orbit directly above them as integral parts of their national territory over which they had sovereign rights. Such claims might be extended to include orbit segments over territorial seas, archipelagic waters, and EEZs as well. There are numerous satellites which contribute to global monitoring of the oceans and are invaluable in Anti-Submarine Warfare (ASW). Still more are under development (Wilkes, 1980: 238; Jaseni, 1985, 1980). If deployed, the Strategic Defense Initiative programme would place weapons in orbit. Satellites also gather scientific research data from the territorial sea and EEZs of Pacific nations without their knowledge or consent, an activity which in theory may be denied under the provisions of UNCLOS.

---

3. Article 3(c) of the Chicago Convention explicitly provides that no state aircraft of a contracting state shall fly over the territory of another state or land thereon without authorization, by special agreement or otherwise, and only in accordance with the terms thereof.

Many of these satellites supply information on weather, waves, wind, sea temperature, and surface vessel traffic, and relay data on currents, temperature, and sound velocity from remote, unattended—free-floating and even submerged—buoys to land stations. New imaging techniques permit the production of precise maps of the sea floor (US News and World Report, 1986). Of more direct application in ASW are satellite-borne blue–green lasers which may be used for communication with or detection of submerged submarines; the mapping of all surface ships so that sound from surface ships of no interest can be distinguished on underwater sound sensing systems from hostile submarines; detection of surface thermal anomalies resulting from the heat released from the reactor; or detection of hydrodynamic signatures that result when turbulence from a submarine's wake mixes water of different temperature, salinity, and biological content into the surface.

In considering taking any of these options, states must also consider the possibilities of enforcing these regimes. There are several possible options of enforcement which, when taken by several states individually or collectively, may create problems for maritime powers. To detect violations of national regimes by, for example, submarines, states could purchase the equipment from like-minded third parties such as Sweden, Japan, or even China. Alternatively, they could play one nuclear power off against another and request the equipment or the intelligence as defence assistance. After all, the United States and its allies often communicate and even publicize the presence of Soviet warships in other countries' waters (Bradley, 1986). And with the Law of the Sea uncertain, the superpowers are competing with each other for influence over strategically located coastal states, particularly those bordering choke points because it is precisely in such choke points that monitoring systems would be most important. Such monitoring might also be placed under the control of a United Nations observation team (Sakamoto, 1984).

Nuclear-free Zones

Like ripples before a fresh wind, the concept and implementation of nuclear weapon-free zones is spreading through Asia and the Pacific. Following it are clouds of confrontation. Outer space, the ocean floor, Antarctica, and Latin America are already nuclear-free zones (Tanter, 1985). Formal multilateral proposals have been

Figure 6.2
The Fisheries Treaty Area, the
Nuclear Free Zone Treaty Area,
and the Environment
Convention Area.

Source: Based on Cicin-Sain and
Knetch (1989), 'The Emergence of a
Regional Ocean Regime in the
South Pacific', Figure 5.

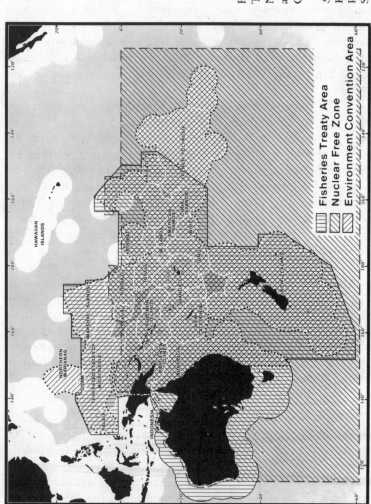

made for an Indian Ocean Zone of Peace and a South Pacific Nuclear Free Zone, and a South-East Asian Nuclear Free Zone is under discussion (Tanter, 1985; Valencia, 1985). New Zealand, Vanuatu, and Palau have individually declared their own versions of such policies (Tanter, 1985) and Vanuatu, the Solomons, and Papua New Guinea would prefer to ban vessels bearing nuclear weapons from their territorial waters (Robie, 1986). China may be considering something similar for its ports and territorial waters[4] (Chanda, 1985; *New Straits Times*, 1985; *Honolulu Advertiser*, 7 May 1985). The declaration of principles by the Philippines' Constitutional Commission states that the Philippines adopts and pursues a policy of freedom from nuclear weapons in its territory (*Honolulu Advertiser*, 26 December 1984; Clad, 1986). The Kanak independence movement is opposed to French militarization of New Caledonia, including the introduction of nuclear weapons (Tanter, 1985). Nuclear-free movements in Japan and Australia are rapidly gathering new momentum (Renfrew, 1985).

These declarations and positions vary considerably in respect to port calls and transit of vessels and aircraft bearing nuclear weapons. The 1967 Treaty of Tlatelolco prohibits the testing, use, manufacture, production, acquisition, storage, installation, and deployment of nuclear weapons in Latin America extending to the 115° W longitude in the Pacific Ocean. Within this area, however, the Treaty covers only territorial sea, airspace, and any other space over which the state exercises sovereignty in accordance with its own legislation. But Argentina, Ecuador, El Salvador, Nicaragua, Panama, and Uruguay claim territorial seas out to 200 nmi. And the Treaty itself is a precedent which may be expanded in content and extended within the Pacific region. On the other hand, the United States, the Soviet Union, France, and the United Kingdom signed the Treaty with the proviso that they accepted no limitations on their rights to freedom of the high seas under then-existing international law. And the Treaty does not explicitly prohibit transit of the zone by ships and aircraft carrying nuclear weapons (Treaty for the Prohibition of Nuclear Weapons in Latin America, 1971; R. W. Smith, 1981).

The South Pacific Nuclear Free Zone Treaty (SPNFZ) was signed at Rarotonga, Cook Islands, on 6 August 1985 (New

4. Although a port visit by US warships was subsequently agreed upon, the conditions of the visit, if any, were not revealed.

Zealand Ministry of Foreign Affairs, 1986). The Treaty entered into force on 11 December 1986, when Australia became the eighth Pacific nation to ratify the treaty. This Treaty of Rarotonga prohibits the testing, manufacture, acquisition, and stationing of nuclear weapons in the territory of the parties to the Treaty. It also prohibits the dumping of nuclear wastes at sea by parties. While the stationing and other aspects refer to the 'territory' of treaty parties (land and internal waters, territorial sea and archipelagic waters, and the seabed and subsoil beneath), the nuclear-free zone itself includes the broader 200-nmi zones of the parties and very extensive areas of high seas as well (see Figure 6.1). It explicitly does not infringe on freedom of navigation on overflight and leaves to each Pacific nation the decision on visits and passage through its territory of foreign ships and aircraft bearing nuclear weapons.

The eastern extent of the South Pacific Nuclear Free Zone reaches to the 115° W longitude where it joins the western boundary of the Latin American nuclear-free zone (the Treaty of Tlateloco) and extends to the south to the 60° S latitude, adjoining the northern boundary of the Antarctic Treaty area (which also contains a nuclear-free provision). The western boundary of the zone is at 115° E longitude. A control system is established for the purpose of verifying compliance with the parties' obligations under the Treaty. The control system consists of reports, the exchange of information, consultations, the application of safeguards by the International Atomic Energy Agency, and a complaints procedure.

Three protocols prepared in association with the Treaty require the nuclear powers (United States, United Kingdom, Soviet Union, China, and France) to commit to abide by the Treaty's provisions in their territories in the region; not to contribute to violations of the Treaty or to threaten the use of nuclear weapons against the parties; and to refrain from testing nuclear devices in the entire nuclear-free zone. To date, only the Soviet Union and China have signed the protocols appropriate to them. The United States has stated that it will not sign the protocols at the present time because the Treaty could undermine its nuclear deterrent capability, disrupt the balance of power in the world, and encourage strategically sensitive areas, such as Western Europe, to create their own nuclear-free zones (US Department of State, 1987). France obviously will not sign, given its strong desire to maintain its nuclear testing programme in French Polynesia. The United Kingdom is presumably following the United States' lead in not signing.

New Zealand and Vanuatu have banned port calls by vessels and aircraft capable of using nuclear weapons; Fiji and Solomon Islands briefly banned such visits and Papua New Guinea and Australia's Labour Party expressed similar intentions until all were persuaded by the United States to reverse these positions (Tanter, 1985). Palau has a nuclear-free constitution which prohibits the use, test, storage or disposal of nuclear weapons within its territorial jurisdiction (Tanter, 1985). The Nuclear Free and Independent Pacific Movement—an influential network of social movements in the Pacific island countries—has proposed a Pacific Nuclear Free Zone which would expand the present Forum proposal to include French territories, Micronesia, the Philippines, and Hawaii and ban all port and airfield visits as well as transit of any part of the zone by nuclear weapon-carrying ships and planes and by nuclear-powered vessels (Tanter, 1985). Although the Law of the Sea Convention appears to recognize the right of innocent passage by nuclear-powered ships and ships carrying nuclear substances (United Nations, 1982: Article 23), three states presently require prior notification for nuclear-powered vessels or vessels carrying nuclear matter to enter their territorial sea (Jin, 1986). A state might impose sea lanes on nuclear-powered ships and ships carrying nuclear substances. If a state should require only ships carrying nuclear weapons to use the designated sea lanes, a warship carrying such weapons would disclose this fact by using such a lane. It is also likely that in order to identify in advance ships subject to these restrictions, special notification may be required by the state from ships in the designated categories (Sohn, 1986). Of course, under the 'neither confirm nor deny' principle, such notification requirements and sea lanes would be an incentive to a nuclear power to avoid such waters.

In September 1984, an ASEAN working group agreed in principle to the establishment of a nuclear weapon-free zone for South-East Asia. An ASEAN official indicated that the agreement referred to warship and aircraft visits. Next, the first port call by US vessels to China since the 1949 revolution was delayed due to China's refusal to allow nuclear weapon-bearing US vessels in its ports. The Philippine opposition in its Declaration of Unity has called for a nuclear-free zone of peace in South-East Asia (*Hono-*

lulu Advertiser, 26 December 1984). The policies would allow transit of ships and aircraft bearing nuclear weapons. Finally, Japan's official government policy—clearly violated and often—is that nuclear weapons cannot and do not enter Japan, including its territorial waters (Nations, 1985).

Increasing superpower belligerence and militarization both globally and in the Pacific, and the US positions in various Law of the Sea matters, have stimulated resentment and the growth of the nuclear-free movement in the Pacific. The exceptions allowing transit of nuclear weapon-bearing vessels and aircraft may only be temporary, at least for the United States. The acceptance of nuclear weapons transit through the region, the deployment of tactical nuclear weapons in the region, and the presence of submarines armed with nuclear missiles (SSBNs) and Tomahawk nuclear-capable cruise missiles on over 100 US surface ships subverts the presumed purpose of the nuclear weapon-free zone—the survival of the South Pacific Forum states in the event of war (Tanter, 1986). Awareness of this contradiction between purpose and content of such zones may spread as a (delayed) reaction to militarization of the region.

Meanwhile, the United States maintains that the navigational provisions of the Law of the Sea are now part of customary international law and that it will use force if necessary to assert this view, especially in the face of 'excessive claims'. The United States has already done so in the Libyan-claimed Gulf of Sidra and in Nicaragua's 200-nmi territorial sea. This strategy may work in the short term against an avowed enemy such as Libya or Nicaragua, but will it work with friends or allies like New Zealand, Indonesia, and the Philippines? (Van Dyke, 1985; *Washington Post Service*, July 1984; *Baltimore Sun*, 1979; *Washington Post*, 14 August 1979).

Third World restrictions on transit of US nuclear weapon-bearing vessels and aircraft could also come as one response to US unilateralism in navigation matters or even in seabed mining (Valencia, 1985; *Honolulu Advertiser*, 27 May 1985). Further, it will be at least several years before the Law of the Sea Treaty comes into effect, and in an environment of acrimony coupled with legal uncertainty, sovereignty on nuclear-free zones may creep seawards, perhaps to the edge of the exclusive economic zone. For example, in response to domestic pressure, Australia moved the splash-down zone of a US nuclear-capable cruise missile test to outside its exclusive economic zone (McDonald, 1985).

As the United States has made desperate and crude attempts to blunt the nuclear-free movement, the concept of nuclear-free zones has increased in electoral popularity. There is a growing perception among developing countries that they must do what they can to avoid involvement in nuclear war and that there is potential for using the international legal system to increase the powers of small states. Production, storage, and passage of nuclear weapons have been banned from Japanese territory since 1968 and now more than 300 local Japanese official bodies, including 5 prefectures, have banned nuclear weapons. The long-standing compromise between Japan's anti-nuclear sentiment and the US nuclear strategy may now be tested by the deployment of the nuclear-capable Tomahawk cruise missiles which are visible on deck (Buruma, 1985; C. Smith, 1985). Such visibility may strain the credibility of the Japanese government's position that a US naval vessel is presumed not to be carrying nuclear missiles if Tokyo has not been informed otherwise in advance by the United States in compliance with treaty obligations (Nations, 1985). Other unexpected developments such as Vietnam joining in a South-East Asian nuclear weapon-free zone or a nuclear-free unified Korea would be of tremendous impetus to the nuclear-free movement. The spread of the belief that the nuclear-free movement is a necessary achievement in the continued evolutionary history of humankind may fuel the growth of a deeply rooted, internationally linked social movement for nuclear resistance capable of seizing the popular imagination and forcing governments through the electoral process or otherwise to enact nuclear weapon-free policies. Such scenarios and their implications place marine space and nuclear weapon-free zones high on the US *realpolitik* agenda for the Pacific.

Conflicts over the Marine Environment

That the islands' marine space constitutes such a large area of the Pacific confers a special responsibility to conserve the resources therein and to protect the ocean ecosystem—another task which requires foresight and careful planning. It is in the vast areas now under the legal jurisdiction of island states that radioactivity has been introduced from American and French nuclear testing in the waters around Micronesia and Tahiti and beyond. There is already evidence of food-chain contamination (Van Dyke, 1985) in this area; there have also been now well-known attempts to deliberately dump both high- and low-level nuclear wastes.

All Pacific island governments have expressed strong opposition to proposals for both dumping of nuclear wastes and testing of nuclear devices in the region. However, there are dangers that this resistance may falter in the face of enticing aid overtures and other actions designed to soften this stance. The disposition of Pacific island states regarding all forms of marine pollution will be a vital factor in preserving the marine environment and in remedying the damage that has already been done. For this reason, the successful outcome of treaty negotiations for the South Pacific Regional Environmental Program (SPREP) is significant. The Convention and the two protocols were completed at the Conference and opened for signature on 25 November 1986 at Noumea, New Caledonia (South Pacific Commission, 1987). The Convention will enter into force 30 days after the deposit of at least 10 instruments of ratification, acceptance, approval, or accession (5 for the protocols). As of July 1988, this had not yet occurred[5] (Anonymous, 1988). This regional environmental protection treaty is an important step for the islands' environment in general and the marine environment in particular, which is one of the Pacific island nations' principal assets.

The Convention requires parties to take all appropriate steps to prevent, reduce, and control pollution emanating from vessel discharges, land-based sources, seabed activities, discharges into the atmosphere, disposal of wastes, storage of toxic and hazardous wastes, and nuclear testing. Parties are also called upon to prevent environmental damage, specifically coastal erosion, caused by coastal engineering, mining activities, sand removal, and dredging. The first protocol—Protocol Concerning Cooperation in Combatting Pollution Emergencies in the South Pacific Region— mandates the adoption of national contingency plans to be co-ordinated with appropriate bilateral and sub-regional contingency plans. The second protocol—Protocol for the Prevention of Pollution of the South Pacific by Dumping—creates a regional agreement consistent with the London Dumping Convention and establishes lists of substances, the dumping of which is prohibited,

5. At the end of 1987, twelve self-governing nations had signed the SPREP Convention and two—Cook Islands and Marshall Islands—had ratified it.

and lists of substances requiring special or general permits. The 'Convention Area' is defined as comprising the 200-nmi zones of twenty-three self-governing island nations (including Australia's East Coast and eastward islands) and island territories and enclaves of high seas enclosed by these 200-nmi zones (Figure 6.1).

There were two controversial issues during the negotiations: (1) inclusion of nuclear weapons testing and (2) inclusion of areas of high seas within the Convention area. A carefully worded provision made it possible for France to become a party to the Convention and yet made it clear that the environmental effects of nuclear testing were of considerable concern to the island nations of the region. The United States was against the inclusion of extensive areas beyond the 200-nmi zones of the participating island nations and territories. However, it eventually agreed to the inclusion of enclaves but not fingers or corridors of high seas.

Conflicting Maritime Claims

In an area as large as the Pacific, with so many islands dotted across its surface and each extending its maritime jurisdiction by 200 nmi, conflicting maritime claims have inevitably arisen. There is no overt conflict at this time. The disputed claims and the principles on which they are based are well known; yet no substantive attempts have been made to resolve the contested issues.

The island states involved in the boundary demarcation problems are American Samoa, Western Samoa, New Caledonia, Vanuatu, Fiji, Tonga, and New Zealand. Details of the various claims and the legal and other principles on which they are based have been meticulously examined and documented (Broder and Van Dyke, 1982). Tonga's territorial claims were first promulgated in 1887, when 'all the islands, rocks, reefs, foreshores, and waters lying between 15° and 23°30' South latitude, and between 177° and 173° West longitude' (Broder and Van Dyke, 1982: 9) were designated Tongan territory. These have come to be known as Tonga's historic claims. They were reaffirmed in 1968 when oil exploration began in this general area. Fiji and Tonga would have a substantial overlap of their respective 200-nmi EEZs if Tonga were to declare the limits of its historical claim as the base from which its EEZ is to be measured.

Recently Tonga has laid claim to the Minerva Reefs (or Teleki

Tonga and Teleki Tokelau), two volcanic formations a few miles apart situated some 180 miles south-west of the nearest Tongan island. A 200-nmi Tongan EEZ around the Minerva Reefs would overlap with New Zealand's EEZ around the Kermadec Islands (a New Zealand dependency). In this case, the pivotal issue would be whether New Zealand would accept Teleki Tonga and Teleki Tokelau as base points.

In 1977 Fiji enacted a Marine Spaces Act (No. 18 of 1977), thus declaring itself to be an archipelagic state. Moreover, in 1965 Fiji had laid claim to a sand cay of 6½ acres called Ceva-i-Ra, which is located 300 miles south-west of Kadavu, the nearest island within the Fijian archipelago. Because Ceva-i-Ra is naturally above water at high tide, it appears that it would be entitled to a territorial sea, contiguous zone, and EEZ. A Fijian EEZ for Ceva-i-Ra would overlap with the EEZ of either New Caledonia or Vanuatu, depending on which succeeds in establishing sovereignty over Matthew and Hunter islands (Broder and Van Dyke, 1982: 39–40). Both Matthew and Hunter islands would generate EEZs of 53,800 sq. nmi (Broder and Van Dyke, 1982: 40). Western Samoa passed the Economic Zone Act of 1977, which set an EEZ of 200 nmi from the baselines described in its Territorial Seas Act of 1971 (Broder and Van Dyke, 1982: 52). Western Samoa's claimed 200-nmi EEZ overlaps with that of Tonga and of American Samoa. Although they are not currently issues for the states concerned, such questions will have to be faced squarely at some point in the future and may provide a focal point for mischief-making by external powers coveting the natural wealth that may be in the disputed area.

In the context of extended maritime jurisdiction, there is a domestic issue that should not be neglected. Traditional land-owning units (clans) in the Pacific often own islands or clusters of islands. In some parts of Fiji, for example, these land-owning units are already demanding fishing fees from local non-indigenous fishermen. Might demands for other kinds of payment, such as for a percentage of the government revenue derived from taxing foreign fishermen, be made in the future by such owners or their representatives? Since these smaller islands or groups of islands are generally the rural, less developed sectors of these underdeveloped island states, might native customary owners demand a percentage of revenues from seabed mining when and if such activity were to begin, particularly if the mining sites were located in areas close to these islands? Speculative as this is (and even conceding its unlikelihood), it is a variation on the conflicting maritime claims theme to which scant attention has been paid. It opens up a domestic political dimension in extended jurisdiction sensitivities, particularly if there should be large amounts of revenue forthcoming from its oil or mineral development.

So far, conflicting maritime claims in the Pacific have two principal characteristics: they are latent, and they deal with what might be called 'demarcation issues', such as establishment of baselines and ownership of islands. It remains to be seen how these issues will be resolved and even when they are settled, other conflicts will no doubt arise, particularly in the wake of seabed mineral exploitation. Reliance on some glamorous slogan like 'the Pacific way' as a means of solving problems may be illusory when the interests of outside powers are threatened and large amounts of money are at stake. In a generation or two, what now appears to be a comfortable consensus may turn out to be paper-thin and brittle indeed.

Conflicts over Pelagic Resources

What might most accurately be described as 'subsistence fishing' has traditionally been and continues to be one of the primary means by which Pacific islanders provide food for themselves. Surrounded by large areas of ocean, Pacific islanders turned to it for a wide variety of marine life for animal protein. Commercial fishing, even on a small scale, was unknown in traditional times. Pacific peoples used a variety of simple but often ingenious means to catch fish, which they shared with kinsfolk and others. That has changed dramatically, and even greater changes are in the offing, particularly as inshore areas are depleted and commercial fishing, both large- and small-scale, becomes more and more the rule. Canned fish, too, has rapidly become a replacement item for fresh fish and shows up in national statistics as an increasingly significant import item.

Island governments have also recognized that within their claimed waters—now extending to areas far beyond where local fishermen dared or were able to venture—there are large quantities of migratory species of fish, mainly tuna. In a protein-hungry world, this constitutes a most important resource (Tables 6.2–6.4). Table 6.2 sets out in aggregate terms 'less-

TABLE 6.2

Less Developed Oceania's Share of the World Catch

Year	Less Developed Oceania's Total Catch (tonnes)	World Total Catch (tonnes)	Less Developed Oceania's Share of Catch (per cent)
1970	42 300	70 696 400	0.060
1971	62 000	71 288 700	0.087
1972	66 000	66 924 000	0.099
1973	90 300	67 677 900	0.133
1974	96 152	71 340 000	0.135
1975	83 811	71 003 700	0.118
1976	110 547	74 717 200	0.148
1977	82 696	73 501 000	0.113

Source: Kent (1980), p. 77.

developed Oceania's' total catch over an 8-year period, 1970 to 1977, and compares it to the world catch. Table 6.3 shows for the same period where individual quantities were caught, by island state. Table 6.4 shows catches in the south-west Pacific by some of the principal distant-water fishing nations. To gain perspective on the quantities of fish being taken from Pacific island waters, it is necessary to determine the percentage of the available fish being taken. The best estimate available is that 0.34 per cent of the stock of skipjack is being harvested from the South Pacific Commission area (Kearney, 1981). If only 17 per cent of the south-west Pacific area is presently being fished for skipjack (Kearney, 1981), there remains a considerable portion of the Pacific within and outside the 30 million sq. km of ocean space now claimed by Pacific island nations where expanded fishing operations might be conducted.

However, its exploitation, as the history of the last decade or so has shown, is controlled by states outside the Pacific islands. The customers for, and fishers of, the Pacific islanders' tuna resources have so far mainly been countries of the Pacific Rim—Japan, Korea, Taiwan, and the United States. To a lesser extent, the USSR, Mexico, the Philippines, and Indonesia are also involved in Pacific tuna exploitation. Pacific island countries have developed a number of different arrangements with foreign fishing states that have sought access to their pelagic resources.

TABLE 6.3

Catches by Territories of Oceania (tonnes)

Territory/Country	Year							
	1970	1971	1972	1973	1974	1975	1976	1977
Less Developed Territories								
American Samoa	0	0	0	100	82	136	113	352
Canton Island	0	0	0	0	0	0	0	0
Christmas Island	0	0	0	0	0	0	0	0
Cocos Islands	0	0	0	0	0	0	0	0
Cook Islands	1 000	1 000	1 000	1 000	1 000	1 000	1 000	1 000
Fiji	3 900	3 900	4 700	4 700	4 805	5 001	5 456	7 881
French Polynesia	2 300	2 200	2 400	2 600	2 386	2 169	2 826	699
Gilbert Islands	500	500	500	500	750	750	750	915
Guam	100	100	100	100	92	122	120	125
Johnston Island	0	0	0	0	0	0	0	0
Midway Island	0	0	0	0	0	0	0	0
Nauru	0	0	0	0	0	0	0	0
New Caledonia	500	500	500	800	868	900	1 000	1 000
New Hebrides	8 000	8 000	8 000	8 000	8 000	8 000	8 000	8 000
Niue	0	0	0	0	0	0	0	0
Norfolk Island	0	0	0	0	0	0	0	0
Pacific Islands Trust Territory	1 000	1 000	400	6 300	3 360	7 795	6 053	4 604

(continued)

TABLE 6.3 (continued)

Territory/Country	Year							
	1970	1971	1972	1973	1974	1975	1976	1977
Papua New Guinea	22 700	37 700	38 200	57 400	61 598	47 326	64 510	39 897
Pitcairn Island	0	0	0	0	0	0	0	0
Samoa (Western)	900	900	900	900	900	1 000	1 100	1 250
Solomon Islands	1 000	5 700	8 800	7 300	11 585	8 711	18 600	15 776
Tokelau	0	0	0	0	0	0	0	0
Tonga	400	500	500	600	726	901	1 019	1 197
Tuvalu	0	0	0	0	0	0	0	0
U.S. Miscellaneous Pacific Islands	—	—	—	—	—	—	—	—
Wake Island	0	0	0	0	0	0	0	0
Wallis and Futuna	0	0	0	0	0	0	0	0
Total	42 300	62 000	66 000	90 300	96 152	83 811	110 547	82 696
Developed Territories								
Australia	101 400	111 400	124 200	129 800	137 798	108 684	111 444	127 839
New Zealand	59 300	66 000	58 300	66 100	68 732	63 752	76 437	110 541
Total	160 700	177 400	182 500	195 900	206 530	172 436	187 881	238 380
All of Oceania	203 000	239 400	248 500	286 200	302 682	256 247	298 428	321 076

Source: Kent (1980), pp. 5–6.
Note: Many of these figures are FAO estimates.

TABLE 6.4

Catches in the South-west Pacific (tonnes)

Country	Year						
	1971	1972	1973	1974	1975	1976	1977
Australia	30 100	31 400	33 800	32 134	32 907	31 053	31 743
Japan	65 100	69 600	74 200	90 526	83 157	134 321	214 097
New Zealand	64 500	56 100	64 700	67 803	64 208	74 869	109 491
Norfolk Island	0	0	0	0	0	0	0
Pitcairn Island	0	0	0	0	0		
South Korea	30 300	40 500	43 600	44 261	38 474	25 165	56 468
Soviet Union	10 400	53 700	74 300	88 800	44 767	78 020	123 009
Others	13 700	14 200	17 800	38 147	37 592	18 472	24 275
Total	214 100	265 500	308 400	361 671	299 305	361 900	559 083

Source: Kent (1980), p. 78.

Purse-seining and super-seining are the trends for the future. 'The purse seine fishery is ... concentrated in the waters bounded by Belau, the Federated States of Micronesia, Kiribati, the Marshall Islands, Nauru, Papua New Guinea and the Solomon Islands.... In 1976, nine purse seine vessels fished in this area and by 1981, this figure had increased to between 50 and 60 vessels, taking in an excess of 100,000 mt' (Ridings, 1983). These statistics and the trends they represent indicate that exploitation of the Pacific islands' fish resources has just begun. As purse seiners and super-seiners replace long-line and pole-and-line fishing for skipjack, albacore, and yellow-fin tuna, the increasing rate of exploitation will have important implications for conservation.

Most of these tuna resources have been and continue to be taken by distant-water fishing nations, which have the necessary capital, expertise, government support, and processing and marketing capability, as well as domestic and foreign markets, for processed fish. Lacking these resources, Pacific island nations—new to commercial fishing and its related activities—have entered into licensing and joint-venture agreements with those wishing to fish in their waters.

The USSR had been seeking fishing rights in the region since the early 1980s, and in 1985 reached an agreement with Kiribati. The US$1.5 million that the Soviets paid for access to Kiribati's EEZ for one year represented 10 per cent of the nation's budget. That agreement expired after one year due to a failure of the parties to agree on a price for a second year of fishing (Doulman, 1986). In 1987, the USSR reached an agreement with Vanuatu on a fishing access contract which allowed the Soviets port rights and landing rights for their fishing crews (Hegarty, 1987). The USSR is currently discussing similar fishing arrangements with other island nations and the possible presence, as well, of one or two diplomatic missions in the region.

The US military establishment became nervous over the growing presence of the USSR in the region. In congressional testimony in September 1986, representatives of the US Department of Defence outlined a wide range of possible motives the Soviet Union could have for establishing the fisheries agreements. These include surveillance of US military activities on Kwajalein; the enhancement of Soviet space and satellite operations, and of Soviet military communications capabilities; the potential establishment of support facilities for deep seabed mining activities; and the attainment of air access and landing rights (Baker, 1986).

Ridings (1983: 5) describes Pacific licensing agreements in the following terms:

Fishery access agreements ... are primarily negotiated with Japanese fishing associations, although agreements between the Trust Territory and Taiwanese interests also exist.... In the central areas of the Southwest Pacific, South Korea and Taiwan have agreements with the Cook Islands and Tuvalu, while France negotiates with Japan for access to all waters under French jurisdiction.... Most Pacific access agreements are based on a lump sum fee, which licenses a specified number of vessels. The Micronesian territories and Kiribati have received part of their payment from the Japanese in the form of goods and services. Papua New Guinea and the Solomon Islands base their fees on both vessel capacity and catch, and the trend in the Western Pacific is this kind of fee. Except in the French territories and the Solomon Islands there is no limit to the catch that may be taken by the foreign vessels.

Specific details of fishing access agreements are given in Table 6.5.

The trend, however, is away from licensing agreements and toward joint ventures. From the standpoint of the distant-water fishing nation, joint-venture agreements are attractive because of cost minimization and the prospects of gaining entry to foreign or domestic markets. Joint-venture agreements with a state like Vanuatu offer the additional attraction of low tax rates. Joint ventures with American Samoa offer the lucrative prospect of foreign catches (unprocessed or processed) entering the American market free of duty or other charges.

For the owners of the resource, the joint-venture arrangement holds the prospect of maximizing returns on minimal investment and the even more lucrative possibility of ultimately replacing the foreign partners and fully exploiting the resource on their own. Ridings (1983: 10) points out that there are three mutually exclusive categories of joint ventures:

1. A foreign company and local private interests have equity in the same company;

2. A foreign company and the host government have equity in the joint-venture company;

3. A company wholly owned by outside interests is registered in the host country.

Table 6.6 shows joint-venture arrangements currently in force. Little reliable data are available on how successful these joint ventures have been, particularly from the standpoint of the island-

TABLE 6.5
Pacific Islands Fishing Access Agreements

Agreement/Owner	Party	Period	Cash Payment (US$)[1]	Other Remuneration[2]	Terms
Signatories to Nauru Agreement					
Belau	Japan	1/79–12/79	$400,000		470 v
		1/80–3/80	$100,000		470 v
		4/80–3/81	$400,000	$150,000	450 v
		4/81–6/81	$100,000		450 v
		12/81–3/82	$150,000		450 v
		4/82–9/82	$225,000		450 v
	Taiwan	1/79–3/79	$60,000		120 v
	ATA	7/80–6/82	$40/t/v		
	Star-Kist	7/81–12/82	$40/t/v		
Federated States of Micronesia	Japan	1/79–12/79	$2 million		900 v
		1/80–12/81	$2 million	$400,000	800 v
		1/81–12/81	$2.1 million	$400,000	800 v
		5/82–4/83	$2.6 million	$180,000	800 v
	Taiwan	1/81–12/81	$60,000		40 v
		4/82–3/83	$24/t/v		6 v

					I v
	Korea	11/80–11/81	$15,000		
	US	see ATA and Star-Kist under Belau			
Marshall Islands	Japan	7/79–12/79	$400,000		400 v
		1/80–6/80	$450,000		450 v
		7/80–3/81	$75,000/m		450 v
		4/81–3/82	$1 million	$160,000	470 v
		4/82–3/83	$1.2 million		470 v
	US	see ATA and Star-Kist under Belau			
Kiribati	Japan	7/79–6/80	$600,000	$150,000	370 v
		11/79–10/82	$950,000	$109,000	370 v
	Korea	10/80–10/81	$185,000		200 v
Papua New Guinea	Japan	5/78–1/79	$1.4 million	$32.7/m/v	contract
		7/79–9/80	3–4.5% fob		contract
		1/80–8/81	3.5–4.5% fob		contract
		8/81–8/82	4–5% fob		contract
	ATA	3/82–12/82	@ $20,000		

(continued)

TABLE 6.5 (continued)

Agreement/Owner	Party	Period	Cash Payment (US$)[1]	Other Remuneration[2]	Terms
Solomon Islands	Japan	10/78–9/79	$300,000	$50,000	$8,000/m
		10/79–9/80	$1,050–4,050/v	$115,000	n.a.
		10/80–8/82	$1,350–5,400/v	$300,000	$12,500/m
	S. Korea	10/80–10/81	$130,000		$1,500/m
	Taiwan	1/80–1/81	$100,000	$100/v	$1,200/m
		5/81–5/82	$100,000	$100/v	n.a.
Central Southwest Pacific Territories					
Cook Islands	S. Korea	11/80–11/81	$82,000		n.a.
		11/81–11/82	$111,000		115 v
	Taiwan	10/81–10/82	$90,000		100 v
French Polynesia	Japan	7/79–4/80	$240,000		225 v
					$2,750/m
		4/80–7/81	$415,000		271 v
					$6,250/m
		7/81–8/82	$310,000[3]		290 v
					$5,600/m

New Caledonia	Japan	7/79–4/80	$126,000	70 v $3,375/m
		4/80–7/81	$270,000	95 v $7,250/m
		7/81–8/82	$195,000[3]	105 v $5,800/m
Tuvalu	S. Korea	8/80–7/81	$99,000	137 v
		8/81–7/82	$92,500[3]	115 v
	Taiwan	11/81–11/82	$84,000	100 v
Wallis and Futuna Islands	Japan	7/79–4/80	$82,000	40 v $1,500/m
		4/80–7/81	$92,500	65 v $1,900/m
		7/81–8/82	$56,000[3]	60 v $1,400/m

Source: Ridings (1983), pp. 6–8.

m = month.
v = vessels.
ATA = American Tunaboat Association.
n.a. = not available.
[1]In US dollars. United Nations average annual exchange rates for the year of agreement are used for conversion and the results rounded.
[2]All dollars are US dollars unless otherwise specified. The United Nations' annual average exchange rates for the year of the agreement are used for conversion, and the results rounded.
[3]Fluctuating fees are a result of the exchange rates.

TABLE 6.6

Tuna Joint-venture Arrangements in the Pacific

Resource Owner	Foreign Involvement	Category	Year
Signatories to Nauru Agreement			
Belau	US/Van Camp	C	1963
	Japan/Hassui Reizo	A	1977
Federated States of Micronesia	Japan/n.a.	A	1980
	Japan/n.a.	A	1980
Nauru	Japan/Hassui Reizo	B	1976
Papua New Guinea	Japan/Kyokuyo	C	1971
	Japan/Kaigai	A	1972
	US/Star–Kist	C	n.a.
Solomon Islands	Japan/Taiyo	B	1973

Central Southwest Pacific Territories			
Fiji	Japan/C. Itoh	B	1963
French Polynesia	Japan/Shin-ei Boki	A	1976
	US/Star-Kist	C	n.a.
	US/Van Camp	C	n.a.
Vanuatu	Japan/Mitsui	B	1957
American Flag Territories			
American Samoa	US/Van Camp	C	1954
	US/Star-Kist	C	1963
Guam	US/Van Camp	C	1974

Source: Ridings (1983), p. 19.

n.a. = not applicable.

Category A: Foreign company and local private interests have equity in same company.

Category B: Foreign company and host government have equity in joint-venture company.

Category C: Company is wholly owned by outside interests and registered in host territory.

nation partners. An impressionistic view is that the economic benefits to governments in the region are minimal. Aside from tax revenues and other income (direct and indirect), little else accrues to the resource owners because of unrestricted repatriation of profits, which is the rule rather than the exception in the Pacific. Neither can it be argued that the joint ventures have been labour-intensive—for the number of jobs created, although important, has not been large.

Kiribati, Tonga, Western Samoa, and Fiji are involved in small fisheries development employing local people using pole-and-line and long-lining techniques. Development of small-scale commercial fisheries has great potential and even greater need in all of the island states, and various programmes have already found their way into official Development Plans (Government of Fiji, 1981: 153–5; Republic of Vanuatu, 1982: 151–3). However, a word of caution is also in order—self-sufficient small-scale commercial fishing enterprises designed to provide fresh fish for local consumption have not thus far been a great success story in the Pacific. Rising fuel and equipment costs, the need to travel greater distances to fishing grounds, and dubious support from home governments are some of the problems they face.

After nearly two decades of experience, the outlines of a division of labour in the Pacific islands' fishing industry is becoming apparent. Large-scale commercial fishing has become the preserve of nations foreign to the region, though by no means strangers to the resources therein. Small-scale fishing for domestic consumption has been relegated to local entrepreneurs. Control—and with it the bulk of the profit—has been firmly held by foreign corporations. This fact is not unrecognized by Pacific island governments, sometimes to their irritation and often to their frustration. The overall Pacific island government approach seems to have been to deal with an unpleasant reality—foreign control of another Pacific island resource—by securing what are in their view the highest licence fees and the most attractive joint-venture terms that can now be gained. They anticipate the day when they might be in a realistic position to modify the present situation and gain a greater share of the total proceeds from this important industry, which has substantial potential for growth.

Sometimes in discussions about the Pacific islands, there is a tendency to give the impression that this small, sparsely populated area of the world can be approached as a whole and that differences between island nations are non-existent. However, differences of view exist on a wide range of issues, including development and access for nuclear weapon-carrying and nuclear-powered ships to island ports. Comparable or greater differences will no doubt emerge over seabed mineral resources when their exploitation becomes ripe for consideration. Indeed, what have so far been muted differences, often painstakingly and laboriously handled so as to avoid confrontation, may have reached a breaking point over some issues. Stresses and strains in island relationships are evident regarding exploitation of tuna resources within the respective maritime zones. These differences are perhaps best reflected in some of the recent subregional groupings that have emerged regarding fisheries management.

The Nauru Agreement

The signatories to what is called the Nauru Agreement, signed in February 1982, were representatives of Belau, the Federated States of Micronesia, the Marshall Islands, Nauru, Papua New Guinea, and the Solomon Islands. The area covered by these states includes waters rich in tuna stocks, particularly skipjack, and it is here that purse-seine fishing by Japanese, American, South Korean, Taiwanese, and Soviet vessels is concentrated. The countries that are signatories to the Nauru Agreement receive the most lucrative benefits from their fish resources of any countries in the region. Six of the nine agreements to which the 'Nauru group' are signatories are joint ventures (Table 6.6). The second group consists of Western Samoa, New Caledonia, French Polynesia, Wallis and Futuna, the Cook Islands, Niue, Tokelau, Tonga, Fiji, and Tuvalu, where the development of local fishery ventures seems to be a high priority. There are few access agreements with foreign fishing interests here; those that do exist are for lesser amounts of money than that paid to countries of the Nauru group. Individual states have also entered into a number of joint-venture arrangements with the Japanese. The US flag territories—American Samoa, Guam, and the Northern Marianas—make up the third group. It comes within the jurisdiction of the United States Fisheries Conservation and Management Act of 1976, which excludes tuna from its management authority (Ridings, 1983: 3).

In addition to these three subregional groups, there is the

overarching South Pacific Forum Fisheries Agency (SPFFA), which was conceived at a meeting of the South Pacific Forum in 1976. However, it was not until the latter part of 1978, after a great deal of debate (some of it quite heated), that the SPFFA was finally established. Membership was restricted to Forum nations (Kent, 1980: 166–72; Van Dyke and Heftel, 1981). Much of the unusually acrimonious debate revolved around the question of membership in the proposed organization and the kind of organization it would be. Kent (1980: 170) describes the alternatives in these terms:

One would aim primarily at ensuring conservation and promoting optimum utilization of the living resources throughout the sea in which they occur.... The other would aim primarily at ensuring maximum benefits for the peoples of the coastal countries in the region and for the region as a whole.
    To be fully effective, the first ... would need participation by all countries in whose waters the resources occur at various stages of their life cycle as well by all the countries which exploit them. The second ..., on the contrary, would comprise only those countries in the South Pacific with a common interest as coastal states.

At the heart of the matter lay the immediate question of whether the United States, which does not recognize exclusive jurisdiction by coastal states over migratory fish, and other non-Forum states ought to be allowed membership in the new organization. When the issue came to a head at the Ninth Forum Meeting in Niue in September 1978, Western Samoa, Niue, the Cook Islands, Australia, and New Zealand supported the broader organization including membership for the United States. Fiji, Papua New Guinea, Nauru, Tonga, Kiribati, and the Solomon Islands took the opposite view. When the decision was finally made, the door to US membership was closed. The Forum went on to adopt a SPFFA Convention that established coastal nations' sovereignty over migratory species of fish within their 200-nmi EEZs and that limited membership to Forum members (Kent, 1980: 169; Van Dyke and Heftel, 1981: 14–15).

The establishment of the SPFFA is in itself significant. Whether, as Kent (1980: 170) argues, 'the agency has been established as a rather weak service agency rather than as anything approaching a management agency', the fact remains that membership in the new organization has been confined to island states. This is important because it maximizes opportunities for the owners of these fishery resources to learn to make their own decisions free from the meddling of outsiders and, in time, from domination by them.

The SPFFA Convention is not perfect; no regional or other agreement ever is. Van Dyke and Heftel (1981: 19–44) have delineated a number of unresolved issues not addressed in the SPFFA Convention and highlighted its ambiguities. These will no doubt eventually be addressed by Pacific islanders acting to solve their own problems on the basis of experience and in the face of changing circumstances and evolving problems. That, after all, is vital for political maturation, as well as for maintaining control over their own destiny. If any complaint is valid here, it is that island states only infrequently resist big-power pressures and chart courses of action consistent with their peoples' own interests.

The area where migratory tuna resources are to be found in the Pacific is so large that it presents problems of surveillance. So far, the available surveillance facilities have been minimal. But despite the lack of such facilities, the SPFFA has made it clear that foreign vessels 'fishing in the South Pacific's 200-mile economic zones without being listed on a register opened at the . . . Agency will be just fishing for trouble. They will be classed as illegals, liable to arrest.' (Keith-Reid, 1983: 51–4.)

There have already been such arrests. In 1982, Papua New Guinea seized the *Danica*, an American super-seiner caught poaching in its waters. The Papua New Guinea government was finally bullied into releasing the vessel after the imposition of a nominal fine (Keith-Reid, 1983: 51). In June 1984, the Solomon Islands government arrested another American ship, the *Jeannette Diana*, for fishing illegally within its EEZ. The ship's captain and the owners were fined, and the vessel itself, valued at US$3 million, was confiscated and advertised for sale. The United States retaliated with a trade embargo against Solomon Islands tuna products worth several million dollars in export revenues (*The Fiji Times*, 1984: 8).

The Forum, drawn into the dispute at the behest of the Solomon Islands, made its position clear. In the official communiqué setting out the record of action taken at its fifteenth session in Funafuti (27–28 August 1984), the Forum 'expressed its continuing concern at the failure of the United States to recognize the applicability of 200 mile EEZ to tuna and at the fact that that country endeavored to enforce its position through embargo legislation'[6] (Fifteenth South Pacific Forum, 1984: 10).

Negotiations on a regional licensing agreement between sixteen Pacific island nations and the United States began in 1984. The US negotiating team was led by the State Department and included advisers from the US tuna industry. Leadership of the Pacific islands negotiating team shifted among the various countries in the region, while major technical and strategic support in formulating the islanders' position came from the Forum Fisheries Agency. After a long and difficult effort spanning ten negotiating sessions, an agreement was finally reached during the tenth round in Tonga in October 1986 (International Legal Materials, 1987: 1048).

The treaty entails a package of approximately US$60 million of financial aid and payments by the United States over a five-year term. About US$2 million a year is to be paid in fishing vessel licence fees and industry assistance and about US$10 million in US foreign aid with supposedly few strings attached. Approximately 85 per cent of these funds are to be allocated among the Pacific island nations according to the amount of fish caught in each nation's EEZ, with the remainder to be divided evenly among all of the participating nations. Significant portions of certain 200-nmi zones, especially in the Solomon Islands, have been excluded to allow development of the local fishing industry. Those nations with the most valuable tuna resources may have forgone for the sake of unity greater financial returns that they could have received had they dealt individually with the United States. The financial terms are substantially more generous than those initially discussed by the US negotiating team. Many believe that it was the entry of the USSR into South Pacific fishery affairs in 1985 that, indirectly at least, was responsible for the US willingness to 'raise the ante' (Wolfe, 1988).

The conclusion of the tuna treaty with the United States signalled a change in the pattern of exploitation of tuna resources. In 1984, distant-water fleets took approximately 600,000 tons of tuna from the region, with an estimated value of US$660 million. But these distant-water fishing nations paid access fees equal to less than 3 per cent of the value of the fish (Kotobalavu, 1988). Under the new treaty, the US$12 million a year which the United

6. The reference to embargo legislation is to the US Fishery Conservation and Management Act of 1976.

States will pay the region is equivalent to about 9 per cent of the value of the 1984 US tuna catch in the region. While this is a step towards redistribution of benefits derived from tuna harvesting, the Pacific island states want a larger return from the use of their resource (Cicin-Sain and Knecht, 1989).

The Forum Fisheries Agency (FFA) is designated to act as 'administrator' on behalf of the South Pacific island nations. It will receive and disburse the payments made under the treaty; receive and distribute reports from licensed vessels fishing in the treaty area; and carry on other administrative functions. The United States is charged with enforcing compliance of the treaty provision on US fishing vessels licensed under the treaty. The agreement extends over a five-year period and can be amended at any time during that period by a unanimous vote of the nations party to the agreement. The United States ratified the treaty and it entered into force on 14 June 1988 (*The Marshall Islands Journal*, 1988: 12).

Whether the conclusion of this agreement will provide 'the satisfactory long term solution to this problem' (Fifteenth South Pacific Forum, 1984: 10) remains to be seen. The FFA is now attempting to negotiate regional access agreements with Japan, South Korea, and Taiwan. There will probably be more such incidents even as surveillance methods improve and the SPFFA takes other steps to ensure that those who fish in member nations' territorial waters do so legally and according to established rules. Perhaps nowhere, in the tangled web of problems associated with this resource, is there more sensitivity and potential for overt conflict and headline-making stories of action and reprisals than over the issue of foreign vessels fishing illegally within island states' EEZs. These incidents have implications both for domestic politics[7] (Fifteenth South Pacific Forum, 1984: 8) and for international relations, including pressures that will be brought to bear on regional organizations such as the Forum and its fisheries arm, the SPFFA.

Conflict over Seabed Mineral Resources

For two days in December 1984 about a hundred individuals from American universities and research organizations, corporations such as Bechtel, Hawaiian Dredging, and Lockheed, and govern-

7. This was evident in the 1984 Solomon Islands elections.

ment agencies from across the United States as well as from the Federal Republic of Germany assembled at the East–West Center in Honolulu to attend a conference on Marine Mining Development in Hawaii. Sponsored by the US Department of the Interior, the Minerals Management Service, and the State of Hawaii Department of Planning and Economic Development, the conference was mainly designed to discuss highly technical matters related to prospective development of cobalt-rich ferro-manganese oxide crusts, which are known to exist within the US EEZ around the Hawaiian Islands.

Although actual mining of these crusts awaits more precise determination of 'abundance, grade, deposit size and setting' (Morgan, 1984: 2; Clark *et al.*, 1984: 163–74) and other information, there is little doubt that serious consideration is being given to this mining. An environmental impact statement is being prepared, and resource data are being acquired by the University of Hawaii, supported by the US Geological Survey and a German consortium of government and industrial interests (Morgan, 1984: 2). The Conference reiterated what is clear from the professional literature on ocean mining: the technology has been developed, and although it is not fully tested, it is available (Anonymous, 1978; Anonymous, 1988; Clark, Johnson, and Chin, 1984). Technology is not the stumbling block to mining of the Hawaiian ferro-manganese deposits.

The problems that lie ahead for ocean mining in and around the Hawaiian archipelago will probably stem from political and environmental objections comparable to those that surfaced over a proposal to mine seabed metallic sulphides located in an area known as Gorda Ridge off the coast of Northern California and Oregon (*Los Angeles Times*, 1984: 18; *Oakland Tribune*, 1984: 4–8; *The Paper*, 1984). Environmental activists in Hawaii and on the West Coast of the United States have closely monitored the mounting plans to begin seabed mining in and around the Islands. When public hearings were held in May 1984 to discuss the related questions of ocean mining and ocean leasing in Hawaii, there was coherent opposition from Hawaiian activists and environmentalists (*Honolulu Advertiser*, 2 May 1984; State of Hawaii, Department of Planning and Economic Development, 1981). The prestigious San Francisco-based Oceanic Society filed a lengthy Memorandum of Opposition against Hawaii proceeding prematurely with plans for an environmental impact assessment, arguing in part that it did 'not support governmental actions that are designed to rush forward with leases in offshore areas when such actions are precipitous, unsound and illegal'. In a detailed four-page appendix to its memo, the Oceanic Society further argued that 'extensive, pre-lease studies should be completed on basic geology/geophysics, geochemistry, chemical and biological oceanography, physiology, ecology, population dynamics, and other considerations that are pertinent to the geophysical areas of interest and onshore support sites' (Oceanic Society, 1984).

Another, although different, example of opposition to seabed mining arose on the first day of the 1984 Marine Mining Development Conference in Honolulu when a small group of Hawaiian women activists bedecked with leis demonstrated their opposition to ocean mining by distributing leaflets. They attempted to speak briefly to the rather startled and embarrassed Conference attendees, who sheepishly accepted the leaflets with as much good grace as the situation allowed.

In addition to the research done in Hawaii, there has been a considerable amount of basic marine-centred geological research conducted within the past decade on the location and availability of seabed minerals and petroleum in selected areas of the Pacific[8] (Recy and Dupont, 1982; Greene and Wong, 1984; CCOP/ SOPAC, 1981; Mizuno and Shujo, 1975). In the early 1970s, the USSR offered to assist the newly emerging island nations in geophysical research to identify possible mineral deposits adjacent to their shorelines. In quick response, the United States, New Zealand, and Australia formed a tripartite consortium to provide similar assistance to the island nations. This activity has come under the aegis of the Committee for the Co-ordination of Joint Prospecting for Mineral Resources in South Pacific Offshore Areas (CCOP/SOPAC), a major regional entity concerned with the mapping and exploration of ocean mineral and hydrocarbon resources[9] (CCOP/SOPAC, n.d.). Considerable petroleum poten-

---

8. Completed and continuing research includes that under the auspices of the Committee for Co-ordination of Joint Prospecting for Mineral Resources in South Pacific Offshore Areas (CCOP/SOPAC), and the hundreds of other studies done by individuals as well as foreign governments and institutions such as those of France, West Germany, Japan, the United States, and the Soviet Union.

9. CCOP/SOPAC was established in 1972 under the sponsorship of the United Nations Economic and Social Commission for Asia and the Pacific (ESCAP) with funding provided by the United Nations Development Program (UNDP) to assist

tial remains to be discovered on the continental shelves and in deeper water on the continental slope and rises of the marginal basins bordering the major circum-Pacific land masses, and perhaps behind the small island arcs in the western and south-western Pacific. Further potential exists in pre-Tertiary sediments underlying already productive basins, and in gas hydrates (gas and water in the solid state) in sediments in deep water. These gas hydrates may also form an impermeable seal capping more gas and oil.

The estimated total gross value of undiscovered oil and gas resources in South-East Asia ranges from US$1.1 trillion to US$11 trillion, in North-east Asia from US$0.4 trillion to US$4 trillion, and in Oceania from US$0.5 trillion to US$6 trillion. This estimate for Oceania does not include resources expected in Tonga, Vanuatu, the Solomon Islands, and most important, Papua New Guinea, all of which could be worth as much as another trillion dollars. By comparison, the United States Pacific area, including Alaska, might harbour $0.3 trillion worth of oil and gas (Valencia and Marsh, 1986; Roland, Goud, and McGregor, 1983; United Nations, Economic and Social Commission for Asia and the Pacific, 1980).

Cobalt-rich manganese crusts have been reported from seamounts in the Hawaiian and Line islands at depths between 1 100 m and 2 600 m. The thickness of crusts reaches 7–9 centi-metres and averages 2.5 centimetres. These crusts contain a mean of 25 per cent manganese, 0.8 per cent cobalt, 0.5 per cent nickel, 0.07 per cent copper, and 0.0005 per cent platinum. A seamount may contain between 2 million and 4 million tons of crust, approximating the amount of ore required for the yearly produc-tion of a commercial deep-sea mine. The concentration of cobalt is about 1 per cent greater than cobalt ores mined on land—and the market price of cobalt (US$27.56/kg) is about five times that of nickel (US4.98/kg) and 15 times that of copper (US$1.77/kg). Total values of cobalt, nickel, copper, and molybdenum in the mid-Pacific Mountains and Line Islands crusts from water depths

island member countries in investigating the mineral and hydrocarbon potential of their offshore areas, in the management of their coastal zones, and in the training of their nationals. CCOP/SOPAC members include the Cook Islands, Fiji, Guam, Kiribati, New Zealand, Papua New Guinea, Solomon Islands, Tonga, Tuvalu, Vanuatu, and Western Samoa.

less than 2 600 m are \$170 to \$202 per wet ton of crust or \$340 million to \$808 million worth of wet ore per deposit, not counting platinum. The exclusive economic zones around the Hawaiian Islands and Johnston and Palmyra islands contain an estimated 10 million tons of cobalt, 6 million tons of nickel, 1 million tons of copper, and 300 million tons of manganese. A prime mine site might contain \$165/tonne of cobalt, \$37.50/tonne of nickel, \$1.32/ tonne of copper, and \$43.57/tonne of manganese for a total of \$247.39/tonne of ore, or perhaps \$4 of gross contained metal value per sq. m (Clark, Johnson, and Chin, 1984; Halbach, 1984; *Honolulu Advertiser*, 12 October 1985: B-1). Additional deposits have been found in the Marshall Islands, the Northern Mariana Islands, and Guam.

Marine polymetallic sulphide deposits are located at 2 000 metres to 4 000 metres around high-temperature hydrothermal vents in sea-floor spreading centres or mid-ocean rift zones. Known locations include the Galapagos Ridge, the East Pacific Rise, the Gorda–Juan de Fuca Ridge System, and the Guaymas Basin. Recently, deposits have been found off Tonga, in the Lau and North Fiji basins, and in the Bismarck Sea; more are expected. Minerals of commercial interest include iron, zinc, copper, gold, manganese, platinum, and vanadium. Some deposits contain up to 21 per cent copper, 50 per cent zinc, and 45 per cent iron (*Honolulu Advertiser*, 7 May 1984: A-6; Cronan, 1983; National Advisory Committee on Oceans and Atmosphere, 1983).

Manganese nodules containing nickel, copper, cobalt, and manganese had long been considered the prime economic mineral resource in the deep sea. There are about 10 trillion tons of nodules in the Pacific. However, only a small portion of these deposits contain the economic cutoff percentage of 2 per cent nickel plus copper plus cobalt and are found in concentrations greater than 10 kg/sq. m over an area sufficient for 20 years' production. The highest concentration of nodules (more than 8 kg/sq. m) with the highest nickel plus copper (at least 1 per cent combined content) are found between 3 200 m and 5 900 m in the North-east Pacific. Mean values of potential mining sites here have the following ranges: manganese 22–27 per cent; nickel 1.2–1.4 per cent; copper 0.9–1.1 per cent; cobalt 0.15–0.25 per cent. Economic-grade nodule fields have also been reported within the exclusive economic zone of Mexico. In the South Pacific, nodule distribution is more irregular; one area of concentration is around the Manihiki Plateau, the Society Islands, Tahiti, and the Tuamotu Archipelago. Further south, nodules occur west of the East Pacific Rise and north-east of New Zealand. Another nodule area lies in the circumpolar region of Antarctica. In the northern Peru Basin, nodule density is 7 kg/sq. m to 14 kg/sq. m up to 30 kg/sq. m with 1.1–1.2 per cent nickel and thus may be of economic interest. Manganese nodules might be mined in the 1990s when economic, technical, legal, and political factors are more favourable. In a first phase of mining, about 0.6 million sq. km in the North-east Pacific nodule belt and 2 million sq. km in the total Pacific may contain fields of sufficient nodule density, weight, and metal content. The *in situ* reserves amount to 16 billion tons of nodules in the first phase, with recoverable reserves of 5.6 billion tons. The area for each mining site would be between 80 000 sq. km and 120 000 sq. km. There would be space in abundance for at least 40 to 45 mining sites in the Pacific during a first generation of deep-sea mining (Halbach, 1984: 42, 45–7, 55–8).

Questions of abundance, grade, deposit size, setting, and economic feasibility aside, there is clear evidence that there are deposits of petroleum, manganese crusts and nodules with nickel, copper, and cobalt components, phosphate and phosphorites, and sulphides (Bramwell, 1977; Halbach, 1984: Figs. 2, 8). For example, in a recently completed, extensive study by the US Geological Survey of offshore areas adjacent to Fiji, Papua New Guinea, the Solomon Islands, Tonga, and Vanuatu, the following findings emerged:

1. An area identified as the southern Tonga platform was found to be a 'source for hydrocarbons [but with] its extent . . . uncertain' (Greene and Wong, 1984: 51);

2. In the Lau Basin, an area between Tonga and Fiji, geologic data suggest 'that massive sulfides may be forming along the spreading ridge from the circulation of mineralizing hydrothermal fluids with consequent precipitation of polymetallic sulfides' (Greene and Wong, 1984: 53–4);

3. In the central basin of Vanuatu, there are preliminary indications of petroleum hydrocarbons, although 'quantity, quality and type of hydrocarbon is unknown, as is the economic prospect of developing such a resource' (Greene and Wong, 1984: 54);

4. The Malakula and East Santo Basins appear to be 'the most promising basins . . . for accumulating hydrocarbons' (Greene and Wong, 1984: 54);

5. The Central Solomons Trough is considered to be the best prospect for the concentration and entrapment of hydrocarbons (Greene and Wong, 1984: 57).

Research on manganese nodules and crusts indicates high-grade and abundant deposits in four areas:

1. The East Central Pacific Basin south-west and west of the Southern Line Islands;

2. The East Central Pacific Basin north and east of the Phoenix Islands;

3. The West Central Pacific Basin west and north-west of the Phoenix Islands;

4. The North Penrhyn Basin north of Penrhyn Island (Gonan, 1984: 16).

Other studies have shown indications of manganese nodule deposits in potentially economically significant quantities and quality in a number of other areas within the EEZs of Pacific island states (Exon, 1982a, 1982b; East–West Center, 1982). Table 6.7 provides summary information on nodule metal grades in various areas.

Complete information about these resources is not yet available, and the search for them goes on—particularly under the auspices of CCOP/SOPAC. Aside from unsuccessful drilling for oil in offshore areas of Fiji and Tonga, there are no serious indications of marine mining in the offing such as in Hawaii. Nor have there yet been feasibility studies or proposals for ocean leasing. In short, compared with what has been accomplished in Hawaii so far, the Pacific islands—although possessed of at least comparable seabed resources—are at a stage of awareness comparable to that of Hawaii about a decade ago.

The island states are not totally unaware of this new resource frontier, however. In the most recent National Development Plans for Fiji and Vanuatu, for example, offshore mineral exploration and related matters figure prominently. There are no detailed overarching policies in place yet, nor are there any indications in the documentary sources examined that consideration is being given to co-operation among Pacific island countries in the future exploitation of their resources.

There are, however, indications of exchange and sharing of information between island states on a fairly regular basis. Concerning seabed mineral exploitation, Pacific island politics differ from Hawaii in one important respect: there are no public environmental interest groups in the Pacific islands. Although there is a

TABLE 6.7

Summary of Nodule Metal Grades in Various Areas

Area		Metal							
		%Mn	%Fe	Mn:Fe	%Ni	%Cu	%Co	%Ni+Cu+Co
Manihiki Plateau (Horn, Horn & Delach, 1973)	Mean	16.9		n.a.	0.30	0.17	0.51	0.98
Samoan Passage (12 samples)	Min.	15.1	13.8	0.74	0.18	0.10	0.25	0.61
	Max.	20.5	20.7	1.33	0.48	0.40	0.66	1.15
	Mean	17.9	18.3	0.98	0.30	0.18	0.40	0.88
Samoa Basin (9 samples)	Min.	13.0	8.1	0.75	0.21	0.11	0.11	0.45
	Max.	18.6	21.2	1.85	0.45	0.28	0.55	1.08
	Mean	16.3	14.6	1.13	0.34	0.20	0.28	0.67
South-west Pacific Basin (18 samples)	Min.	12.2	14.7	0.57	0.15	0.11	0.20	0.61
	Max.	21.2	25.8	1.20	0.70	0.33	0.52	1.47
	Mean	16.2	18.6	0.87	0.43	0.24	0.40	1.07

South Penrhyn Basin (48 samples)	Min.	7.9	5.6	0.50	0.11	0.07	0.22	0.54
	Max.	23.0	22.5	2.12	1.08	0.69	0.56	2.02
	Mean	15.2	15.4	0.99	0.41	0.22	0.36	0.99
North Penrhyn Basin (10 samples)	Min.	7.5	5.3	0.58	0.20	0.09	0.09	0.48
	Max.	24.1	16.6	4.46	0.99	0.95	0.43	2.10
	Mean	16.3	10.1	1.61	0.57	0.38	0.23	1.18
Equatorial North Pacific[1] Red clay	Mean	17.4	11.4	1.53	0.76	0.50	0.28	1.54
Siliceous ooze	Mean	22.4	8.1	2.76	1.16	1.02	0.25	2.43

Source: Exxon, *South Pacific Marine Geological Notes*, Vol. 2, No. 4, June 1981.

n.a. = not applicable.

[1] Data from D. R. Horn, B. M. Horn, and M. N. Delach (1972), *Ferromanganese Deposits of the North Pacific*, Tech. Rep. Off.

Int. Decade of Ocean Expl. 1, Washington, DC, 78 pp., and D. R. Horn, M. N. Delach, and B. M. Horn (1973), *Metal Content of Ferromanganese Deposits of the Oceans*, National Science Foundation Tech. Rep., No. 3, NSF GX33616, 51 pp.

commitment on the part of every government in the region to environmental protection, legislation is almost non-existent. For example, nowhere is there better testimony to concern about the protection of the environment than in what has come to be known as the Rarotonga Declaration (Appendix), adopted by almost all the Pacific island nations in March 1982. 'The Action Plan for managing the natural resources and environment of the South Pacific Region' (UNEP Regional Seas Programme, 1983), which is based on the Rarotonga Declaration, is even more detailed and comprehensive, particularly with respect to the marine environment. The South Pacific Regional Environmental Program Treaty (SPREP), designed to effect the aims of the Action Plan, has been negotiated. Even after the Treaty is implemented, however, there will still be enormous problems of enforcement. When and if the prospect of seabed mining reaches the state it has in Hawaii, no amount of legislation will by itself protect the marine environment without the involvement of well-informed environmental interest groups as well as other organizations whose activities are designed to hold governments accountable.

As pressures and enticements increase to develop both land-based and marine resources, there will be temptation for some anxious governments to short-circuit whatever exists in the corpus of environmental law in the interests of securing contracts from prospective developers.

The potential seabed minerals are those the major industrial powers are likely to focus their attention on—cobalt, manganese, nickel, copper, chromium, platinum group metals, molybdenum, and vanadium—either because they need them or because they might want to control access to them as part of a strategic minerals denial policy (Boczek, 1984). It is difficult to escape the impression that competition for and the prospect of conflict over the mineral resources of the Pacific are already in the making. For many reasons, the United States considers the Pacific more important than the Atlantic (Anthony, 1984). With its dependence on outside sources (mainly the Third World) for certain strategic minerals—which may not now be critical but could become so in the near future—the United States may want to ensure access to what is available within the marine zones of Pacific island states for one important reason: having chosen not to sign the Law of the Sea Treaty, the United States, as long as it remains a non-signatory to that Treaty, will find it difficult to obtain access to seabed minerals outside the island EEZs. If seabed minerals in which the United States has an interest can be mined within the EEZs in co-operation with island governments, there will be even less reason to submit to the requirements of the International Seabed Authority and, consequently, no reason to sign the Law of the Sea Convention. All other things being equal, US companies may even find it more attractive to deal with the resource-poor but flexible Pacific islands, which have less power to insist on transfer of mining technology and other requirements that have been an irritation to the United States.

Conclusions

Added to the mounting evidence of the existence of seabed minerals within the claimed waters of Pacific island states, the existence of land-based commercial mineral deposits including bauxite, copper, nickel, gold, chromite, and possibly petroleum as well as a number of minerals of lesser importance such as magnetite sands and manganese, is better established (Exon, 1982a; 1982b; East–West Center, 1982). Indeed gold, copper, nickel, silver, and manganese have for many years been commercially exploited. The importance of the Pacific islands as a source of mineral wealth is clear. When this is added to potentially available mineral resources outside of the EEZs and the pelagic resources of the region, the resource significance of the whole region emerges. But the importance of the region—indeed its strategic importance—is due not only to its resource base, but also to such other factors as the attractiveness of the islands as possible military communications/command/control bases and ports of call for a wide variety of military surface and sub-surface vessels, which are being increasingly deployed throughout the region by both superpowers. If one accepts the 'defence of the sealanes' argument of the United States and its Pacific Soviet threat thesis (Arkin and Chappell, 1984), the role of the region in the bigger picture comes into even sharper focus.

With increasing superpower tensions in the North-west Pacific, the re-militarization of Japan, the importance of submarine nuclear capability in the nuclear strategies of the superpowers, the militarization of the region looms larger and 'strategic denial' (Anthony, 1984: 3–6) takes the form of an extension of the Monroe doctrine into the Pacific. In operational terms, strategic denial means even more now than its original intention on the part of the United States to deny 'access to the islands to any present or potential enemy' (Anthony, 1984: 4). It now includes denial of the region's strategic minerals, marine space, and anything else of strategic value to present or potential enemies of the United States or their allies. Like it or not, the Pacific Ocean has now become an American lake; its island states are protected by the American nuclear umbrella whether they want to be or not. Strategic denial is a policy that invites conflict and confrontation—between the superpowers; between island states unwilling to become client states and those with a different disposition; and between island states and the superpowers, which try to entice them into entangling alliances. One outgrowth of such conflict is that inevitably island states are pitted against each other. Considered in systemic/ linkage terms, strategic denial, whether of resources, territory, marine space, or of island governments to freely choose allies, is the fuel that is likely to feed the fires of conflict and to exacerbate all of the uncertainties that accompany instability.

'Pacific' means 'peaceful', but that has already lost a lot of meaning to those who have watched with growing apprehension and frustration almost a half century of nuclear testing in the region and its concealed or underreported effects—on people, the food chain, and the environment in general. At one end of the spectrum, the arms buildup in the Pacific leaves the region open to possible naval nuclear war, conveniently far away from the major metropolitan powers' population centres. At the other end of the spectrum lies the festering prospect of increasing nuclear pollution, foreign interference in domestic politics, collaboration of élites with foreign interests, and consequential political repression and corruption (already much in evidence and growing).

It is difficult to sustain the view that mineral and other resources are at the heart of the newly emergent importance of the Pacific. The more defensible proposition is that the Pacific islands' mineral resources together with such less tangible resources as marine space, a commodious environment, and friendly people, make the islands especially important in a world dominated by technological advance, great power rivalry and new offensive postures in the name of defence, a dramatic shift in trade patterns, and new patterns of international interdependence.

These small islands thus face problems, challenges, and opportunities that call for unusually creative action. These problems and challenges will test the collective genius of Pacific islanders, whose fragile cultures have already begun to fray and decline. The opportunities that lie ahead can only be seized by political leadership willing and able to move in new directions—at times in concert with each other, at other times by lone trail-blazing. They will need caution as well as cunning, much as their ancestors did when they followed the stars and braved the uncertainty of uncharted waters, venturing boldly from many directions towards these now strategic islands.

There is potential for conflict at different levels and between different actors at the level of regional organizations. What happens in the SPFFA and in the Forum itself with respect to fisheries will be vital. Given the 'creative tension' that already exists in the SPFFA, issues related to conservation, rates of exploitation, fees for licences, approaches to surveillance, and types of joint venture and other arrangements with distant-water fishing nations are all bound to generate friction. It is not conflict *per se* that is of so much concern as conflict that becomes destructive, getting in the way of orderly resolution of larger or more fundamental problems. So far, a particular kind of collective approach has worked well in the pelagic resources area, in the sense that differences over key issues such as non-Forum country membership in the SPFFA have not affected the basic solidarity of island states. SPFFA would be negligent, however, if in addition to gathering basic data on pelagic resources, it did not pay some attention to the delicate question of considering means that might be used to address conflicts between members, as well as those that involve member nations in their relationships with the increasingly complex array of customers with whom they will be doing business.

Assuming even a small measure of continuing orderly political development within each island state, it is probable that issues pertaining to pelagic resources will become the subject of domestic political debate. This has not happened so far, partly because the fledgling opposition parties and what pass for interest groups in the region have shown little interest in challenging the slender assumptions on which present government policies are based. This is bound to change, and when it does there are likely to be repercussive effects on governments and on regional organizations. In turn, such changes will undoubtedly affect bilateral and sub-group relationships among governments and their distant-water fishing counterparts as well as the network of foreign clients with whom they do business. What has so far been a fairly stable situation could tend to a disequilibrium not previously known. For these reasons, the Pacific has become an area of multiple uncertainties.

Selective offers may soon be made to individual island states for mining rights, ocean leasing, and oil and gas prospecting licences. In the absence of sufficient data or broad consultation, regrettable decisions might be made that could be avoided. Perhaps the establishment of a South Pacific regional centre for minerals policy, data collection, and analysis would be appropriate (East–West Center, 1982: 19); however, yet another regional organization may overload the circuits and overtax the capacity of island governments to fund it. But it is precisely a regional focus on marine minerals development that is needed, and no less urgent is the need to sift and analyse what data have been collected and to direct the future course of data collection and analysis. There is still time to attend to these urgent preparatory tasks, as actual marine mining is not likely to begin yet (Johnson and Clark, 1985). There is also an urgent need to train a wide range of marine scientists who have a firm grasp of the petroleum and mineral fields. In the absence of composite information, a substantial amount of regional consultation, and indigenous or trusted expertise, it would be best for the islands to adopt a wait-and-see attitude.

Equally important, there is an urgent need for what might be called 'information self-sufficiency'. Pacific islanders must become knowledgeable about the great industrial powers by whom they are surrounded and with whom they are likely to be increasingly involved. Not only is there a need for a core of Pacific islanders to become proficient in the major languages of the wider Pacific region—Japanese, Mandarin, Korean, Russian, and Indonesian—but they must also learn their modes of negotiation and become familiar with their cultures, their histories, and the underpinnings of their economic theories. The Pacific islands must develop a common strategy that would protect their marine, seabed mineral, and other resources. This calls for a sophisticated and co-ordinated foreign policy framework—diplomatic, political, and economic—not unlike ASEAN, designed to prevent them from becoming hostages or pawns of any larger power. (The larger powers include not only the United States and the Soviet Union, but Japan, China, Korea, the European states, and the ASEAN nations.) There is much that Pacific islanders can learn from these countries, but they will have to decide what they most want to learn; that means co-ordinated regional planning and the ability to discern what will be important in their national interests.

Both in the long and in the short run, these achievements will require investment in what might be the scarcest of their natural resources—their own people. Unless Pacific island states can provide for their own development the necessary army of technicians, technocrats, and trained personnel in a variety of twenty-first century skills, they will be left behind in the race for control of their newly discovered frontier resources, for the second time since their rediscovery. Perhaps even more fundamental is the urgent need to shift cognitive gears: no longer are the resources of the world limited to land, labour, and capital. Pacific islanders must recognize that the resources of their world are land, labour, capital, and the ocean that surrounds them. They must acquire the knowledge and skills to use all four.

It is easy in an exercise such as this to be prescriptive, to specify from the ivory tower of speculative and analytical thought the direction public policy ought to take, what should be done, and in what sequence, without acknowledging the existence of the harsh political realities that constitute the fundamental framework within which public policy must be made. All of the suggestions made here are by their very nature political. As is the case in any state, almost all of the political decision-making in these micro-states is controlled by those in charge of the key mechanisms of the state—that is, by a power élite of elected politicians and what is usually a small coterie of local bureaucrats and trusted community influentials. These are polities that have few effective countervailing forces capable of holding the power élite accountable. By and large, even opposition parties are poorly informed, particularly about some of the complex issues raised here. In these circumstances, the only interest groups that prevail are those representing their own special interests—business, banking, transnational corporations (TNCs), foreign governments—which usually control the commanding heights of the economy.

Given these structural features of the decision-making process, the power élite has few constraints on its use of state power. Crucial decisions are made without any public participation, or, as is also often the case, without even any public knowledge. Whatever 'political development' has meant for these states, it has not entailed much in the way of political education designed to prepare and encourage people to participate in the making of political decisions.

The track record of the recent past engenders pessimism about the future of marine resources policy. Dominant state élites seem to be fundamentally unprepared to deal effectively with great issues confronting them. They are hampered by information insufficiency and a singular lack of vision about the future. Their choice of foreign experts is often seriously flawed. Put more pointedly, the islands are vulnerable to being dispossessed of their ocean resources just as they were dispossessed of their land-based resources—gold, nickel, manganese, copper, sandalwood, timber, phosphate, and the land itself. The Japanese, the Americans, the South Koreans, the Chinese, the Canadians, some Latin Americans, the West Germans, the French, and a number of ASEAN nations now talk with monotonous regularity about the Pacific Century. When the Pacific Century is over, will it be said that islanders slept through it all while those who controlled the mechanisms of power in island states, with few exceptions, danced late into a long and weary night, celebrating plunder disguised as development?

Plunder disguised as development in the exploitation of the natural resources which have been here identified will be serious enough where the impact is immediate—on the islands and on islanders. On reflection, however, this is far too narrow a view and this arises because of an epistemological flaw: the very conceptualization of *natural resources* in this essay has itself been too narrow. Starting from the perspective of the Pacific Islands, the concept of *natural resources* must be enlarged to include:

1. those that have been opened up by advances in science and technology, e.g. outer space, including particularly the geo-stationary orbit;

2. those that go beyond the traditional physical resource concept, e.g. climate, weather and culture, including archives of traditional knowledge;

3. those that do not lend themselves to physical appropriation, e.g. the radio frequency spectrum; and

4. those that require a long-term perspective, e.g. environmental quality (Anthony, 1988).

Once one accepts this expanded definition, it becomes immediately apparent that resource exploitation has inescapable *global* consequences and quite serious implications for future generations of humankind. Indeed one is brought face to face with two compelling notions: that of intergenerational equity, that is matters related to 'problems of equity between generations arising from such factors as depletion of resources, degradation of the quality of resources, impoverishment of resources or foreclosing options for future generations' and the 'common heritage or patrimony of humankind' (Anthony, 1988: xvi).

The tools, the mechanisms, the procedures, indeed the corpus of international law by which these resource realms are to be protected, are, where they exist, weak—and often unenforceable (particularly when immediate action is necessary)—and more often than not, non-existent. There are time and spatial dimensions involved in the management of these resource realms. The time dimension is relevant to intergenerational equity because implicit in it is the concept of the responsibility of this generation to those of the future. One highly immediate and pertinent example of the 'spatial dimension' is the well-publicized problem associated with the ozone layer and the host of issues related to it. The ozone layer problem, for example, has a particularly pernicious consequence for many islands: that of rising sea-levels, which, if this were to eventuate, would submerge a significant number of atolls in the Pacific and elsewhere.

The flip side of the entire resource realm coin is what can be described as 'anti-resources' such as pollution, acid rain, and nuclear waste. For the Pacific, the major 'anti-resource' is pollution of the marine environment and possibly human gene pools resulting from nuclear testing: by the Americans in the Northern Pacific; the French in the South-west Pacific, and the British in Australia. The extent of food-chain contamination may be more serious than suspected. Few scientists have undertaken the empirical research that cries out to be done on this subject and the reason is clear enough—the issue is too politically controversial. Radiation contamination of humans in the Pacific has been extensively documented (Danielsson and Danielsson, 1986; Alcalay, 1988) but the damage, primarily from testing, by a series of French governments, encouraged by the acquiescence of the United States, continues unabated. The substantive point is simply this: an issue such as contamination of the marine food chain in the Pacific is not miraculously contained there any more than a major nuclear disaster at Chernobyl is confined, by some magic of science, to that city and its immediate environment. And, of course, the same argument applies to the 'greenhouse effect': the burning of fossil fuels in North America, the destruction of large forest areas in South America and elsewhere (Cockburn, 1989), and the degradation of soil through intensive cultivation. All have cumulative *global* consequences which affect life on this planet. The 'greenhouse effect' cannot be contained by those who contribute most to creating the problem. Thus many resource problems in this extended definition are man-made and constitute an attack, in short, on the common heritage of humankind or that part of it which is left to us.

It is imperative, therefore, to see conflict over natural resources as an issue that also has global implications, and not merely for one geographical unit. The issues raised are of such far-reaching importance to human life that action and education on many fronts is urgently needed at a pace and on a scale far exceeding any brought to bear on any issue before. But it is precisely this collective approach that humans have been so ill adept an accomplishing. In the search for development, growth and diversification, we may have already plundered humankind's common heritage—irreversibly.

References

Alcalay, G. (1988), 'The Islands of Micronesia: Captives of U.S. Nuclear Strategy', *Covert Action Information Bulletin*, Vol. 29 (Winter), pp. 11–14.

Alexander, L. M. (1986), 'Geographical Perspectives on International Navigation', Paper presented at the East–West Center/Law of the Sea Institute Conference on International Navigation, January, Honolulu.

Anand, R. P. (1986), 'Transit Passage and Overflight in International Straits', Paper presented at the East–West Center/Law of the Sea Institute Conference on International Navigation, January, Honolulu.

Anonymous (1978), *The Deep Seabed and Its Mineral Resources*, Proceedings of the 3rd International Ocean Symposium, Tokyo.

Anonymous (1988), 'Pacific Impact: Quarterly Review of the South Pacific Commission', Vol. 1(1), March, p. 32.

Anthony, J. M. (1984), 'Great Power Rivalry and Emergent International Conflict in the Pacific: Implications for Pacific Island Micro States', Paper presented to a Conference on Peace and Transformation in the Asia–Pacific Region, 26–29 March.

—— (1988), 'Introduction', in Ranginui Walker and William Sutherland, eds., *The Pacific Peace: Security and the Nuclear Issue*, London: Zed Press, pp. xiii–xvii.

Arkin, William M. and Chappell, David (1984), 'Forward Offensive Strategy: A Look at Pacific Military Politics', Paper presented to Okinawa International Conference against Military Bases and Blocs, 26–30 April.

Baker, B. Jr. (1986), 'Statement before the Subcommittee on East Asian and Pacific Affairs Committee on Foreign Affairs', United States House of Representatives, 10 September.

Baltimore Sun (1979), 'Navy Ordered to Contest Sea Claims of Over 12 Miles by Other Nations', 1 August, p. 2.

Boczek, B. A. (1984), 'Resource Rivalry in the Third World', Paper prepared for the Conference on NATO, Warsaw Pact and the Third World, Kent State University, 11–12 April.

Borgese, E. M. and Ginsburg, N., eds. (1982), *Ocean Yearbook 3*, Chicago: University of Chicago Press, Appendix G, Table G1.

Bradley, I. (1986), 'Submarine "Scare" Much Ado About Nothing', *The New Zealand Herald*, 4 April, p. 6.

Bramwell, M., ed. (1977), 'Pacific Mineral Resources', in *The Rand McNally Atlas of the Oceans*, p. 164.

Broder, S. and Van Dyke, J. (1982), 'Ocean Boundaries in the South Pacific', *East–West Center Environment and Policy Institute Report*, No. 41, Honolulu.

Burke, W. T. (1986), 'Changes Made in the Rules of Navigation and Maritime Trade by the 1982 Convention on the Law of the Sea', Paper presented at East–West Center Law of the Sea Institute Conference on International Navigation, January, Honolulu.

—— (1988), 'Law School', University of Washington, Oral Communication.

Buruma, I. (1985), 'We Won't Tell You about Our Nuclear Weapons if You Don't Ask', *Far Eastern Economic Review*, 11 July, p. 51.

CCOP/SOPAC (1981), *Proceedings of the 10th Session*, October.

CCOP/SOPAC, 'South Pacific Marine Geological Notes', various dates.

CCOP/SOPAC (n.d.), 'Summary of CCOP/SOPAC Activities 1975–1985', *Miscellaneous Report*, No. 23, Suva, Fiji.

Chanda, Nayan (1985), 'No Boat to China', *Far Eastern Economic Review*, 30 May, p. 14.

Christol, E. Q. (1978), 'Unilateral Claims for the Use of Ocean Space', in J. K. Gamble, *Law of the Sea: Neglected Issues*, Proceedings of the Twelfth Annual Conference of the Law of the Sea Institute, Law of the Sea Institute, pp. 122–33.

Cicin-Sain, B. and Knecht, R. W. (1989), 'The Emergence of a Regional Ocean Regime in the South Pacific', East–West Environment and Policy Institute, Working Paper No. 14, January.

Clad, James (1986), 'Constitutional Conundrums', *Far Eastern Economic Review*, 2 October, p. 15.

Clark, A., Johnson, C., and Chin, P. (1984), 'Assessment of Cobalt-rich Manganese Crusts in the Hawaiian, Johnston and Palmyra Islands' Exclusive Economic Zones', *Natural Resources Forum*, Vol. 8, p. 163.

Cockburn, A. (1989), 'Unto Dust: Scorched Earth, Mercury Poisoning and the Greenhouse Effect', *Interview*, Vol. XIX, No. 1, pp. 66–9, 87, 91.

Coquia, J. (1989), 'National Development of Ocean Law, Policy and Management', Paper presented to SEAPOL Conference on Ocean Regime Building in Southeast Asia, Phuket, Thailand, May.

Cronan, D. S. (1983), 'Metalliferous Sediments in the CCOP/SOPAC Region of the Southwest Pacific with Particular Reference to Geochemical Exploration for the Deposits', 4 CCOP/SOPAC Technical Bulletin 8.

—— (1984), 'Criteria for the Recognition of Areas of Potentially Economic Manganese Nodules and Encrustations in the CCOP/SOPAC Region of the Central and Southwestern Tropical Pacific', *South Pacific Marine Geological Notes*, Vol. 3, No. 1, January, p. 16.

Danielsson, B. and Danielsson, M. T. (1986), *Poisoned Reign French Nuclear Colonialism in the Pacific*, London.

Doulman, D. J. (1986), 'Some Aspects and Issues Concerning the Kiribati/Soviet Union Fishing Agreement', *Pacific Islands Development Program*, East–West Center, Honolulu, Hawaii, May.

East–West Center (1982), *Resource Potential and Implications of Mineral Development in the South Pacific*, Honolulu.

Exon, N. F. (1982a), 'Manganese Nodules in the Cook Islands Region, Southwest Pacific', *South Pacific Marine Geological*

Notes, Vol. 2, No. 7, June.

―――― (1982b), 'Manganese Nodules in Kiribati Region, Equatorial Western Pacific', *South Pacific Marine Geological Notes*, Vol. 2, No. 6, May.

Fifteenth South Pacific Forum (1984), 'Communique', Funafuti, Tuvalu, 27–28 August, p. 10.

The Fiji Times (1984), 'U.S. Tuna War Key Role in Solomons Elections', 5 September, p. 8.

Gamble, J. K. Jr. and Frankowska, M. (1984), 'The Significance of Signature to the 1982 Montego Bay Convention on the Law of the Sea', *Ocean Development and International Law Journal*, Vol. 15, pp. 121–60.

Government of Fiji (1981), *Eighth Development Plan 1981–1985*, Suva: Government Printing Office, pp. 153–5.

Greene, H. G. and Wong, F. L., eds. (1984), 'Executive Summary' in *Geology and Offshore Resources of Pacific Island Arcs—Fiji, Papua New Guinea, Solomon Islands, Tonga and Vanuatu*, Suva, CCOP/SOPAC.

Hailbronner, K. (1983), 'Freedom of the Air and the Convention on the Law of the Sea', *American Journal of International Law*, Vol. 77(3), July, pp. 490–520.

Halbach, P. (1984), 'Deep-sea Metallic Deposits', *Ocean Management*, Vol. 9, p. 35.

Heller, P. P. (1978), 'Air Space over Extended Jurisdictional Zones', in J. K. Gamble, ed., *Law of the Sea: Neglected Issues*, Proceedings of the Twelfth Annual Conference of the Law of the Sea Institute, Law of the Sea Institute, pp. 135–57.

Hegarty, D. (1987), 'Soviet Bid to Catch the Winds of Discontent', *Pacific Defense Reporter*, 1987 Annual Reference Edition, pp. 13–17.

Honolulu Advertiser (2 May 1984), 'Ocean Mining Opposed at Lease Proposal Hearing'; (7 May 1984), 'Pacific Island Notes', p. A-6; (26 December 1984), 'Marcos Foes Sign Unity Document', p. A-18; (27 May 1985), 'Marijuana on Rise', p. C-1; (7 May 1985), p. D-1; (October 1985), p. B-4; (12 October 1985), p. B-1; (14 October 1985), p. B-1.

International Legal Materials (1969), *Vienna Convention on the Law of Treaties*, Vol. 8, p. 679.

―――― (1987), *Treaty on Fisheries between the Governments of Certain Pacific Island States and the Government of the United States*, done at Port Moresby, Papua New Guinea, 2 April.

Jaseni, B. M. (1980), 'Ocean Surveillance by Earth Satellites', in

E. M. Borgese and N. Ginsburg, eds., *Ocean Yearbook 2*, Chicago: University of Chicago Press, pp. 250–69.

—— (1985), 'A Note on Ocean Surveillance from Space', in Elisabeth Mann Borgese and Norton Ginsburg, eds., *Ocean Yearbook 5*, Chicago: University of Chicago Press, pp. 240–53.

Jin Zu Guang (1986), 'Conflicts between Foreign Ships, Innocent Passage and National Security of the Coastal State', Paper presented at the East–West Center/Law of the Sea Institute Conference on International Navigation, January, Honolulu.

Johnson, C. and Clark, A. L. (1985), 'Potential of Pacific Ocean Nodule, Crust and Sulfide Mineral Deposits', unpublished paper, East–West Center, January.

Juda, J. (1986), 'The Exclusive Economic Zone: Compatibility of National Claims and the UN Convention on the Law of the Sea', *Ocean Development and International Law Journal*, Vol. 16, p. 12.

Junko, Yamako (1984), 'Fisheries in Asia and the Pacific—Japan's Involvement and Its Problems', *AMPO*, Vol. 16, Nos. 1–2, pp. 82–104.

Kearney, R. E. (1981), 'Some Economic Aspects of the Development and Management of Fisheries in the Central and Western Pacific', *South Pacific Commission Fisheries Newsletter*, No. 22, New Caledonia.

Keith-Reid, R. (1983), 'A Red Letter Deadline', *Islands Business*, June, pp. 51–4.

Kent, G. (1980), *The Politics of Pacific Islands Fisheries*, Colorado: Westview Press, pp. 166–72.

Kimball, L. (1984), 'Preparatory Commission: The Long Road to Success', *Marine Policy*, Vol. 8, pp. 363–6.

Kotobalavu, J. (1988), 'Extended Maritime Jurisdiction in the Pacific: Maximizing Benefits from Marine Resources', in J. P. Craven and J. Schneider, eds., *The International Implications of Extended Jurisdiction in the Pacific*, Honolulu: Law of the Sea Institute.

Lowe, A. V. (1986), 'Some Legal Problems Arising from the Use of the Seas for Military Purposes', *Marine Policy*, Vol. 10(3), July, pp. 171–84.

Los Angeles Times (29 February 1984), 'Plan to Mine Ocean Ridge Cut Back', p. 18.

The Marshall Islands Journal (24 June 1988), Vol. 19, No. 26, p. 12.

McDonald, H. (1985), 'Hawke in the Draught', *Far Eastern Economic Review*, 14 February, pp. 12–13.

Morgan, C. L. (1984), 'The Hawaii Manganese Crust Project', unpublished paper, Department of Planning and Economic Development, Honolulu, 29 October, p. 2.

Mizuno, A. and Shujo, J. (1975), *Deep Sea Mineral Resources Investigation in the Eastern Central Pacific Basin*, Hisamoto, Takatsu: Geological Survey of Japan, Tokyo.

United States National Advisory Committee on Oceans and Atmosphere (1983), *Marine Minerals: An Alternative Mineral Supply*, Washington, DC: National Oceanographic and Atmospheric Administration.

Nations, R. (1985), 'Chores of Deterrence', *Far Eastern Economic Review*, 11 April, pp. 36–7.

New Straits Times (21 March 1985), p. 11.

New Zealand, Ministry of Foreign Affairs (1986), *South Pacific Nuclear Free Zone Treaty*, done at Rarotonga, 6 August 1985 (in force 11 December 1986); and Protocols 1, 2 and 3, done at Suva, Fiji, 8 August 1986; *New Zealand Treaty Series*, No. 7.

Noegroho Wisnoemoerti (1986), 'Archipelagic Waters and Archipelagic Sea Lanes', Paper presented at the East–West Center/Law of the Sea Institute Conference on International Navigation, January, Honolulu.

Oakland Tribune (17 February 1984), 'Mineral Leasing Opposed', p. A-8.

Oceanic Society (1984), Letter to the Department of Planning and Economic Development, Honolulu, 30 May, p. 2, and Appendix attached to the letter.

The Paper (24 February 1984), 'California Says "No" to Ocean Strip Mining'.

Prescott, J. R. V. (1983), 'Maritime Boundaries in the Southwest Pacific Ocean', in Edward L. Miles and Scott Allen, eds., *The Law of the Sea and Ocean Development Issues in the Pacific Basin*, Honolulu: Law of the Sea Institute, University of Hawaii, p. 495.

Prescott, J. R. V. and Morgan, J. R. (1983), 'Maritime Jurisdictions and Boundaries', in J. Morgan and M. Valencia, eds., *Atlas for Marine Policy in Southeast Asian Seas*, Berkeley: University of California Press, pp. 40–54.

Recy and Dupont (1982), *The South-west Pacific; Structural Data*, Paris.

Renfrew, B. (1985), 'New Zealand's Nuclear Ban', *Honolulu Star Bulletin and Advertiser*, 14 January, p. A-10.

Republic of Vanuatu (1982), *First Development Plan*, Port Vila: Government Printing Office, pp. 151–3.

Ridings, P. J. (1983), 'Resource Use Arrangements in Southwest Pacific Fisheries', unpublished paper, East–West Center, Honolulu, p. 19.

Robie, D. (1986), 'Nuclear Free Treaty No Nearer Solution', *New Zealand Times*, 22 June.

Roland, R., Goud, M., and McGregor, B. (1983), 'The U.S. Exclusive Economic Zone—A Summary of Its Geology, Exploration, and Resource Potential', *U.S. Geological Survey Circular*, No. 912.

Sakamoto, Y. (1984), 'Reversing Militarized Proliferation in the Asia-Pacific Region', Paper presented at the United Nations University Tokyo Seminar on Peace, Science and Technology, April.

Smith, C. (1985), 'No More Nukes', *Far Eastern Economic Review*, 18 April, pp. 38–9.

Smith, R. W., ed. (1981), 'National Claims to Maritime Jurisdiction, 4th Revision', US Department of State, Bureau of Intelligence and Research, Office of the Geographer, Washington, DC, Department of State (May).

Sohn, L. B. (1986), 'International Navigation Interests Related to National Security', Paper presented at the East–West Center/Law of the Sea Institute Conference on International Navigation, January, Honolulu.

South Pacific Commission (1987), 'Report of the High Level Conference to Adopt a Convention for the Protection of the Natural Resources and Environment of the South Pacific Region', South Pacific Commission, Noumea, New Caledonia, February.

State of Hawaii Department of Planning and Economic Development (1981), *The Feasibility and Potential Impact of Manganese Nodule Processing in the Puna and Kohala Districts of Hawaii*, Honolulu, Hawaii.

—— (1984), *Ocean Leasing for Hawaii*, Honolulu.

Surace-Smith, K. (1984), 'United States Activity Outside of the Law of the Sea Convention: Deep Seabed Mining and Transit Passage', *Columbia Law Review*, Vol. 84, No. 4, pp. 1032–58.

Tanter, R. (1985), 'Nuclear Free Zones as a Demilitarisation Strategy in Asia and the Pacific', Paper presented at the United Nations University Meeting on Regional Peace and Security in Asia and the Pacific, Tashkent, USSR, 27–29 April.

Treaty for the Prohibition of Nuclear Weapons in Latin America

(1971), *Treaties and Other International Agreements*, Vol. 22, Part I (TIAS 7137), pp. 754–86.

United Nations (1982), *Convention on the Law of the Sea* (7 October), Article 30.

United Nations Economic and Social Commission for Asia and the Pacific (1980), *Symposium on Petroleum Potential in Island Areas, Small Ocean Basins, Submerged Margins and Related Areas*, Wellington: New Zealand Department of Scientific and Industrial Research.

United Nations Environment Programme, Regional Seas Programme (1983), Reports and Studies No. 29.

US Department of State Press Release (4 February 1987).

US News and World Report (3 March 1986), 'Mapping the Ocean Floor by Satellite', p. 74.

Valencia, M. J. (1985), 'ZOPFAN and Navigation Rights: Stormy Seas Ahead', *Far Eastern Economic Review*, 7 March, pp. 38–9.

Valencia, M. J. and Marsh, J. B. (1986), 'Southeast Asia Extended Maritime Jurisdiction and Development', *Marine Resource Economics*, Vol. 3, No. 1, pp. 3–27.

Van Dyke, J. (1985), 'U.S. Hurt Itself in Spurning Law of Sea Pact', *Honolulu Star Bulletin and Advertiser*, 26 May, p. E-3.

Van Dyke, J. and Heftel, S. (1981), 'Tuna Management in the Pacific: An Analysis of the South Pacific Fisheries Agency', *University of Hawaii Law Review*, Vol. 3, pp. 1–65.

Van Dyke, J., Smith, Kirk, and Suwatibau, Suliana (1984), 'Nuclear Activities and Pacific Islanders', *Energy*, Vol. 9, No. 9/10, pp. 7–8.

Washington Post (1979), 'Government Sails Different Courses on Offshore Limits', 14 August, p. 17.

Washington Post Service (1984), 'U.S. in Freedom-of-Navigation Exercise', July.

Wilkes, O. (1980), 'Ocean-based Nuclear Deterrent Forces and Anti-submarine Warfare', in E. M. Borgese and N. Ginsburg, eds., *Ocean Yearbook 2*, Chicago: University of Chicago Press, p. 238.

Wolfe, E. E. (1988), 'Comments', in J. P. Craven and J. Schneider, eds., *The International Implications of Extended Jurisdiction in the Pacific*, Honolulu: Law of the Sea Institute, p. 131.

Appendix

SOUTH PACIFIC DECLARATION ON NATURAL RESOURCES AND THE ENVIRONMENT

This Conference:

Having regard to the Declaration of the UN Conference on the Human Environment adopted in Stockholm in 1972 and the desirability for regional declaration within the South Pacific framework;

Noting the World Conservation Strategy;

Recognizing that the environment of the South Pacific Region has features such as tropical rain forests and small island/lagoon/reef ecosystems which require special care in responsible management;

Taking into account the traditions and cultures of the Pacific peoples which incorporate wise management, born of their long history of living successfully in the region, as expressed in accepted customs and rules of conduct;

Seeking to ensure that resource development for the benefit of the people shall be in harmony with the maintenance of the unique environmental quality of the region and the evolving principles of sustained resource management, particularly in view of increasing population densities;

Building on the established processes of regional co-operation based on independence, consultation and consensus;

Declares that:

1. The resources of land, sea and air which are the basis of life and cultures for South Pacific peoples must be controlled with responsibility, and safeguarded for the benefit of present and future generations, through sustained resource management.

2. Integrated environmental, economic, social and resource planning and management is essential to ensure sustainable rational use of the land and sea resources of the region, and the greatest enhancement of human well-being.

3. An effective programme of public information, education and training is necessary to promote basic environmental understanding by the people, as well as the skills necessary for effective environmental assessment and management.

4. Appropriate and enforceable legal instruments and institutional arrangements are a necessary basis for effective integration of environmental concern with the whole development process.

5. A system of specially-designated areas such as national parks and reserves is essential for the protection of traditional use of resources, and should be included in resource use planning.

6. The economic utilization of resources, particularly forests and fisheries, should be based upon reliable information to ensure sustainable production without over-exploitation or damage to the environment and affected peoples.

7. Management of the growth and distribution of population should be encouraged to ensure adequate management of natural resources and to maintain adequate standards of human well-being.

8. The rate and nature of discharges of non-nuclear wastes shall not exceed the capacity of the environment to absorb them without harm to the environment and to the people who live from it.

9. The storage and release of nuclear wastes in the Pacific regional environment shall be prevented.

10. The testing of nuclear devices against the wishes of the majority of the people in the region will not be permitted.

11. The vulnerability of much of the region to environmental and economic damage from natural and man-made disasters requires the development of national and regional contingency plans and prevention programmes.

12. Regional co-operation should be further developed as an effective means of helping the countries and territories of the South Pacific to maintain and improve their shared environment and to enhance their capacity to provide a present and future resource base to support the needs and maintain the quality of life of the people.

13. Traditional conservation practices and technology and traditional systems of land and reef tenure adaptable for modern resource management shall be encouraged. Traditional environmental knowledge will be sought and considered when assessing the expected effects of development projects.

14. Involvement and participation of directly affected people in the management of their resources, including the decision-making process, should be encouraged.

Source: *Report of the Conference on the Human Environment in the South Pacific*, March 1982.

Index

Tertiary sedimentary basins, 95
Terumbu Layang-Layang (Da Hoa Lau)
(Spratly Islands), 106
Thailand: agribusiness, 29; commercial
farming, 29; fish exports, 116; fishing
disputes with Malaysia, 116; mineral
reserves, 135; naval bases, 135; naval
fleet, 133; peasant unrest, 35; rice
exports, 13, 28; rice industry, 33–4;
tuna exports, 13
Third World see Developing countries
Timber industry: foreign investment,
18; forest exploitation, 18; production
and export, 25; reforestation, 20;
South-East Asia, 24; stockpile, 25
Timor Sea: boundary disputes, 102;
conflict over continental shelf, 102;
hydrocarbon potential, 102
Tin, 36
Tonga: boundary disputes, 201;
hydrocarbon potential, 226;
overlapping territories, 202;
territorial claims, 201
Trade disputes, 38–9
'Trash' fish, 159
Trawler fishing: conflict over fishing
areas, 156–8; conflict with small-scale
fishermen, 156–8, 160–8; impact on
small-scale fishing, 110; regulations
and policies, 162
Treaties, nuclear-weapon, 195
Treaty of Amity, Commerce and
Navigation, 38
Treaty of Tlatelolco, 195
Tribal peoples: Bontocs, 44;
displacement of, 19–20, 43–6; effect
of development on, 43; effect of
logging on, 19–20, 45; Kalingas, 44;
Kayan, 44; Kejaman, 44; Kenyah,
44; Penan, 44; Tingguian, 45; Ukit,
44
Tuna exports, 13
Tuna fishing, 214, 217–21

UNCLOS (UNITED NATIONS
CONVENTION ON THE LAW OF THE
SEA), 118, 119, 140, 189–93; air

defence, 119; innocent passage,
190–1; military zones, 119; the
United States, 119; legal contention,
119, 189–91
UNDP Project on Regional Offshore
Prospecting in East Asia, 129
United Kingdom, military co-operation
with ASEAN, 135
United States: military bases in: Japan,
127, South-East Asia, 127–8; military
co-operation with ASEAN, 128
United States Pacific Fleets (Third and
Seventh), 127
Uruguay, territorial claims, 195
Usiminas (Brazil), 80

VANADIUM, 225, 230
Vanuatu: boundary disputes, 201;
nuclear-free zone, 195
Vietnam: claim to Spratly Islands, 103,
106; conflict over: Natuna Sea,
102–3, Paracel Islands, 106, 107,
Spratly Islands, 103, 105–6; naval
fleet, 133; Soviet naval outposts in,
128

WASTE MATERIALS, HAZARDOUS, 75,
88, 146; effect on environment, 41;
effect on health, 88
Water pollution, by hazardous
chemicals, 146
Western Samoa: boundary disputes,
201; overlapping territories, 202
WESPAC (Programme Group for the
Western Pacific), 129
Wood industry, 22–3; conflict between
producers and consumers, 23–6

YAWATA STEEL see Nippon Steel

ZINC, 36, 38, 225
ZOPFAN (Zone of Peace, Freedom and
Neutrality), 126, 136